Brexit, Kant & Othello - S. James

All Rights Reserved. No reproduction, copy or transmitted or made without written permission. No paragraph or section may be transmitted save with the written permission or in accordance: Act 1956 (as amended). Copyright 2021 of the author. The author of this work has been asserted in accordance with the copy of this book is deposited with the British Library.

ISBN: 9798464350892

#BK&O

(REV230102)

First published June 30th 2022

Foreword

Here are sections two, three and four of my four-part book on Brexit. Section 1 was a book already published. I had intended to bundle them all up and publish it here all together; the first book as a second edition with some light revisions, and then these three sections as a sort of addendum. But at the last minute I balked. The first book identifies me and some people may find this work controversial, so to protect myself and my family, I deleted the Section 1 book which I will reluctantly leave as is, and just publish sections two, three and four here under a pen name.

Hi Frank,

hope this is of interest. Let me know what you think, any criticism, however harsh always welcome.

Best regards.

Sebastian.

Outline

I am defending the proposition that we should be an independent democracy. That because peace is good, a large number of small democracies is preferable to a small number of power blocks. That borders should be derived from geographical observation rather than imposed by cultural beliefs. That anyone should be free to question and vote about anything, and that laws should be applied equally to everyone. I will be looking at the modern tendency to impose beliefs and undervalue empiricism. I'll propose a couple of possible solutions and wander off on a few of tangents. Nothing too controversial – enjoy!

Section 2.0 (Preamble)

In the months that followed the publication of my first Brexit book, as events unfolded, I reappraised my view of certain people and thought of various things I wish I had put in the first edition (as well as spotting a couple of embarrassing typos) but my main failing with the first book was that in order to keep it brisk I had omitted virtually all of the arguments from my blogs saying *'there's no point in regurgitating pre referendum arguments in a post referendum world'*. On that point I could not have been more wrong. To my astonishment, far from subsiding, arguments about whether Britain should leave actually intensified! Despite the matter being settled fairly, freely and openly, our decision to leave was attacked in every way imaginable, and I found myself having to endlessly re-run arguments I had thought were done and dusted. Clearly I had made a mistake to have written a 'how' book rather than a 'why' book.

So it did cross my mind to write a revision, but initial sales were poor, so much so that, out of embarrassment, I stopped contacting my wonderful agent (Michael) and wonderful publisher (Lionel). I joked that I had out-sold David Hume but I did feel deflated that they had shown confidence in me that I hadn't repaid with bumper sales. And as Brexit once again took over my life there was no time to promote a book about *how* we won when there were more important battles to be fought against 'the People's Vote' and 'Chequers'. So I came to see the first edition as the latest in a long line of well written SJ flops, and shrank back from bothering them with any talk of a second edition.

Michael observed that in my eagerness to get the book out before the anniversary of the vote, the ending of the first book was inconclusive and unsatisfying. In terms of literary criticism he was obviously right about this, but as a record of political events an inconclusive, unsatisfying ending was actually an accurate portrayal of the anguish which the country descended into. But still he had got me thinking about having another bite of the cherry.

Then in September 2018 Lionel informed me there had been a mini surge in sales. Other writers like Will Podmore, Julie Burchill had referred to my book in their work, and in October 2018 they kindly asked if I would consider a second edition. That night I barely slept as my mind whirled through all the scores I could settle and all the wrongs I could right. The next morning my long-suffering wife asked why I hadn't slept. I told her. She was unimpressed.

But in the hope that a truthful worm's-eye account of the counter-revolution may result in a better future I will now complete the story. I will leave the first book as the best I could do at the time. I will assume (hopefully wrongly) that this still isn't settled and start with a section about why Brexit is necessary then there will be a section about the philosophical background to the issues, then in the last section of the book there are some supplementary rants that I hope are of interest. So herewith I proudly present ... B2: This time it's personal!

2.1 Preamble to Examples

In the next few chapters I'm going to go through the main Brexit arguments one by one and I'm going to adapt these arguments from my blogs. In the years when I was writing these the situation seemed on a knife edge, and still even now as I pull these notes together in 2020, it's by no means certain what way things will go, so the manner in which I wrote these blogs constantly changed. Some were written with an optimistic voice to raise people's morale, while others had an angry tone. Sometimes I referred to membership in the present tense and sometimes in the past. People who to me now are 'Remainers' to you in your time may be 'Rejoiners'. And in some places I may appear to be arguing about things that, with your benefit of hindsight, appear to have been inevitable. Where possible I'll retain the voice used in the original essays to help convey the prevailing mood at the time, but to you reading in your time this variation of tone may seem inconsistent. This is all I ask the reader to indulge. History is a moving target.

2.2 We didn't vote to become poorer
First up is the idea that EU membership made us richer. The Office for National Statistics (ONS) regularly publishes economic data. Below is the complete dataset for GDP growth. There are various ways of measuring economic data and people disagreeing for political reasons will always say they prefer a different measure, but the GDP figures all show basically the same pattern and this particular measure is good because it goes way back to 1956 allowing us to observe the general trends.

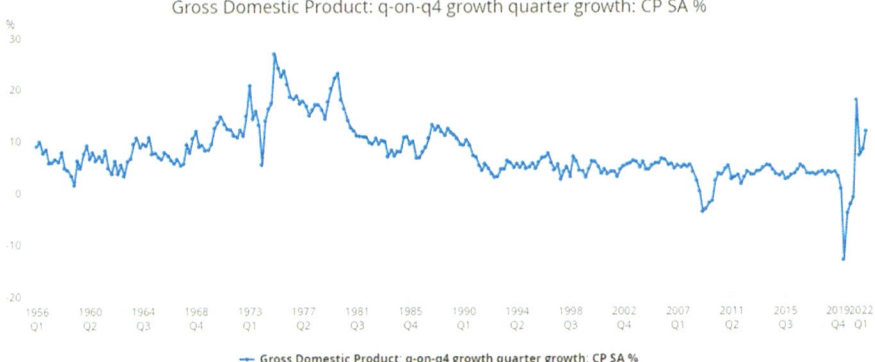

The ONS website has a handy tool allowing us to generate graphs for specific periods. Heath joined the EEC (without a referendum) in 73, there was a referendum vote to remain in 75, and the oil crisis of 73 will have distorted the figures somewhat, but the general trend is clear – before integrating GDP growth was consistently above 5% and trending up. Below is the graph for this period:

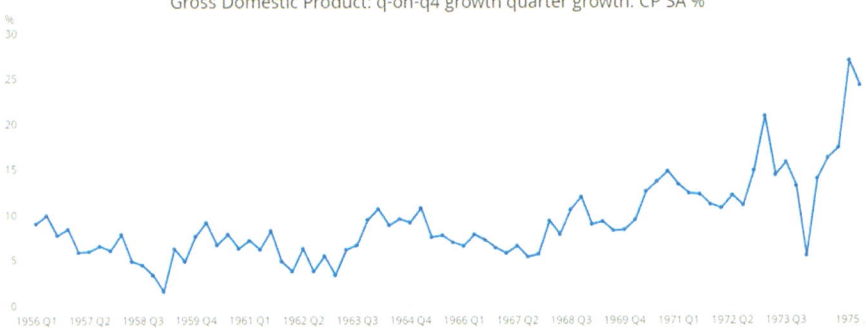

I see a line going from bottom left to top right. And here (below) is the graph from the 1975 referendum to remain up to the 2016 referendum to leave:

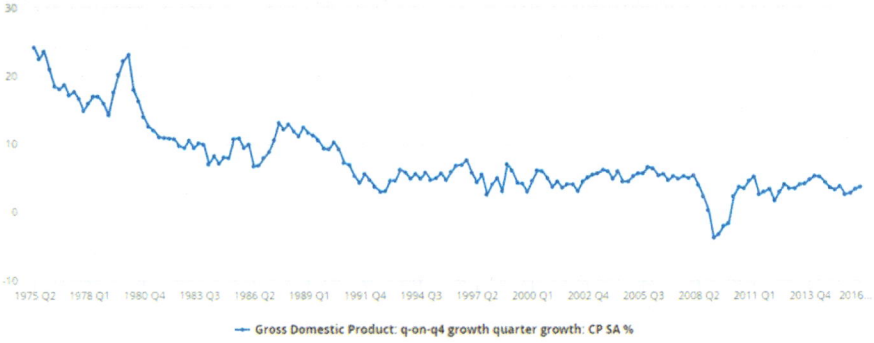

I see a line going from top left to bottom right. That's a collapse from 24.2% to 3.7%. And below is the graph from the vote to leave to now (mid 2022):

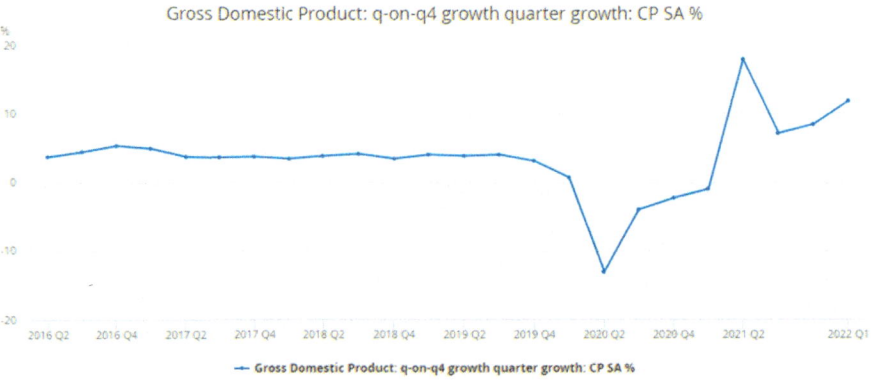

We see the dip and pump caused by Covid in 2020-21 which we can ignore, but the general upward trend is clear. At the time of going to press GDP growth is at its highest levels for 33 years. When we voted to leave it was flat-lining at sub 4%, now it's about triple that.

Summary:
Before joining = Good.
Membership period = Collapse.
After leaving = Improvement.

Next, let's look at balance of payments; here (below) is the full dataset:

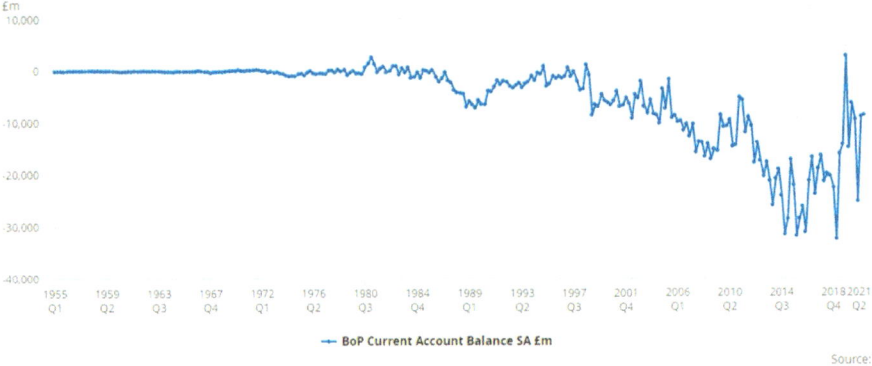

(ONS dataset)

If ever there was ever a history of EU membership in one line then this is it. This graph tells us that:

1, Britain had relatively balanced trade (equal imports and exports) for decades prior to EU integration.

2, Then in 1986 Margret Thatcher signed the Single European Act and our trade balance began to collapse. By the time we voted to leave we had gone from balanced trade to a deficit of minus £32,540 million! Here is the graph for that time period:

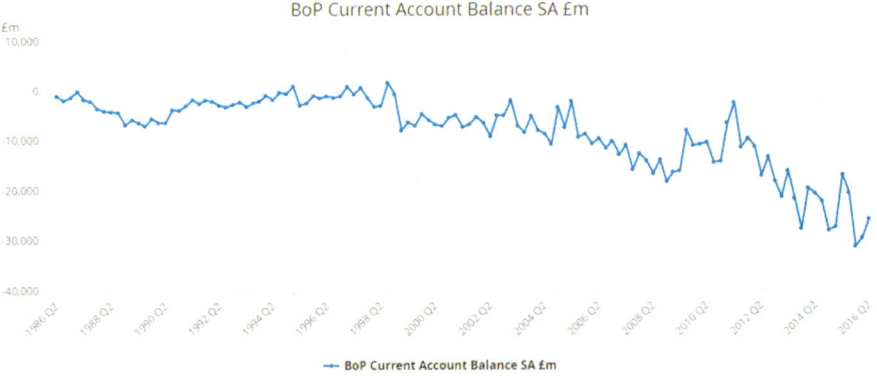

I see a line from top left to bottom right.

3, At the nadir of Theresa May's attempt to destroy our democracy (Q1 2019) the trade deficit reached record levels of minus £34,541 million!

4, The departure of Theresa May coincided with the biggest improvement of our trade balance in history. In Q1 2019 we had the worst trade balance ever. Just 8 months later we achieved balanced trade again for the first time in over twenty years!

5, Since our vote to leave, despite Covid and despite being governed by venal, incompetent Tories, our trade deficit has gone from minus £32,540 million to minus £7,300 million. Here is a close up of that section of the graph:

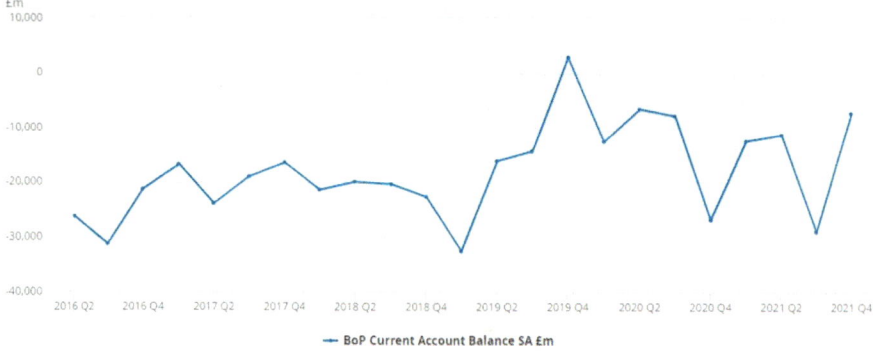

I see a line that goes from bottom left to top right. Obviously Covid could be a black swan, but the current trend indicates we should return to a permanent trade surplus by 2023.

So ... before we joined we had balanced trade, after we joined it went down and after we left it went back up. Clear? These figures don't show a coincidence but a correlation, when more people have more democratic control over more power, more people become more prosperous. But as society becomes less democratic there is decline. Next wages. Here is the full ONS wages dataset from when records began in 1955:

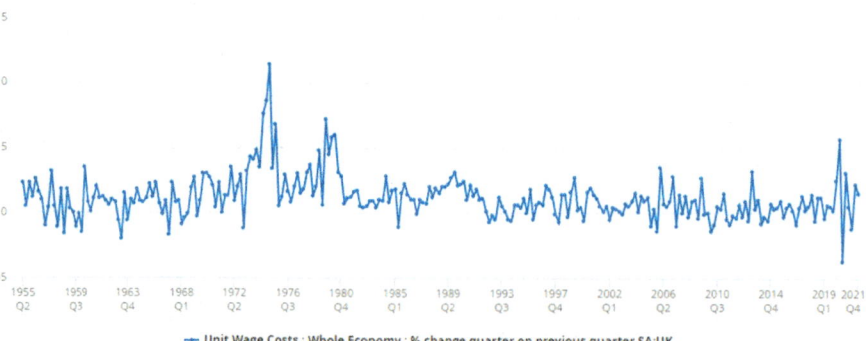

Because the wages dataset is about the percentage change from quarter to quarter this graph looks deceptively subtle but when we look closer we see it tells pretty much the same story as the GDP figures. This graph (below) shows that before 1975 wage rises were generally above 1% per quarter and trending up:

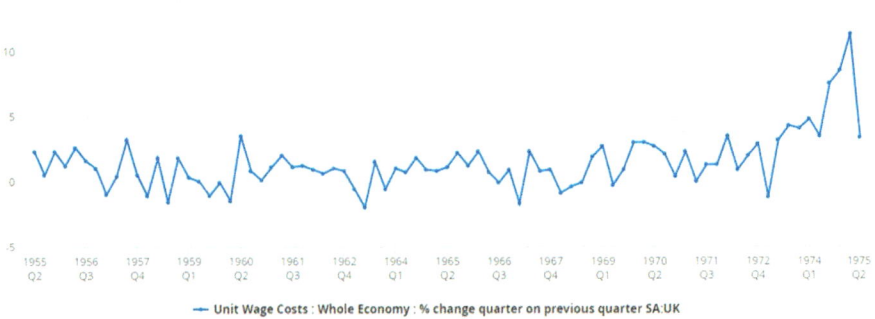

… But this graph (below) shows what happened next:

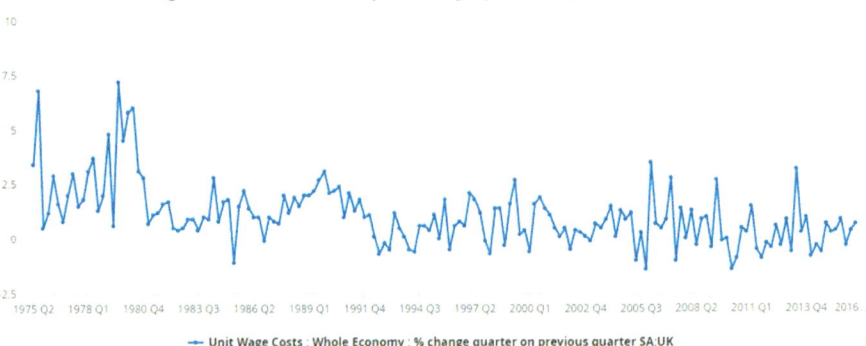

We went from wages growth averaging above 2% per quarter to sub 1% and flat-lining. The calculation method for this dataset makes the change look subtle but the actuality was brutal - wage increases more than halved. That's why we left. Next here is the wages graph from the vote to leave to now (mid 22):

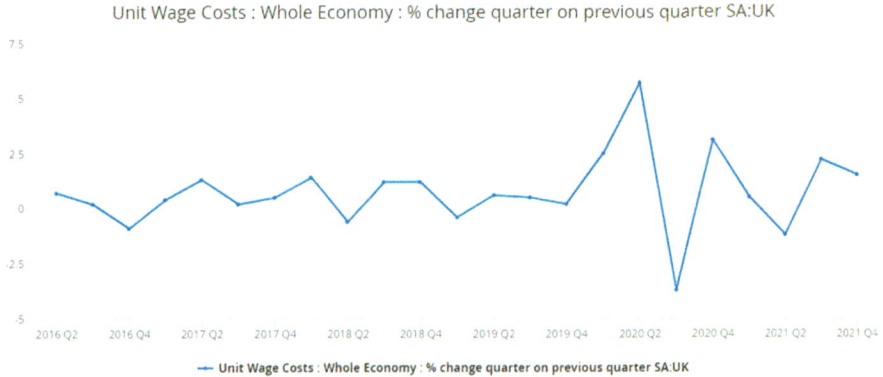

It may not look like much because we have a shorter time series to analyse, and obviously Covid has distorted the figures, but we have gone from averaging 0.7% (when we voted to leave) to double that and trending up. So once again it's a case of:

Before membership = Good.
During membership = Collapse.
After membership = Improvement.

Not convinced? OK. The graph below shows wages over a five year period (two and a half years before and after the vote to leave).

(ONS dataset)

We can clearly see that wages were more erratic <u>before</u> the referendum and more stable <u>after</u>. Coincidence? They rose by less than 1% in the 30 months <u>before</u> and by over 1.5% in the 30 months <u>after</u>. Coincidence? Now let's look at wages as a percentage of GDP:

(CP SA Employee compensation as % GDP)

This graph shows wages as a percentage of GDP over a 60 year period. For 25 years <u>before</u> we joined it was about 58% whereas for 40 years <u>after</u> it was consistently about 6% lower and declining. Coincidence?

(Note: Incidentally the above undermines the notion of a Thatcherite economic miracle. The sixties and seventies were the real boom decades - not the eighties).

This next graph shows the correlation between GDP growth and EU integration over a fifteen year period.

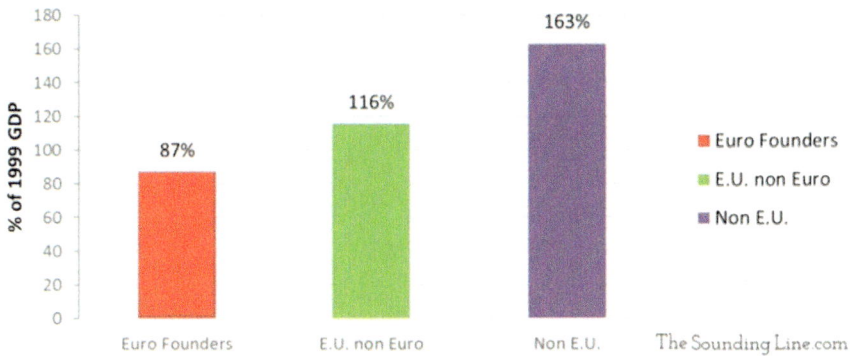

The red bar represents the EU founders, the green bar represents member states that are in the EU but not the Eurozone (eg UK, Sweden, Poland and Denmark). The purple bar represents European countries that are not members of the block (eg Switzerland, Greenland and Iceland). There is clearly a correlation between democracy and prosperity. Countries in the Single Market cannot vote to amend laws (re goods, services, labour or capital) so naturally they decline. Whereas the countries that can democratically revise the laws they live by, prosper. This is surely a statement of the obvious, no political system in history succeeds more and fails less than democratic self-rule. Which probably explains this:

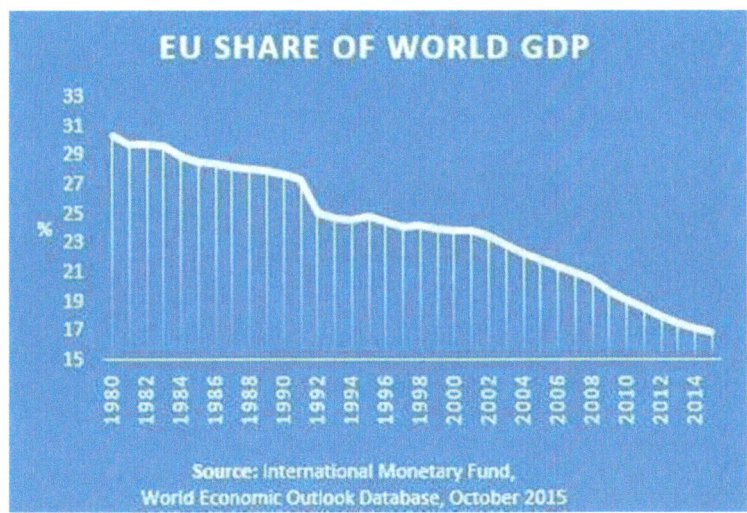

Next, unemployment, before the referendum the Nostradamuses of Remain tried to terrify everyone with lurid conjecture that half a million people would lose their jobs if we dared vote to leave. George

Osborne put the figure at 820,000. This graph (from the Guardian) shows the actual steady decline of UK unemployment:

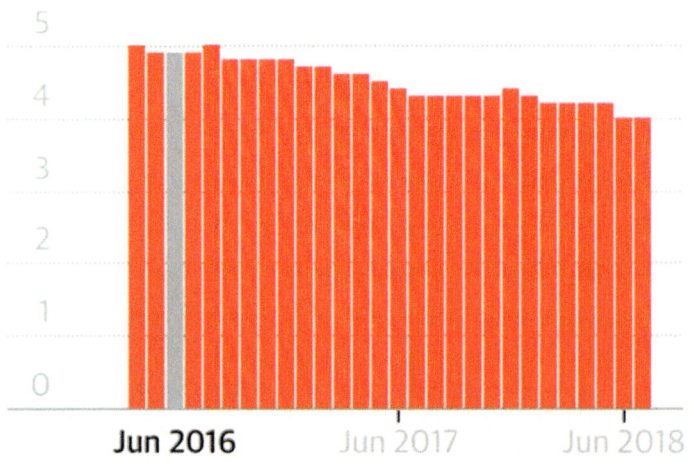

Source: ONS

(The grey line represents the date of the vote to leave). Now let's look at that in a broader context:

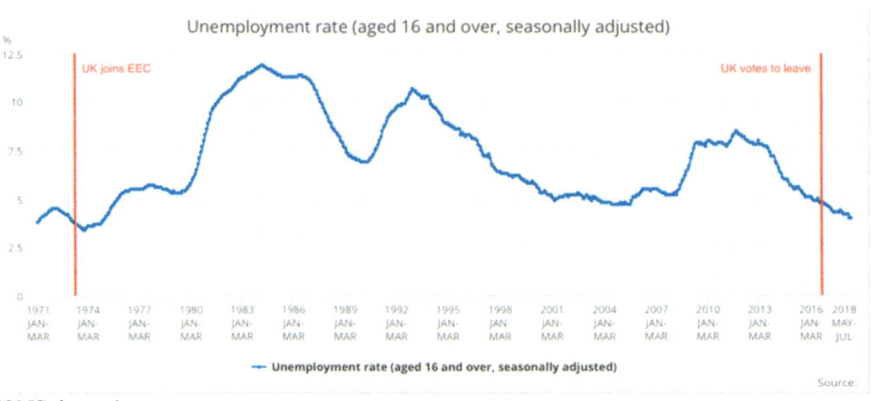

(ONS dataset)

The red line on the left is the date when Heath signed us up for the EEC. The red line on the right is the 2016 vote to leave. In 1973 we had 3.7% unemployment, we joined and it tripled; now we are leaving its back at 3.7%. Coincidence? Next, employment. Fell off a cliff did it? Nope, it hit record levels:

12

Figure 3: UK employment rate (people aged 16 to 64 years), seasonally adjusted

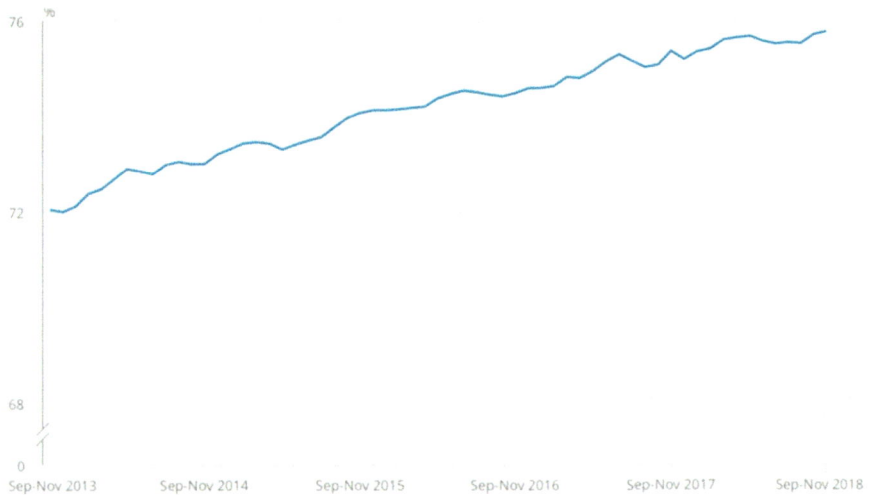

September to November 2013 to September to November 2018

Source: Labour Force Survey, Office for National Statistics

Let's look at that over the longer term shall we? ...

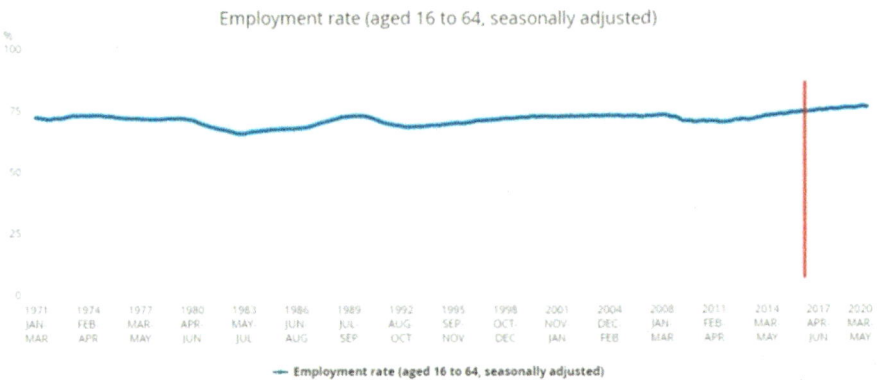

Above is the ONS dataset for employment since records began in 1971. Guess what! Since our vote to leave (red line) it's gone above 75% for the first time ever! Next up, government borrowing, this graph (Guardian) shows it fell every year after the vote to leave:

Government borrowing, £bn

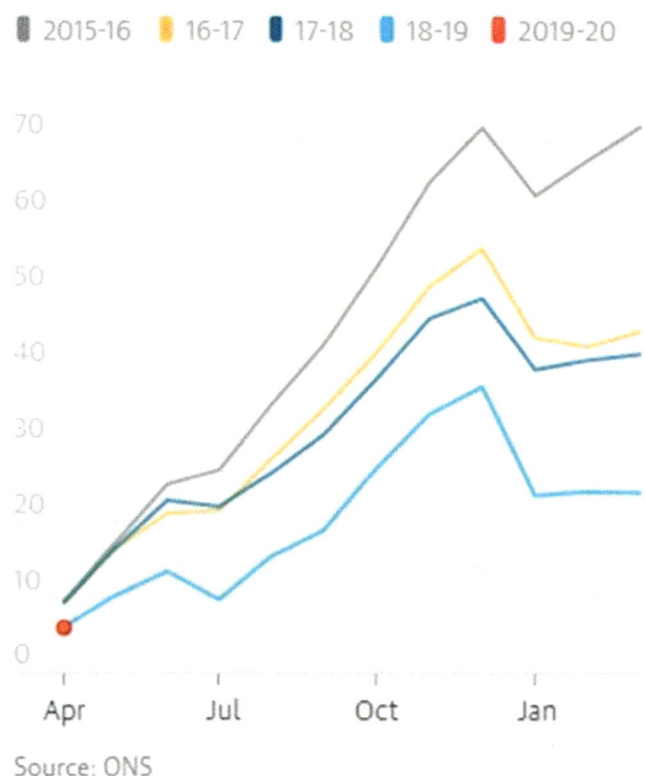

Source: ONS

On 21st February 2019 the Telegraph reported: "The Government delivered a record budget surplus in January … A surplus of £14.9bn in January, the largest since records began in 1993, put public sector borrowing on track to comfortably undershoot the Office for Budget Responsibility's forecasts. Borrowing in the financial year-to-date is at its lowest level in 17 years."

Could the reality be any more different from the hysterical predictions of the Remainiacs? The next two graphs show how leaving the Single Market would make us richer. This first one shows the long term decline of global tariffs:

Figure 11: Tariff liberalisation since 1947: RTAs, MTNs and unilateralism.

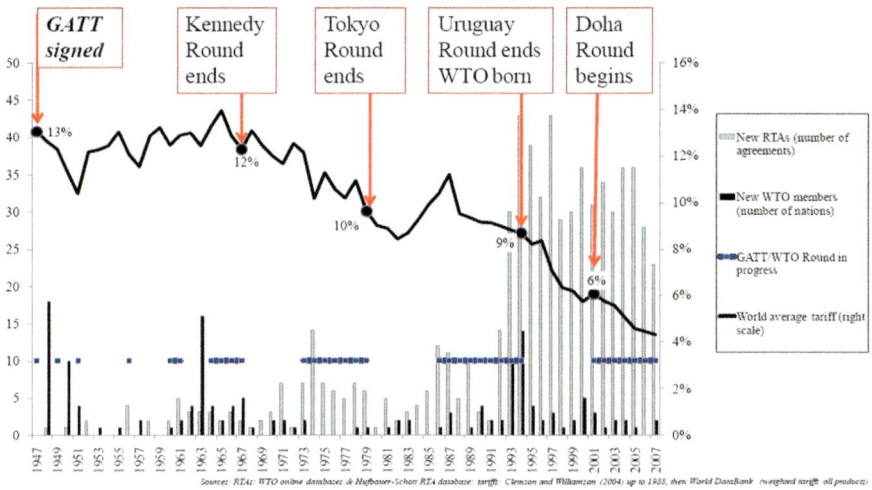

So, tariffs are clearly in a death spiral. Now here is a graph showing our EU membership contributions going up and up…

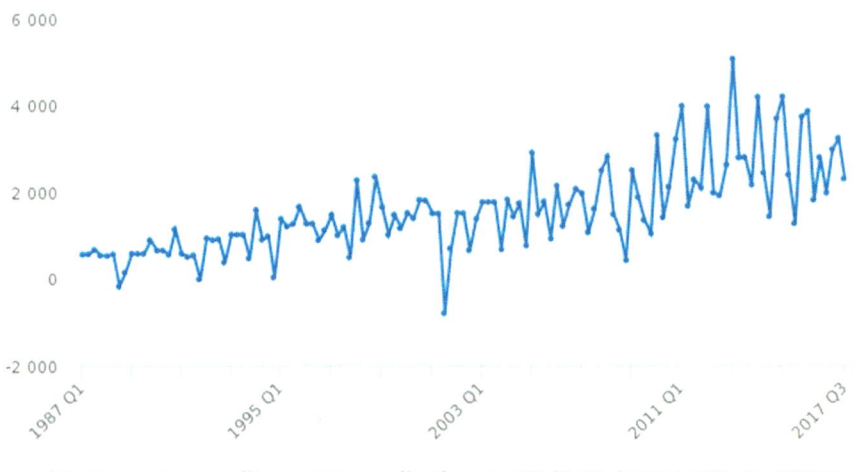

There is no such thing as free trade with the EU. We either:

A, Pay a membership fee and no tariffs. Or …
B, Pay tariffs and no membership fees.

It's one or the other. So why would we want to pay membership fees that are going up and up when we could pay tariffs that are going down and down? The obvious answer is that we wouldn't - unless of course we wanted to make ourselves poorer for the sake of some irrational ideological belief. Clearly paying tariffs would make us richer than paying EU membership fees. Doubly so when we consider that the whole of society has to pay the membership fees whereas no one is obliged to pay any tariff; the only people who would pay them are the 6% of British companies that export goods (not services) to the EU. EU tariffs would amount to less than half of UK membership contributions which would mean an automatic saving of around £5bn per annum. Could there be a more clear-cut argument for paying tariffs rather than membership fees? But all the while the Remain side tried to get people to conflate membership with prosperity by repeating phrases like "We want tariff-free trade". It was an exercise in deception. In March 2019 Phil Radford published his analysis of UK exports on Brexit Central. It featured this graph:

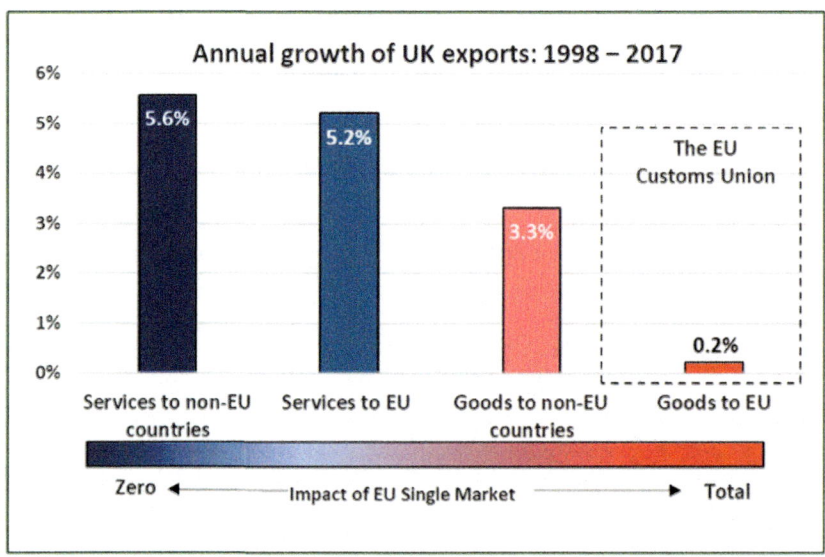

He observed: "The UK's slowest-growing export trade since 1998 is goods exports to the EU, which have grown by just 0.2% per year since 1998 (3.7% over 20 years) Yet this is precisely the sector that is supposed to benefit from tariff free trade within the Customs Union ... Conversely, the UK's fastest growing exports are services exports outside the EU, unimpacted by either the Customs Union or Single Market ... Since 1998, the track record of the Customs Union has been to take a trade relationship that was balanced and turn it into a £95 billion deficit, which is larger - per head - than the US trade deficit with China."

Next, here is a map I knocked up in my lunch break.

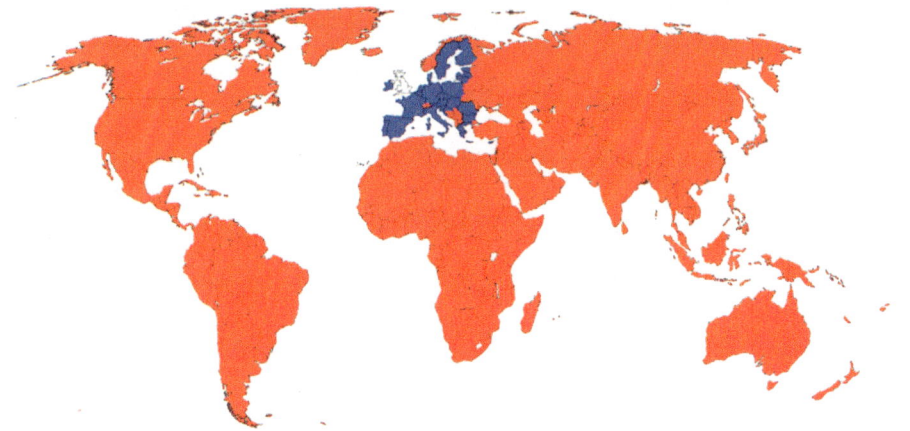

Which market should we be concerned about? The small one with low growth, or the big one with high growth? We could either:

A, Lock ourselves into the small, low growth market which will make goods from the world market more expensive and prevent us from doing any trade deals. Or…
B, Not lock ourselves into the EU market, in which case we can trade freely with whoever we like whenever we like.

It's not a tough choice.

2.2.1 EU GDP Decline
Not convinced? Ok. Here is a graph I put together illustrating the general economic decline of EU member states:

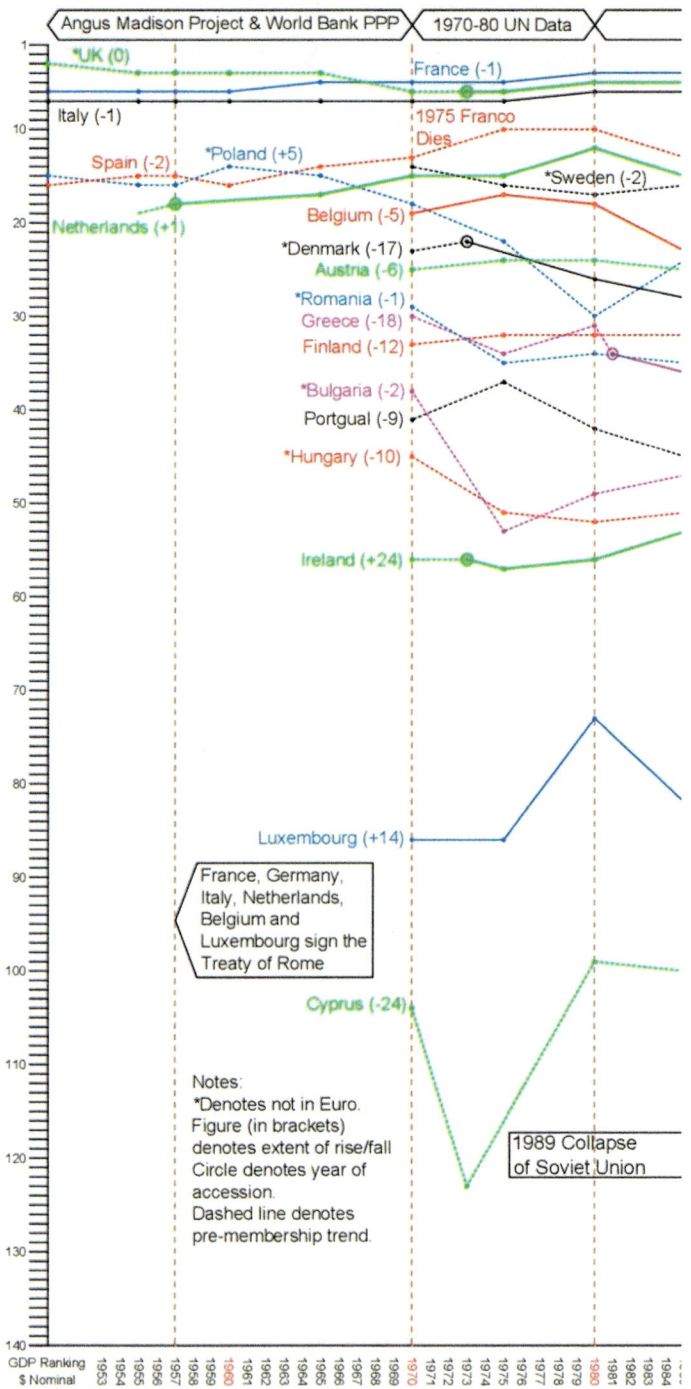

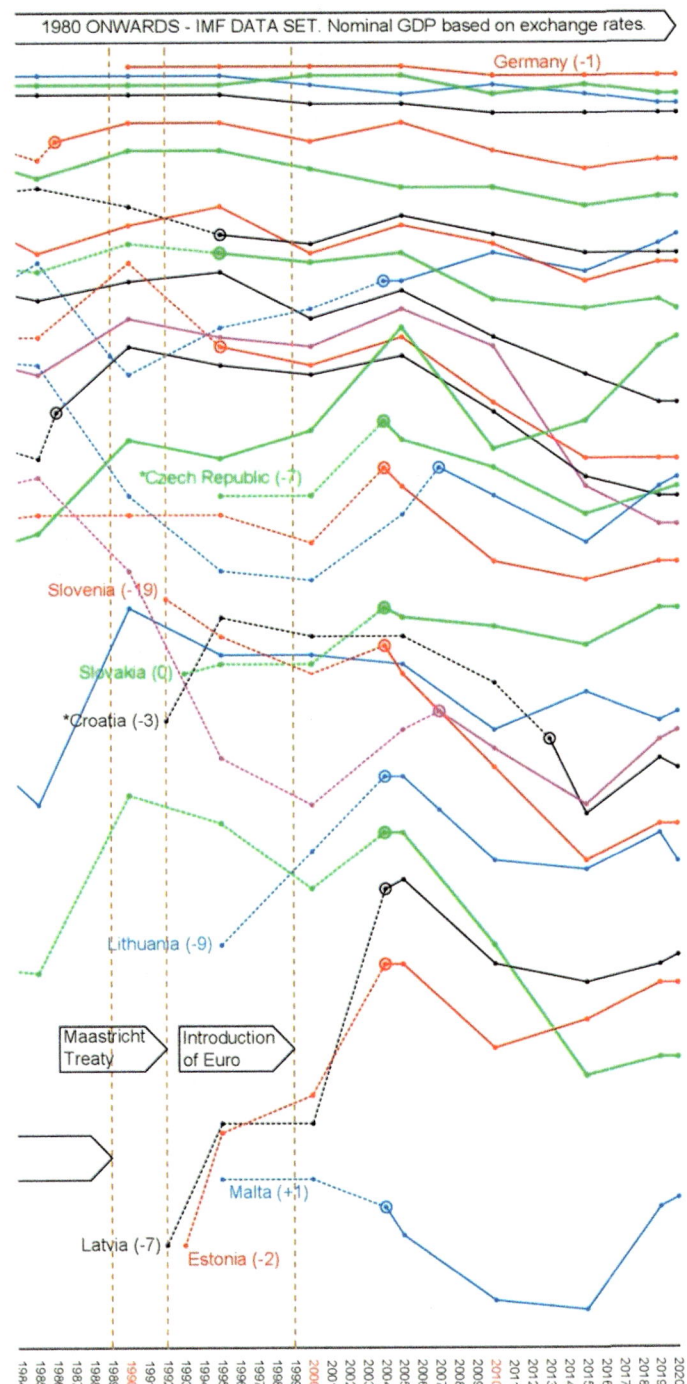

To establish general correlations I have used the longest-term economic data I could find. The data up to 1970 is Angus Madison Project & World Bank PPP. The dataset from 1970 to 1980 is from the UN and from 1980 onwards I used IMF GDP based on exchange rates.
The lines represent the world ranking of member states by GDP.
The dashed lines show the trend before accession.
The joining dates are circled.
The continuous lines show the trend after accession.
By the name of each country I noted the number of places it rose or fell during membership.
We see the general decline from left to right. As member states became more integrated (less democratic) they tended to drop down the table. If you can't see the detail at this scale I will talk you through the data. From top to bottom:

Since unification, **Germany** (red) has declined from 3rd to 4th place.
Since the Maastricht Treaty, **France** (blue) has declined three places.
Italy (black) has dropped from 6th to 8th over the same period.
Spain (red) was doing well in 1985. After joining in 1986 it carried on growing, but at a slower pace. Since Maastricht Spain has fallen from 9th to 13th.
Since Maastricht, **Holland** (green) has dropped from 12th to 17th.
Since joining **Sweden** (black) has dropped from 21st to 23rd.
In 1950 **Poland** (blue) was 15th and on the way up the rankings! But from 1960 it steadily declined until the fall of communism in 1989. 1990 was its lowest point. After 1990 Poland steadily rose up the rankings. It joined the EU in 2004 and the ascent slowed slightly. But clearly the thing that transformed Poland's economy was leaving the Soviet Union, not joining the European Union. Also Poland has not been damaged so much by EU membership as it is not in the Euro, and is a net recipient of EU funding.
Denmark (black) was on the up before joining in 1973, it then crashed 17 places.
Austria (green) was also on the up until it joined in 1995, then it crashed 6 places.
Romania (blue) declined under communism, revived after communism and has declined one place since joining.
Greece (magenta) has crashed 18 places since joining.
Finland (red) has crashed 12 places since joining.
Bulgaria (magenta) is similar to Romania, it declined under communism, revived after communism then fell two places since joining.
Portugal (black) dropped 9 places since joining.
Hungary (red) was steady for 34 years before joining, but dropped 10 places in the 16 years after.
Then **Ireland**! (in green obviously) The one country to totally buck the trend! On a rollercoaster, but up 24 places since joining! When the one country that is part of the Anglosphere does so much better than the countries that are not, we have to wonder whether it is membership of the Anglosphere that made the difference rather than membership of the EU.
Czech Republic (green) up 8 places in the 9 years before joining, and down 7 places in the 16 years after.
Slovenia (red) down 19 places since joining.
Slovakia (green) up 7 places in the 11 years before joining. No change in the 15 years after joining.
Croatia (black) down 3 since joining.
Luxembourg (blue) up 14 places, good. But it should be noted that Luxembourg started from a low point when the dataset began in 1970. Over the last 30 years as integration accelerated it has dropped 11 places.
Lithuania (blue) went up 18 places in the 9 years before joining. Went down 9 places in the 16 years after joining.
Cyprus (green) went up 19 places in the 34 years before joining. Went down 24 places in the 16 years after.
Latvia (black) up 38 places in the 12 years before joining and down 7 in the 16 years after.
Estonia (red) up 30 places in the 11 years before joining and down 2 in the 16 years after.
And finally **Malta** (blue) is still 2 places below where it was before joining.

The general approximate conclusions we can draw, from these empirical observations of many countries over many years, are as follows:

1, In virtually every instance EU member states are going down the rankings.
2, Membership of the block does not generate prosperity.
3, If there is any political event that has generated prosperity for the countries shown, it was leaving the Soviet Union, not joining the European Union.

It's all very very simple: as EU member states became less independent and less democratic, they became poorer. THEY'RE. GOING. DOWN.

2.2.2 Causation

Obviously, establishing causation is notoriously difficult in economics as we can never directly compare the effect of two different policies applied to the same people at the same time. But let's try to be as empirical as possible by contrasting many countries over a couple of decades. Here are two groups of countries:

Group A: India, Japan, South Korea, Canada, Australia, New Zealand, USA, Switzerland, Greenland, Iceland, Moldova.

Group B: France Germany, Italy, Spain, Belgium, Luxembourg, Greece, Portugal, Holland.

The Group A countries can directly elect representatives who can revise ANY law (re goods, services, labour or capital) so I call them 'independent democracies' Group B countries can't so I call them 'member states'. Over the last 20 years Group B countries have had about 9.5% unemployment and 1% GDP growth. That is worse than any of the Group A countries. When a pattern holds up this consistently over many countries over many years, it places the burden of proof on those who advocate us being a member state to explain why the greater success of Group A countries has nothing to do with their greater democratic control of their laws.

Above are two economic ignoramuses, George Osborne and Liz Truss in 2016 arguing that if we voted to leave, we would somehow be the first country in history to become more democratic AND less prosperous!

Conclusion
Overall it's hard to imagine a more clear-cut case for leaving. Before we joined we had balanced trade, higher wages, high GDP growth and low unemployment. After we joined, our trade balance collapsed, GDP growth declined 80% unemployment tripled, pay rises stopped; inequality increased and so did debt. EU supporters endlessly asserted that the EU had given the UK prosperity when it was clearly the other way round. We imported their goods which damaged our manufacturing base. We imported their unskilled labour which depressed wages, we imported their skilled labour (which was good but) which meant our employers could close their training schemes. And finally we paid ever increasing membership fees. And for what? To save a diminishing tariff on a diminishing number of exports! But all the while EU supporters swore blind it was the Brexiteers who were economically illiterate. They were stuck stuck stuck in an oxymoronic alternative reality in which we could somehow have the pre-admission flourishing society with the post-admission shit political system.

In the years after the vote to leave, despite the fact that we were governed by a manifestly incompetent and corrupt government, implacably opposed to making a success of Brexit, our economy slowly but surely debunked all of the ludicrous predictions of the Remainiacs. No one who values empiricism can read the above and ridicule the economic case for leaving. But of course, that is the whole point - the people we are dealing with are not empiricists.

2.3 EU don't like the vote
EU supporters are fundamentally opposed to democracy.

1, The apologists for the EU did everything they could to prevent us from having a referendum in the first place. When they could no longer prevent the referendum they complained it shouldn't have been allowed because it was 'destabilising'. Once they lost the referendum they marched through the streets calling for the result to be ignored.

2, When their march against democracy failed they proposed a 'second referendum' that was a sham: *"We the undersigned call upon HM Government to implement a rule that if the remain or leave vote is less than 60% based on a turnout of less than 75% then there should be another referendum"*. Britain's electorate is 46.8 million so a 75% turnout would be 35.1 million. 60% of 35.1 is 21.06 million. So according to their formula Leave could amass a record-smashing 21 million votes, but Remain would only require 14 million votes to keep their system in place! Or to put it another way – Leave could win by over 6.9 million votes but we still would not actually leave! So upon closer inspection the 'second referendum' EU supporters advocated was not an exercise in democracy at all, but a war against it, a pseudo-democratic travesty in which the method of counting was fixed to retain the existing system. They realised they didn't rig the vote enough the first time so they sought a re-run in which nothing was left to chance. They called it a 'people's vote' but it wouldn't be a meaningful battle of ideas at all, just a procession, after which no vote we ever cast again would be allowed to change any substantive issue. It was a campaign for authoritarianism masquerading as its antithesis.

Incidentally, The European Commission for Democracy Through Law (Venice Commission) has issued a code of good practice on referenda. Section 7.A states there should be no minimum threshold and 7.B states that referenda should be decided by a simple majority. So Remain's proposals for the second referendum contravened their own precious European rules!

3, The 'People's Vote' campaign was always coy about what actual question their referendum would ask. Sometimes they mooted the idea of a three-way choice, other times a two-stage questionnaire. Guess what? Both of those are also prohibited under the Venice Commission Code which requires a simple binary choice! When they finally confirmed what question they wanted put to the people, apparently it was to be a 'choice' between remaining in the EU … or continuing to be ruled by the EU under the terms negotiated by Theresa May. Being an independent country with democratic control over all our laws would not even be option under their proposals!

4, Why do you suppose Leave campaigned before the vote but Remain campaigned after? Because Leave respected democracy whereas Remain didn't.

5, For Leave it was all about the referendum where everyone could participate and every vote counted equally, whereas Remain constantly sought to move the process to smaller, less representative institutions like the High Court, the House of Lords, the Civil Service, Electoral Commission or Supreme Court because those bodies were stacked with unelected EU Stooges. They won where there was least democratic representation, we won where there was most.

6, When the UK is independent we can have whatever laws we like, laws identical to EU laws if we want. The only precondition will be that we will actually have to vote for them first. Why are Remainers so opposed to that? The answer is obvious – they favour laws that people wouldn't vote for. It is the democratic system *itself* they are opposed to.

7, Let's contrast the European Parliament and the European Commission. The Commission are appointees but they have the power to draw up laws, whereas the European Parliament is elected but only have the power to amend law. So it's like the Lords and the Commons but switched around – the elected chamber is subordinate to the appointed chamber. Why? Because the EU doesn't believe in the supremacy of democracy.

8, The EU removed democratically elected leaders from office in Greece and Italy.

9, Every referendum held specifically on membership of the Euro resulted in rejection, so it was simply imposed elsewhere without a referendum.

10, Treaties, laws and economic policies democratically rejected by the voters of France, the Netherlands, Denmark and Greece were imposed on them anyway. So for example, France and Holland rejected the European Constitution in a referendum so it was renamed the Lisbon treaty and imposed without one. Denmark rejected the Maastricht Treaty in a referendum but it was largely, gradually imposed anyway without referenda. Greece rejected the EU bailout in a referendum which was imposed anyway through coercion.

11, Countries in the Eurozone have no democratic control over monetary policy or interest rates.

12, Where does the opposition sit in the European Parliament? Nowhere. Because there isn't one. To be in the European Parliament is to participate in the project.

13, If the electorate in Single Market/Customs Union countries vote for better laws (re goods, services, labour or capital) the ECJ can simply strike down those laws.

14, Who did Ursula von der Leyen defeat in the election to become commissioner? No one. She was the only candidate!

15, There are five EU presidents, how many are elected by us? None.

16, Notice how powerful people in the EU are never voted *out* of office? Instead their term ends and they are succeeded by the next appointee, but democracy is never used to correct previous errors.

17, EU supporters mendaciously conflate voting with democracy when these are not the same thing. Democracy comes from two words: 'Demos' (people) and 'kratos' (rule), but it's perfectly possible for people to have votes whilst remaining powerless. Tyrannies rarely ban voting altogether. If we look at the Soviet Union under Stalin, China under Deng Xiaoping, Iran under Ayatollah Khomeini or Iraq under Saddam Hussein, we see these societies indeed held elections, but only on the precondition they were meaningless. What meaningful votes can the electorate in the EU hold? If the European Court of Justice (ECJ) think we have voted for a law that affects goods, services, labour or capital they can strike it down. And what law could not hypothetically be considered to affect those? So … er … we are free to vote for whatever we want … so long as the ECJ don't think it has anything to do with goods, services, labour or capital! The local councillors we elect are not permitted to alter any law regarding goods, services, labour or capital. Referenda results are not implemented if the people vote the wrong way. So what about national elections? Well, certainly within the UK the voting system is rigged to ensure small parties are permanently excluded; and the big parties generally only select EU stooges as candidates. Result? Hobson's choice. You can vote for whatever the hell you like so long as the existing order is completely unaffected. Under our pre-1973 system a little old lady could go into a voting booth, put an X in a box and overthrow the government. But after four decades of EU membership British voters had the same control over the EU that Hong Kong residents have over the Chinese Communist Party. None. The one time we voted for real change it quickly became obvious our 'democracy' had become a sham - there was a ruling elite who simply refused to implement the result. Obviously they sought to pass this off as procedural technicalities but it was nothing of the sort. Previous votes had only been implemented because we had been presented with a Hobson's 'choice' between more of the same or more of the same. The moment we voted to dispense with the existing system itself, those who profited from it revolted back. Shocked at our ingratitude they attacked the vote and the voters in every way imaginable. Apparently we were stupid, mad, evil, misinformed etc. We will be coming back to this later.

18, The EU's idea of confronting any problem is for the leaders of member states to meet and decide a common policy - Greek crisis, migration crisis, environmental crisis, Euro crisis etc. The negotiations duly take place (in secret) and the leaders then emerge to assure us they have haggled a terrific deal. Let's pretend this is actually true and they really have done a brilliant bit of negotiating. Whether they have negotiated a good deal or not is immaterial – it should be us telling them the policy not them telling us the policy! Why shouldn't we have a vote about those things? Their system is designed to explain rather than listen, it assumes things are improved by international talks rather than local actions. Does their system work? You tell me. How many of the above crises has the EU successfully resolved?

19, EU supporters have adopted a curious way of speaking which they use to convince themselves there is virtue in authoritarianism:

"The solution is to be more European" (Translation: 'the solution is to be less democratic').

"Populist" (Translation: 'democratic').

"Harmonise" (Translation: 'remove from democratic control').

"Align" (See 'harmonise').

"Dynamic alignment" (See 'harmonise')

"Level playing field" (Them ruling us).

"People's vote" (Something that permanently excludes people from having meaningful votes)

"Meaningful vote" (A vote that is meaningless if they don't like the result).

Conclusion
So we see EU supporters' contempt for democracy isn't just some isolated incident, it's not a freak blip, it's a default setting. At every turn they take the path that minimises the democratic control of the powerful.

In a good system the maximum number of people have the maximum democratic control over the maximum power. In a bad system the minimum number of people wield the maximum power in secret. I can prove that with the following statement: Democracy involves a larger number of stupid people in decision making than theocracy, bureaucracy, plutocracy or autocracy, but it *still* achieves better outcomes. Why? Because it involves more scrutiny of more power by more people. (This idea of publicly cross-checking will become important as we go on).

There are two types of nation on planet Earth: ones where the people tell the government what to do, and ones where the government tells the people what to do. The EU favours the latter. Their dream is for a Soviet / Islamic / Chinese style pseudo-democracy in which their superior values are projected on us inferior people, and voting only exists to confirm decisions already made by the ruling elite. They trot out lofty rhetoric about 'progressive values', but what tyrant in history hasn't claimed they were doing shit for the greater good? We are assured with a nudge and a wink that although the EU may have shortcomings, its lack of democracy is there to favour the good guys over the bad guys. Even if that were sincere, in practice it means that the person deciding who is good and bad - is king. The EU and the war against democracy are the same thing. To campaign for one is to campaign for the other.

2.3.1 Quick recap.
So the above two mini essays have been about economics and democracy, and I maintain there is a relationship between the two. When lots of people have lots of democratic control over lots of power they have lots of prosperity. Whereas when a small number of appointees exercise power in secret there is decline. I base this on many observations of many countries over many years. As the UK became increasingly integrated within the EU our votes became meaningless, so our economic decline continued. Similarly the decline of the EU is caused by the declining democratic control EU citizens have over laws. Specifically laws re goods, services, labour and capital. But that's the EU's problem; so far as the UK is concerned we should revert to the superior pre EU system because it's greater correlation of votes to power generated social improvement.

2.4 EU can't even argue
Now we come to the argument that Brexit was simply a mass irrational spasm. It was – by Remain! Here I want to look at the type of arguments Brexiteers and Remainers used, because they were fundamentally different, and to do that I need to talk about Karl Popper. I mentioned him before (in Part 1) but I want to recap here because I want to knock down each of the main arguments.

Karl Popper maintained that science is about falsification rather than confirmation; that knowledge is established by testing ideas. For example, Marxists always argued that theirs was a scientific analysis of history - everything that happened was determined by class struggle, so a workers' revolution was inevitable. But when the workers failed to revolt, rather than take this as a refutation of their theory Marxists suggested workers were victims of 'false consciousness' unable to see the situation as it truly was. Popper fulminated against this way of dealing with counter evidence, claiming it immunised Marxist hypotheses (which were originally testable) turning them into irrefutable pseudo-science. There was no conceivable observation that could prove they were wrong. If the workers revolted it showed the Marxists were right, if they didn't revolt it showed they were *still* right. It was win/win. An argument is unfalsifiable if lots of facts can support it, but no fact can disprove it.

Another example. What if I were to claim that we are about to have a recession? If the economy goes up then I can claim there is an economic bubble which vindicates my prediction; conversely if the economy goes down I can claim the downturn has already started. Again, it's win/win. Any fact can be cited as vindication of my prediction, whereas no fact can be said to refute it.

A forecast is just a guess about the future, and because the future doesn't exist yet it contains no facts that can be checked. So any argument based on a forecast is an argument without facts. Naturally it's tempting to make unfalsifiable arguments because they can't be disproved, but ultimately unfalsifiability is a weakness rather than a strength because theories that can't be tested are basically just opinions so they're not very useful; worse still because they appear scientific they can be used to give gravitas to opinions that might not deserve it. Karl Popper compared the theories of Marx, Freud, Adler and Einstein and concluded that only one of them presented theories that could be subjected to objective testing – Einstein.

So what on earth has that got to do with Brexit? Well, if we go through the various Remain arguments made during the Brexit referendum, guess what they all have in common? …

1, Vote Remain or there will be an economic crash.
2, Vote Remain or you will lose your job.
3, Vote Remain or there will be a war.
4, Vote Remain or you are racist.
5, Vote Remain or you won't be safe.
6, Vote Remain because it's trendy.
7, Vote Remain or there will be uncertainty.
8, Vote Remain or we will lose prestige/influence.
9, Vote Remain or we will lose our seat on the Security Council.
10, Vote Remain because Boris and Farage are evil.
11, Brexit could lead to spread of infectious diseases such as super-gonorrhoea (seriously!)

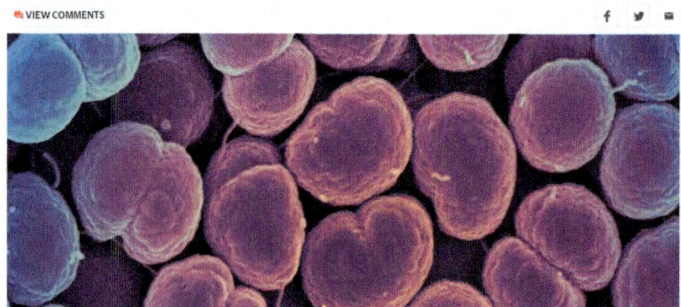

Spot the pattern? All those Remain arguments were either guesses about the future, opinions about people's character or appeals to our sentiment. There is no empirical observation I can make right now that could disprove any of the above. They were all unfalsifiable. Similarly 'We are worse off than if we had stayed' is a fallacy because it attempts to compare what can be observed with what can only be speculated.

No facts could substantiate the Remain claim that Britain would be worse off as an independent democracy, because no external body could give us better laws than we could write for ourselves. So instead of making a positive case for EU membership Remain relied entirely on character assassinations and predictions, which are unfalsifiable.

Now let's look at the main Leave arguments. Basically there were two, one geographical and one historical:

1, India, the USA, Canada, Australia, New Zealand, Japan, South Korea, Switzerland, Norway, Iceland and Greenland are independent democracies and they are doing pretty well. EU member states are not independent democracies and they are in decline. So we should become an independent democracy.

2, In the 40 years before the UK joined the EU we confronted fascism, defeated fascism, set up the NHS, set up the welfare state, set up the green belt, passed the Race Relations Act, the Equal Pay Act, the Clean Air Act, rebuilt our shattered cities, decriminalised homosexuality and abolished the death penalty. We had higher growth, higher wages, lower unemployment, lower inequality, lower debt, less waste and balanced trade. Our achievements in the 40 years *after* we joined are not comparable, so we should revert to the superior pre-EU system.

Now, whatever you think about the above two arguments my point is that any amateur could go onto Wikipedia and check to see if I was making it up. Some of them may be decent arguments, others less so, but they all involve talking about numbers, dates and events which actually exist and are observable. Brexit was falsifiable. If the Remain side had demonstrated, with facts, that more people having more democratic control over more power resulted in worse outcomes then Brexit would have been debunked. But they never did.

So superficially the Leave arguments tended to be amateurish and badly spelt, whereas the Remain arguments appeared professional and authoritative. But on closer inspection it was the Leave arguments that tended to involve empirical observation whereas the Remain arguments were deliberately uncheckable, conjectural pseudo-science. They asked us to take their forecasts on trust, we didn't, and sure enough all their lurid predictions turned to dust. They had been making it up all along. Why did Remain depend entirely on conjectural arguments? Reason was against them, so they turned against reason. For all their histrionics that we were irrational vandals, the reality was Brexiteers were simply advocating a mundane, benign system called 'democratic independence' that could be seen functioning pretty well around the world for decades.

Now let's flip it around and look at the empirical argument in another way. Let's pose three practical questions:

1, What good laws can't we have as an independent democracy?
2, How are independent democracies disadvantaged by their ability to vote for better laws?
3, Which countries became independent democracies and then declined?

If the Remain campaign had been empiricism-based they would have relentlessly addressed these points, but they never did. Bottom line - Leave said 'look', Remain said 'listen'.

Note: Often when I make this point I am told to drop it as apparently there are heaps of failed democracies in Africa, but which ones exactly? Which African country was an Arcadian paradise, which then introduced genuine open democracy, and consequently went down the pan? Names? And even if such a country does exist I doubt any downturn could be causally attributed to democracy. Still I am persuadable if the evidence is there, and being a

Brexiteer has taught me patience, so I look forward to eventually being given a factual counter-argument. Outside of Africa Haiti, Ukraine, Bosnia and Argentina have been suggested. The experience of the first thrFee suggests a correlation between war and decline, not democracy and decline. Regarding Argentina, it should be remembered that before 1983 critics of the Junta got pushed out of helicopters. The idea that pre-democracy Argentina was better doesn't have a lot going for it.

2.5 EU Believe
EU supporters regularly sought to portray Brexiteers as some sort of loony religious cult. On this issue Brexiteers didn't help themselves, often coming out with idiotic phrases like 'Believe in Britain' as if a lump of land sticking out of the sea was something we should worship.

But, when we look beyond these silly choices of words the astonishing thing was the extent to which the EU position was belief-based whilst the Brexit position was not.

In the above section about Karl Popper I argued that, for all the froth about 'Believe in Britain' the Leave position was actually pretty empirical. We could see that countries with democratic control over laws (about goods, services labour and capital) were doing well and that countries that didn't were not. And we could see that we were better governed before 1973 than we were after. We could see these things. With our eyes. It required no belief whatsoever. I admit, lots of Brexiteers prattled on about patriotism (I never did) but I suspect they were carelessly using 'patriotism' as a synonym for 'good government' they weren't really that bothered about Elgar, the Windsors or Trooping the Colour, they just wanted democratic control of power for fairly pragmatic reasons. But when we look at the EU side we see the opposite: A set of highly emotive arguments, but which were presented in a very business-like way.

1, Just like a religion Remain relied heavily on unfalsifiable arguments. Why didn't they make a positive factual argument for remaining? Because there wasn't one.

2, The EU flagellates itself with the Euro despite its obvious failure. They don't stick with it because of the empirical evidence - there isn't any - it's an article of faith.

3, Just like a religion the geniuses at the top direct the rabble. It is inconceivable to them that those at the top should listen to those at the bottom.

4, The EU parliament is not like the US congress where there are two opposing groups, it is more like a church where there are various different factions, each with their own outlook, but who are all ultimately committed to the same project.

5, The offer of the EU is a system in which a small number of ideologically pure appointees decide things in secret. We have a word for this type of institution: 'church'. Also note that failed leaders are never voted *out* of office, but superseded by appointment.

6, Just like a religion there is an elite who know better, their every utterance assumes moral superiority.

7, Naysayers are considered heretics, their arguments denounced as thought crimes.

8, When religion prospered, much of the mass was held in Latin which the peasants could not understand, the only parts that they could understand were the bits where they were told they were unworthy sinners who should seek redemption and listen to their enlightened betters. The Remain campaign bore uncanny similarities to this. They besieged us with incomprehensible gobbledygook about how the sky would fall down if we dared take control of our lives; the only part of their campaign intelligible to the layman was the bit about how those who disagreed were sinners; racist, far-right, bigots … and that redemption entailed submission to their rule.

9, Notorious atheist Christopher Hitchens would often argue with theists that there was no good action they could do as theists which he could not also do as an atheist. Brexiteers could make a similar point - that there was no good law the EU could give us that we couldn't vote to give ourselves. The EU position here was classic theism – to assume goodness comes from allegiance to a group rather than the way we conduct ourselves.

10, We have already seen that EU supporters think democracy is only legitimate when it confirms their prejudices. This was also the case with economics; when the economy did well it was claimed it was because Brexit hadn't happened yet, but when the economy did badly, apparently it was because we were about to fall off the edge of the world. Remainers had taken on the characteristics of a doomsday cult, endlessly spewing out Nostradamus-like claims that vindication was just around the corner 'any day now' they would say 'any day now'.
The Treaty of Rome was Genesis, The Commission were the saints, the Troika was the Trinity, Farage was the serpent, Remain were the virtuous, Leave were the sinners, Brexit was the original sin and Brex-pocalypse would be the Rapture.

11, Just like a religion, every action of the EU is designed to achieve one of two things: Increasing ideological domination, and expanding territorial domination. Brexiteers desired the opposite. Brexiteers wanted the will of the people to control the powerful institutions, and Brexiteers had no interest in seizing control of neighbouring territory.

12, Their conjectural arguments were prophecies.

13, Surely the most wonderful thing about being in government is the power to simply create fiat money from nothing. Who wouldn't want that? John Major. In a single day (06.09.92) his government spent £3.3 billion of government reserves in a desperate attempt to prevent the UK government from having any control over monetary policy. This is not normal behaviour, it is ideological fanaticism.

14, Just like a religion Remain sought to retain control by creating anxiety about what is unknown and unknowable:

15, In case c-274-99 the EU's Advocate General stated, "Criticism of the EU is akin to blasphemy and can be restricted without affecting freedom of speech". (Thanks to WP for bringing that one to my attention!)

"Brexit could be the beginning of the destruction of not only the EU but also Western political civilisation in its entirety." – Donald Tusk.

"The job you do, the home you live in are at risk." – David Cameron.

"A vote to leave would tip our economy into a year-long recession with at least 500,000 UK jobs lost." – George Osborne.

"Infectious diseases such as super-gonorrhoea could spread more rapidly if the UK leaves the European Union" This quote was attributed to 'health chiefs' by the London Evening Standard (Editor George Osborne) on 28.07.18 although no specific source was given.

…and a week before the referendum, the head of the (EU funded) IMF, Christine Lagarde, said the outcome of a decision to leave would range from "pretty bad to very very bad"

The above statements show a pattern. None of them appeal to reason or contain facts. All of them are emotive statements seeking to bring about a fearful, unthinking spasm of rejection. My point here is that going right back to Galileo and Spinoza it was essentially the same strategy believers have always used against empiricists: 'don't fuck with the established order you will burn in hell!'

Conclusion
So when Farage exhorted people to 'believe in Britain' it was a stupid move because Brexit was little more than a pragmatic choice to adopt a functional system. I don't need any belief in anything to see that more democracy is more good. But I <u>would</u> need belief to think less democracy is good – lots of it! So when Tony Blair called on EU supporters to 'rise up in defence of what we believe' it was the obvious argument for him to make. Of course he supported the EU because of his beliefs – no one would advocate membership on the basis of the evidence! And in the 2017 General election who was the most pro-EU national party leader? Tim Farron (Liberal Democrat and Neo-Christian) who throughout the campaign repeatedly refused to say whether he thought homosexuality was a sin. This was no coincidence; he was simply restating the standard position of the conservative religious right: he was a believer so he was for the belief-based system.

Brexit was a classic example of believers V empiricists…

Archbishop of Canterbury says second Brexit vote may be needed and brands no-deal a 'moral' failure

By **Steven Swinford,** DEPUTY POLITICAL EDITOR
9 January 2019 • 7:44pm

…well he always has believed that humanity should submit to omnipotent power…

2.6 Racism

In the Brexit debate, the most devastating argument put forward by EU supporters was that their opponents were racist. Brexit = racism is a weak argument for reasons I'm about to go through, but it's not a totally baseless argument because some Brexit supporters have indeed posted some disgraceful things that I have no interest in defending. So from the get-go I want to make clear that racism is totally unacceptable and must <u>always</u> be confronted. I want to take issue with bad arguments, not provide a shield for odious people to hide behind.

1, I advocate Britain being an independent democracy. If I hold that view it does not necessarily follow that I am racist. This is a point of basic logic. The former is about how laws are made and applied; the latter is about irrational hatred. Gandhi advocated independence for India. He was not racist. Tom Paine campaigned for American independence. He was not racist (Paine wrote *The Rights of Man* and campaigned against slavery all his life). So it's perfectly possible to be *against* racism and *for* living in an independent democracy, EU supporters are mischievously conflating two separate things.

2, A common argument I hear is 'there should be no borders' but every country has a border. If believing yourself to be a citizen of this or that country makes you racist then who is not guilty?

3, A similar argument I often hear is that nationalism = racism. But the EU is a nation. It has its own flag, anthem, currency, president, judiciary, legal system, parliament, border, Common Defence Policy and a fence in North Africa that Donald Trump would be proud of! EU supporters consider themselves to be citizens of a nation called the European Union. They are patriotic nationalists. So on closer inspection, the Remain argument is actually: "It is racist to want to be part of this or that nation – unless that nation is called the European Union."

Here is a picture of some EU supporters…

…but that's not nationalism right?

… and here are some angry patriots at the March for Europe…

…down with nationalism yeah?

Obviously a pro-EU supporter could produce equivalent disturbing images of Brexit demonstrations (not that we had many) but the point is these images are obviously and emphatically about nationalism. They represent pride, patriotism and a romanticised view of what they consider to be *their* country. These are values which EU supporters claim to reject, but somehow their passions have overwhelmed their ability to recognise nationalism in this instance.

4, During the referendum campaign EU supporters repeatedly claimed that if we voted for Brexit then we would 'lose influence' but what is 'influence' if it isn't the power to impose our will on outsiders? If EU supporters crave influence, then implicit in that is the assumption that we should desire some measure of control over others because we know what's best for them. Could there be a more illiberal argument?

5, EU supporters favour giving preferential treatment to 27 predominantly white European nations, whilst charging the Common External Tariff on imports from the poorest farmers in the world. Brexiteers don't.

6, Another common argument runs something like this: "Milo, Farage and Robinson are racist, they like Brexit, therefore Brexit is racist". This argument seems strong at first because (unlike most pro-EU arguments) it begins with empirical observation, but its fallacy lies in drawing general conclusions from specific examples. It's mixing up deductive and inductive reasoning. Inductive reasoning (from Francis Bacon) is about identifying general correlations to which there are some exceptions (e.g. winter is colder than summer) whereas deductive reasoning (from Aristotle) is about irrefutable truth (e.g. all men are mortal, Socrates is a man, therefore Socrates is mortal). For inductive reason to be valid it needs to be based on the broadest possible range of observations, not just one person's opinion about a few oddballs.

7, Does anyone really think the people who set up The Schengen Area (European free-movement area) had no racial agenda? That they were completely disinterested in race-based social engineering? How is it possible to be in favour of preserving indigenous cultures <u>and</u> have free movement?

8, When Europeans arrived in America, Australia and New Zealand, those places went from being monocultural to multicultural. It was a catastrophe for the indigenous peoples concerned. It is hypocritical (of both sides) to claim that free movement and multiculturalism were good in one instance but bad in another.

9, Remain referred to Brexiteers as 'gammon'. Gammon is cooked pink pig. The image that instantly springs to mind is Ray Winstone in the film Sexy Beast. A more blatant racial stereotype is difficult to imagine.

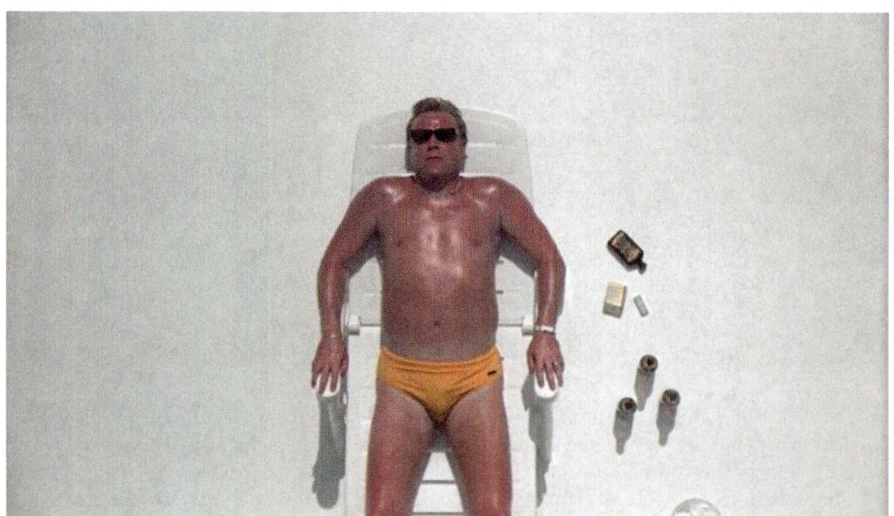

10, I advocate the British, Kurds, Palestinians and Tibetans all having their own homeland, and being able to democratically decide their own affairs. If you think only three of those four are entitled to that, then you need to explain how you're not making a race-based judgement of your own. Remainers appear to favour self-determination for every people that ever existed – except us.

11, So we see EU supporters have a tendency to see racism only where it confirms their own prejudices. Similarly they also have a tendency to be blind to racism when it doesn't confirm their prejudices. For example they never acknowledge that the murder of Lee Rigby, the Manchester bombing or the mass rape of girls in Telford, Rotherham and Rochdale could have been racially motivated. To campaign against racism and for your particular group is contradictory not complementary, the whole point is we should treat people equally.

So if I wanted to I could easily cobble together a fairly convincing argument portraying EU supporters as pantomime villains in exactly the same way they have done to us. But why waste your time and mine countering one dodgy argument with another?

The accusation of racism is 'scientifically unfalsifiable' which means it is easy to prove guilt but not innocence. For example – what if I were to wrongly accuse someone of racism? If they are seen helping someone of another race then I could claim it is a cunning ruse to conceal their inner depravity, but any odd choice of words or eccentric behaviour could be assumed to indicate guilt. So it's an easy accusation to make, and easy to prove, but virtually impossible to disprove. Consequently racism is an accusation that can be lazily rolled out against lots of people without much thought or evidence. Additionally the accuser appears to be a champion of decency, so what is to stop a mischievous person going round willy-nilly, accusing everyone who disagrees with them of racism? The answer is, not much. So they do.

Clive Lewis MP ✓
@labourlewis

Replying to @MrAlecMoss

I'm conflating nothing. Leave was an inherently right wing, deregulatory and racist project. If you can't accept that then there really is little to discuss?

8:01 AM · Mar 24, 2019 · Twitter for iPhone

951 Retweets   **334** Likes

I like Clive Lewis, he is in favour of a 'Green New Deal', proportional representation and abolishing the House of Lords, also he is against neoliberalism so I hoped he would win the Labour Leadership in 2020; but I take issue with him here. For Lewis, simply to accuse someone of racism is to win the argument. His opponent cannot win by proving they are not racist, and they certainly cannot win by proving that they are! And once their character has been besmirched it naturally follows that their opinion on anything else has no credibility either. There is 'little to discuss' unless we first admit racism? He has framed it so we either admit to being monsters or remain silent - it's win/win for Lewis! Obviously he won't see this as a problem at all, but I do because he is seeking to pre-emptively silence legitimate counter-argument; and he is basing it on his opinion of others. It's an authoritarian argument dressed up as an ethical argument. Worse still, by casting this allegation around so carelessly, he risks making us numb to the seriousness of racism. Lost the argument? Lost the vote? Short of facts? Never mind, just trot out the 'R' word and you are a hero. This isn't the way to a better world.

So what are we to do? Because racism does exist, it demeans us all, and we must be able to confront it without getting tangled in a miasma of existential doubt. I suppose I'm just asking for everyone to draw a deep breath, to accept that we all bring a certain amount of baggage to this issue, and to not use this serious accusation to silence legitimate debate. The question must be firmly repeated: 'Why do you think one person should be treated differently to another?'

Note: Incidentally Lewis' claim that Brexit was a deregulatory project bit the dust when, just weeks after leaving, Johnson introduced regulations that had hitherto would have seemed unimaginable. During the Covid pandemic the government introduced a lockdown, regulating how many people could meet in public. Was it strict? My auntie Jackie died and only 16 people were allowed to attend her funeral! Call that a 'deregulatory project'? Additionally, when it comes to Brexit Lewis seems to be for the few not the many.

2.7 EU didn't give us peace

One of the key arguments for the EU was that it had given us peace. There are several objections to this:

1, In 1940 there were 106 countries in the world, today there are 195. As the number of countries increased, obviously political union has declined accordingly. Have nationalist wars increased over that period? No. Over the last 80 years planet Earth has gone from the most nationalist wars ever to the fewest nationalist wars ever. The EU argument is that political union generates peace, but if that were the case then as the number of countries increased, we would expect the amount of war to increase accordingly, but precisely the opposite has happened. So if we look at the empirical evidence of the whole world over the last century, the patterns suggest that independent democracies generate peace, not war, and that political union generates war not peace. Or to put it another way, a small number of large countries generates more war than a large number of small countries.

2, The Second World War ended in 1945. In 1957 six countries signed the Treaty of Rome, there are now 27 countries in the EU. There are 50 countries in Europe. Yet the EU claims credit for <u>all</u> the peace enjoyed by <u>all</u> of Europe since 1945! So they are claiming credit for developments outside the EU geographically, and before the EU historically.

3, What about the ethnic cleansing in former Yugoslavia which the EU simply allowed to happen? Or the mass murders in Paris, Brussels and Manchester? Call that peace? Do those deaths somehow not count? Are we not discussing that particular *genre* of mass murder today? Here is a picture of the civil war in France.

... but ... but ... that's 'peace' right? In London in 2018 one person is being stabbed to death every three days. Call that 'peace'? At the time of writing there is at least one bomb/hand grenade attack in Sweden every 3 days. But that's peace? What is war about? It is surely about the total suppression and domination of people. Well sorry, but that is precisely what just happened in Greece and Catalonia. Wasn't the whole point of the EU to prevent the powerful imposing themselves on the weak? Again, that's exactly what's happening. In order to make their claims, EU supporters use highly selective definitions of 'peace' and 'war' that exclude any facts that don't confirm their prejudices.

4, In Kenneth Waltz's '*Theory of International Politics*' he argues "The most destructive wars of the hundred years following the defeat of Napoleon took place not among states but within them … Estimates of deaths in China's Taiping Rebellion … range as high as 20 million. In the American Civil War some 600,000 people lost their lives. In more recent history, forced collectivization and Stalin's purges eliminated five million Russians, and Hitler exterminated six million Jews." Yes to place these conflicts wholly in the domestic realm is questionable, but no more questionable than conflating war with nationalism.

5, "The world of tomorrow is a world of empires in which we Europeans, and you British, can only defend your interests, your way of life, by doing it together, in a European framework and in the European Union." - Guy Verhofstadt. Here Verhofstadt is making no attempt to conceal his desire for an empire. He wants his empire to govern us, and to increase in size and power. When is he against the domination of the weak by the strong? When it's by someone else! Incidentally he made the above statement at the Liberal Democrat conference in the UK in 2019 and was cheered by the delegates. When is a liberal democrat not a liberal democrat? When they are a Liberal Democrat! Also, notice how he is deliberately conflating 'defending our way of life' with membership of a club committed to the annihilation of our way of life?

6, If the EU gave us peace then why do we live in fear? Why the terror of speaking out? Why were their arguments fear-based?

7, EU supporters conflate nations with war and political union with peace, but wars are no longer about nationhood – they're about religion. In the mercantilist age nations had wars to get rich (to loot their neighbour's wealth) but today going to war is very expensive, so it makes nations poorer not richer, consequently over the last 75 years war between nations has declined globally. Here is a map from Wikipedia (2017) showing the ongoing conflicts of the world.

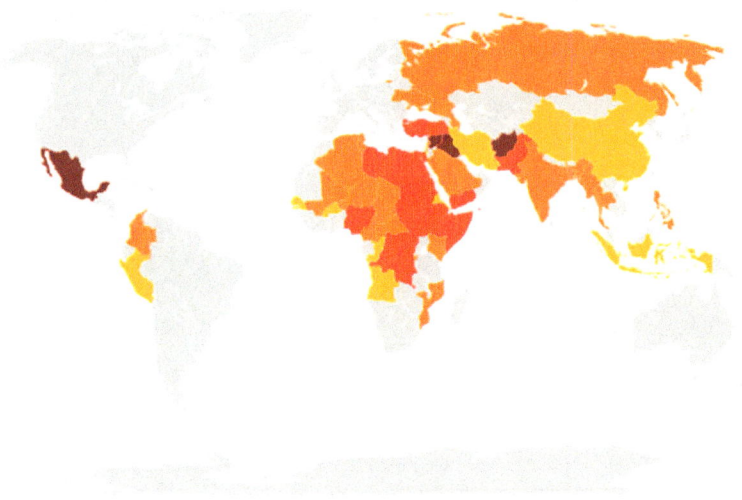

…and here is a map showing all the Islamic territories in the world:

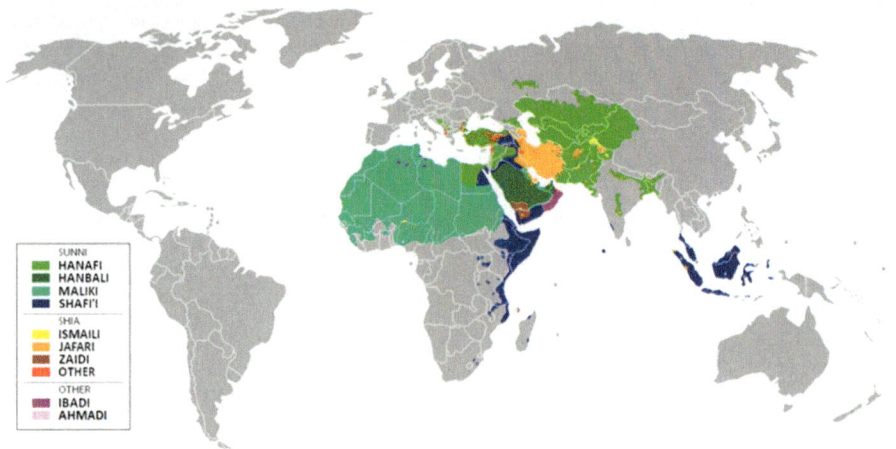

We see there is an approximate correlation between the two maps. This correlation becomes even more obvious when we consider that the conflicts Russia and China are involved in are largely to do with where they border with Islamic states. Now here is the same information expressed as a list of conflicts in which more than 100 people were killed in the last 12 months (as of summer 2017).

Over 10,000 deaths:
War in Afghanistan.
Mexican Drug War.
Syrian Civil War
Iraqi Civil War

1000 – 9,999 Deaths:
Kurdish / Turkish conflict.
Somali civil war.
Communal conflicts Nigeria.
Darfur / Sudan.
Boku Harem insurgency.
Libyan civil war.
Yemeni civil war.
Sinai insurgency Egypt.
South Kordofan conflict / Sudan.
Sudan / Ethiopia conflict.

100 – 999 Deaths:
Kashmir conflict.
Balochistan conflict (Pakistan / Iran).
Internal conflict Myanmar.
South Thailand insurgency.
Insurgency in North East India.
Israeli / Palestinian conflict .
Colombian conflict.
Naxalite insurgency India.
Moro conflict Philippines.
Cabinda war, Angola.
Armenia / Azerbaijan.

Sectarian conflict Pakistan.
Internal conflict Bangladesh.
Oromo conflict Ethiopia.
Ogaden conflict Ethiopia.
Congo insurgency.
Algeria / Tunisia.
Congo / Burundi.
War in North West Pakistan.
Sudanese nomadic conflicts.
Insurgency North Caucasus.
Central African Republic conflict.
Northern Mali Conflict.
Insurgency in Egypt.
Renamo Mozambique.
Donbass / Ukraine.
Burundian unrest.
Turkey / Islamic State.

You will notice I have given these different colours. I have coloured red each conflict in which one side is seeking to make more territory more Islamic. I have coloured in blue all the conflicts where Islam does not seem to be a contributing factor. In that year there were 42 ongoing armed conflicts. 36 of these (and most of the biggest wars) involved a set of belligerents fighting for an Islamic cause. If we take those out of the equation, then the biggest war in the world was the Mexican drug war (which isn't about nationalism). So religion and drug trafficking are factors in the 34 bloodiest conflicts in the world; the biggest war that's about nationalism (number 35) is the Ukrainian conflict (in Europe).

Obviously conflicts by their very nature are in constant flux, and by the time you read this some of the above will have diminished whilst others will have escalated, but the point is that, although it represents only 23% of the human race, this particular religion is a factor in 85.7% of the world's conflicts, and 36 of the worst 42. At the time of writing a string of countries stretching from Nigeria to China are involved in ongoing armed conflicts. Muhammad was the leader of an army, and it's only natural that a belief system written by a soldier should be inclined towards the domination of territory. Sure enough conflicts seem to occur where the philosophy of the soldier predominates. And of course it doesn't take much imagination to see these, not as separate conflicts at all, but as separate skirmishes in a single intergenerational, international religious war against the rest of humanity. For example, in your society, where is there the most war? In the rural areas where there are the fewest police? Or where the philosophy of the soldier predominates?

To summarise:
1, The EU are claiming to have saved us from nationalist wars, but nationalist wars have been declining worldwide for the last 80 years. Generally, today wars are caused by belief not nationalism.

2, The EU are claiming political union generates peace, so how come as political union has declined over the last 80 years the world has fewer military conflicts? Generally, today peace is caused by reason, not political union.

There is a final point I would like to make before moving on to less depressing subjects. In the mercantilist age we bought and sold stuff, commodities and resources had value, so there was a motive to extend borders. In the modern age we buy and sell information so there is no reason to extend borders outwards. That's why border disputes have declined, nothing to do with political union. Unfortunately looking at it through this prism it could also be argued that Europe's attempt to take over

Britain never really ended, it simply shifted from being an industrial war 80 years ago to being an information war today.

2.8 EU are Conservative
EU supporters sought to *conserve* the current system. Even the two words 'Leave' and 'Remain' demonstrate my point - one is about change, the other is about not changing.

Remain wanted to extend the transition period, stay under EU rule, retain the maximum number of EU laws, stay in the Single Market and remain under the ECJ. Any change they could not prevent they fought to make as small and as slow as possible. The word we use to describe this sort of behaviour is ... 'conservative'. But Remain weren't just conservative because they sought to conserve the existing condition – they were conservative because the system they sought to retain was itself specifically designed to have no reverse gear.

Naturally we all wish to conserve the good and dispense with the bad, so conservatism isn't necessarily bad when it's the conservation of good things like rainforests. The architects of the EU considered their project to be good. It therefore followed that the more power the EU had, the better everything would be; and that relinquishing that power would be bad. And naturally, it's important to have a system that prefers the good to the bad right? So a highly complex structure was established which had the appearance of being democratic and rules-based, but which had the ability to switch between being radical in its seizure of power, and conservative in its relinquishing of power. So when Denmark voted against the Maastricht Treaty, France voted against the EU constitution or Greece voted against austerity no ground was given, but when opportunities arose to seize control of countries, suddenly the project was the opposite of conservative, and advanced very efficiently (Common defence policy, expansion of 1994 etc). Of course Europhiles won't consider this to be a problem at all, because for them there is moral virtue in a system impervious to democratic errors. But once a system has been created that can disregard votes it considers to be wrong, what if there is a problem with the system itself? If advancing the project is considered to be the same as being good, how do we condemn a bad event that advances the project? or acknowledge a good event that doesn't? And once implementing votes has become optional, what objective measure could the EU check itself against to determine whether it's succeeding? Comparative debt levels? Unemployment levels? Inequality, lifespans, birth-rates or pollution levels? Well no, none of those would be valid, because for the EU, to succeed is to integrate.

So with the best will in the world a type of neo conservatism (in the Burke-ian sense) has been established. The EU is a self-conserving, democracy-proof labyrinth, which cannot appraise itself because to simply exist is to be good. But conservatism is only good when it conserves the good (polar ice caps and wildlife etc) when people seek to conserve a system without democratic oversight of power it is a thing to be confronted.

2.9 EU didn't give us human rights
Remainers endlessly claimed that the EU lavished us with lots of wonderful human rights, but if human rights are about anything they are surely about people not having to submit to rules they didn't vote for, passed by people we didn't vote for, sitting in an institution we actually voted to leave! But this was precisely the abuse of human rights the EU supporters were happy to embrace.

Article 1 of the UN Covenant of Civil and Political Rights states: 'All peoples have the right of self-determination. By virtue of that right they freely determine their political status and freely pursue their economic, social and cultural development.'

Why do EU supporters disagree with that? If EU supporters gave a crap about human rights then why were they utterly opposed to us 'freely determining our political status and our economic, social and cultural development'? External rule was imposed on us against our will, and the perpetrators had the audacity to masquerade as champions of human rights!

(Guardian. Patrick Stewart sketch: What has the ECHR ever done for us?)

Just before the 2016 referendum the Guardian made a short film in which Patrick Stewart played a foul-mouthed nationalist bigot who asks: 'What has the European Convention on Human Rights ever done for us?' The answer comes: "the right to a fair trial … the right to privacy … freedom from torture and degrading treatment … freedom of religion … freedom of expression … freedom from discrimination … freedom from slavery … domestic violence … and freedom from torture." If you want to sneer at people for being ignorant of the facts, it's generally advisable to check the facts yourself before sneering. Here I will go through how the UK enjoyed those rights prior to the ECHR being incorporated into UK law in 1998:

The Right to a Fair Trial.
The 39th clause of Magna Carter (1215) gives all 'free men' the right to justice and a fair trial. This was extended by the Habeas Corpus Act of 1679.

The Right to Privacy.
Privacy is a broad term so by its very nature is difficult to define. There is no single privacy law in the UK, instead it was covered by several acts of Parliament. The earliest example I can find of British law protecting someone's privacy was Thompson v Stanhope (1774) which granted an injunction preventing the publication of private letters. This case was followed by various others, and by the mid-twentieth century the modern tort of 'breach of confidence' was established.

The Theft Act (1968) made blackmail a crime.

The Protection from Harassment Act (1997) created both criminal sanctions and civil remedies for harassment.

Freedom from Torture.
English common law has always, in principle prohibited the use of torture. Indeed one of the distinguishing features of English common law writing from its inception was its rejection of torture as a method of proof, and the House of Lords has accepted that this can properly be said to be a defining characteristic of English common law, and as such a true constitutional principle.

Freedom from Degrading Treatment.
The English Bill of Rights criminalised 'cruel and unusual punishments' in 1689.

Freedom of Religion.
The 'Declarations of Indulgence' were a pair of proclamations made by James II of England (VII of Scotland) in 1687 and 1688. It was the first step in establishing freedom of religion in the British Isles.

Freedom of Expression. (See also later section on Foucault)
Free expression is a very broad subject which encapsulates many aspects of life. Whilst none of Magna Carta's clauses make reference to free expression, by curbing royal powers and strengthening individual protection they extended liberties to the 'freeman of England'.

In the civil war (1642-51) the Levellers used early print technology to produce pamphlets. One of them William Walwyn petitioned in 1647 that 'no man for preaching or publishing his opinion on religion in a peaceable way, may be punished or persecuted as heretical by judges'.

The 1689 Bill of Rights granted free speech for MPs in the confines of Parliament.

Between 1765 and 1769 Sir William Blackstone published his landmark common law texts stating that any book or pamphlet need not be subject to prior approval by a government before it was published, but that if it contained 'improper, mischievous or illegal' words the author could be prosecuted thereafter.

In 1872 the Government introduced the Parks Regulation Act that gave people the legal right of 'public address' at Hyde Park.

From Thomas Paine's The Rights of Man, right up to DH Lawrence's Lady Chatterley's Lover the state has often sought to censor certain types of expression, and even today 'hate speech' is a crime, however as publication has become easier, censorship has been abandoned incrementally. Admittedly this is as much to do with the impossibility of enforcement as the passing of any specific law, however many UK courts in the 1980s and early 1990s were already applying a free speech principle in many common law cases such as libel, and saw it as their duty where possible, to maintain free speech. So even before the HRA (Human Rights Act) judges were willing to provide legal protection for what they saw as the foundational tenets of free speech.

Freedom from Discrimination.
Discrimination is obviously a very broad term and over the centuries we have passed several laws prohibiting many types of it:
The Papists Act (1778) addressed discrimination against Catholics.
The Reform Act (1867) gave the vote to every male householder irrespective of race or religion.
The Representation of People Act gave women equal voting rights (before France, Spain or Italy and slightly before Germany in 1918).
Britain passed the Race Relations Act in 1965.
Britain decriminalised homosexuality in 1967.
Britain passed the Equal Pay Act in 1970.
Britain passed the Sex Discrimination Act in 1975

Freedom from Domestic Violence.
The Married Woman's Property Act (1870) meant any money earned or inherited by a woman while married stayed hers.

The Matrimonial Causes Act (1878) made it possible for women in the UK to seek legal separation from an abusive husband.

The Matrimonial Causes Act (1923) allowed divorce on the grounds of adultery for women as well as men.

The Sexual Offences Act (1956) extended the definition of rape to include incest, sex with a girl under 16 and the use of drugs.

The 1976 Domestic Violence and Matrimonial Proceedings Act specifically addressed domestic violence and gave survivors new rights, by offering civil protection orders.

The 1977 Housing Act acknowledged women and children at risk of violence as homeless and therefore entitled to state-funded temporary accommodation.

In 1991 Marital Rape was criminalised.

The Family Law Act Part IV (1996) gave police automatic powers of arrest where violence had been used or threatened.

Abolition of Slavery.
Somerset V Stewart 1772 bestowed freedom on any slave once they set foot on British soil.
Britain passed the Slavery Abolition Act in 1833.

The film ends with an enlightened expert explaining to Stewart:

"…After the war British legal experts did draft a bill of human rights to help Europe sort itself out, you know, to help protect people from abuses of state power, that kind of thing…it's called the European Convention on Human Rights…" Defeated, Patrick Stewart then explodes into a quivering mass of idiocy and everybody laughs at him. But hold on … here the film makers have shot their own fox by admitting that _we_ wrote _their_ human rights laws!

Basically the film was propaganda seeking to establish a lie that the EU bestowed human rights on us. But as usual, when we drop the hysteria and check the facts, we find, actually, once again, it's the other way round.

2.10 EU Capitalists
The popular misconception about Brexit was that those in favour were 'the Right' and those against were 'the Left'. That was a narrative that EU supporters worked hard to establish, because it was much easier to induce an unthinking spasm of rejection by depicting someone as 'far-right' than by depicting them as 'far-left'. Unfortunately, leading Brexiteers (if you accept that we actually had leaders) walked right into this trap. Time and again Farage and Johnson screwed up our campaign by saying that we had to get out of the EU in order to implement some type of Thatcherite agenda and reduce immigration. Remain supporters were not being unfair when they pointed this out.

There are two things I would say in response. Firstly if we have democratic control over laws (about goods, services, labour and capital) then who is to say we won't vote for left-wing laws? We did before 1973. In the 40 years _before_ 1973 socialism was triumphant, in the 40 years _after_ 1973 Capitalism was triumphant. And yet Remainers insisted that reverting to the pre '73 system would somehow result in more post '73 legislation! Farage and Johnson stupidly conflated Brexit with a Thatcherite agenda because they assumed there was political capital in it, and maybe because they really did think they were the same thing; but in doing this they were making exactly the same mistake that many Remainers made – confusing _how_ laws were made with _what_ laws were made. The second point I would make is that a subjective opinion about the character of a couple of eccentrics is hardly a good basis for choosing a political system for the long term.

Instead of looking specifically at the character of this or that politician, why not look generally at the capitalist and Marxist organisations? Every Marxist organisation in the country was for Brexit: The Morning Star, The Communist Party, The Socialist Party, The Communist Party of Britain Marxist Leninist, Sp!ked (formerly Living Marxism) and the Socialist Workers Party. Yes the TUC were for the EU but that is easy to explain - the EU funded them. Now let's look at the Capitalists. The CBI was for Remain, as was the Bank of England, the Chambers of Commerce and the Department of Trade and Industry. Yes the Bruges Group (Thatcher fan club) was for Brexit but again that is easy to explain – they were against a political system that delivered crappy levels of growth and high unemployment.

Now let's look at the class makeup of the vote. According to an Ipsos MORI poll on the 5th September 2016 it was as follows:

Class	Remain	Leave
AB	54	46
C1	51	49
C2	35	65
DE	36	64

Overwhelmingly it was the lower classes who voted leave and the upper classes who voted remain. But here I am just saying who was in each camp when the important point is why were they so aligned.

Generally Marxists supported Brexit not because Marxism is right or Brexit is wrong, but because Marxists had sufficient confidence in their arguments to assume that, any system which gave more control of more power to more people had to be good. Conversely the neo-liberals, bosses and super rich were opposed to Brexit because they favoured a plutocracy in which goods, services, labour and capital could be moved independent of inconvenient democratic events. They had prospered under the existing condition so naturally assumed that the existing condition was benign and meritocratic, so why change it?

Here are some quotes from some of the leading left-wing commentators at the time.

"The left wing case for Brexit is strategic and clear. The EU is not - and cannot become a democracy. Instead it provides the most hospitable ecosystem in the developed world for renter monopoly corporations, tax-dodging elites and organized crime. It has an executive so powerful it could crush the left wing government of Greece; a legislature so weak that it cannot effectively determine laws or control its own civil service. A judiciary that...subordinated workers' right to strike to an employer's right to do business freely. Its central bank is committed, by treaty to favour deflation over growth. State aid to stricken industries is prohibited ... austerity...is written into the EU treaty as a non-negotiable obligation."
-Paul Mason. Guardian 16.05.16

"the Euro is such an insanely right-wing project it is a wonder British Tories aren't endorsing it ... Europe brings peace. Is that so? It is becoming obvious that you cannot have the economics of the Great Depression without having the politics of the Great Depression."
-Nick Cohen, Spectator 06.07.15

"The EU and its basic treaties and institutions ... were designed to serve big business and minimise the potential for democratic intervention by national governments or parliaments in favour of the people against profits."
-Morning Star editorial (Ben Chacko) Jan 2015

Neoliberalism is hardwired into the Lisbon Treaty. The EU is adamant that no democratic event should impede the movement of goods, services, labour or capital. A more insanely right-wing arrangement is difficult to imagine.

As we all know, Marx claimed that the revolution would involve the proletariat seizing control of the means of production; and all through my life this seemed a pretty fanciful notion, conjuring up images of scruffy students storming B&Q or chaining themselves to the NatWest. But hold on a minute, what do todays workers actually produce? The chances are you and most of the people you know don't actually produce physical stuff like cars, ships, steel or coal - you sell your skill, not your stuff. Maybe you are a graphic designer, a structural engineer, a hairdresser or a teacher. Most people today buy and sell their knowledge. So in the modern world the Marxist revolution would be one in which the proletariat seized control of the means of producing information. But that's exactly what has just happened with Twitter and Facebook! Isn't it strange that the moment ordinary people could freely disseminate information with their phones on the internet a political earthquake took place! There is a serious argument to be made that Brexit *was* the Marxist revolution, but that everyone was so anxious to deride it as being right-wing that they missed it!

There is another argument I would like to include here which was suggested to me by Will Podmore. It is this: The arguments Remain used against Brexit closely resembled arguments by capitalists against socialists: working class movements were not based on workers' genuine needs and demands but derived only from cynical manipulation by corrupt and demagogic elites ('trade union bosses', dastardly extremists etc)

2.11 EU are the far-right
For the last 5 years EU supporters have manically sought to depict Brexiteers as 'the far-right' as if repeating a falsehood often enough would somehow make it true.

The real far-right impose crushing austerity. The real far-right are for a system that delivers mass youth unemployment. The real far-right are neoliberals. The real far-right are for a system that reduced wages. The real far-right are the ones who seek to insulate power from democracy at every turn. The real far-right propose sham referenda where the outcome is rigged. The real far-right have 'elections' with only one candidate. The real far-right think our votes should be meaningless as a tiny elite of ideologically pure appointees decide things in secret. The real far-right employ gobbledygook terminology to exclude the maximum number of people from the debate. The real far-right advance their system through small secretive bodies stacked with appointees. The real far-right base their positions on belief rather than empiricism. The real far-right seek to shut down legitimate debate with accusations of thought crimes. The real far-right seek to retain power through fear and psychological abuse. The real far-right attack people rather than ideas. The real far-right deny the correlation between belief and war. The real far-right crave the expansion of territory and the extension of their powers. The real far-right favour preferential trading terms for 27 predominantly white European nations. The real far-right discriminate against the poorest farmers in the world with their 'Common External Tariff'. The real far-right crave influence over their neighbours. The real far-right desire an empire. The real far-right delineate borders on the basis of ideology rather than geography. The real far-right seek to conserve a conservative system. The real far-right are against our human right to democratically determine our laws. The real far-right are against a return to the political system that defeated fascism and set up the National Health Service and Welfare State. The real far-right are against returning to the system that passed the Clean Air Act, the Race Relations Act, set up the Green Belt, passed the Equal Pay Act, decriminalised homosexuality and abolished the death penalty. The real far-right are for the system that increased unemployment, pollution, debt, terrorism and inequality. The real far-right presided over the re-criminalisation of blasphemy and the decriminalisation of bigamy. The real far-right invite the advance of an Islamic religion that is anti-gay, creationist, patriarchal, mercantilist, supremacist, mono-cultural, expansionist, censorious, authoritarian, socially conservative, coercive and segregated. The real far-right want to stick with a system that has militarised our police and increased powers of surveillance. The real far-right are *against* the lower classes and *for* the elite. The real far-right want to stick with a system that has monetised everything. The real far-right assert their moral superiority over their inferiors. EU supporters were everything they claimed to reject. They claimed to be progressive but how exactly is it possible to 'progress' to an undemocratic, conservative, neo-liberal, nationalistic, theocracy that imposes its will through fear?

Conversely although Brexiteers were derided as 'the right' (and often, stupidly accepted this caricature) but when we look at the empirical reality, again, it's the other way around.

Brexiteers were generally the lower classes whereas Remainers were generally the upper classes. Brexiteers were the outsiders, whereas Remainers controlled the established order. Brexiteers were against a political system that depressed wages. Brexiteers were against discriminatory tariffs on the poorest farmers in the world. Brexiteers sought a return to the system that pioneered human rights. Brexiteers wanted more people to have more democratic control of more power, whereas at every fork in the road Remainers chose what would insulate the most power from the most voters. Brexiteers sought control of the executive by the people, Remain sought control of the people by the executive. Brexiteers were empiricists, they wanted a return to a pre-1973 system that could be seen to work whereas Remainers were a religion who believed external rule was virtuous despite the evidence. (When Remainers sought to be empirical they tried to draw general conclusions from specific examples - Johnson is amoral, Farage is evil etc). Brexiteers could see the parallels between less democracy and worse laws, whereas Remainers constantly conflated bad laws with a good system and good laws with a bad system. Brexiteers were radicals who wanted to adopt a functional system, Remainers were conservatives who sought to retain a failed system. Brexiteers wanted to control their locality democratically, whereas Remainers sought expanding control over neighbouring territory through coercion. Remain claimed to be for free speech but in reality sought to halt all debate with state sponsored propaganda consisting of psychological abuse and hysterical conjecture (see also later section on Foucault and 'normalising power'). I could go on, but you get the picture. After losing the referendum Remain supporters manically repeated the phrase 'lurch to the right' like a mantra, but by every conceivable measure the real 'lurch to the right' happened during our EU membership.

The great genius of the EU was its ability to pass itself off as its antithesis. The EU is a nationalist project that claims to reject nationalism, a neo-capitalist project that claims to be for the common man. They are the polluters who pass symbolic environmental laws. The haters of indigenous cultures who claim to reject racism. The practitioners of 'power-play' who claim to have a 'rules-based' system. The 'democrats' who decide things in secret and isolate power from democratic oversight. The 'defenders of human rights' who impose external rule in Greece, Italy, Catalonia and the UK. The 'rules-based open society' who bribe their useful idiots to campaign for external rule. The EU are the far-right that got away with it.

We have been attributing nouns like 'left' and 'right' on the basis of solipsistic emotional responses, but when we attribute them on the basis of sound empirical observation, again and again we see that actually, it's the other way round.

Overall it is hard to imagine a social conflict that's more of a clear cut case of left against right than Brexit, with the Brexiteers being the left and Remain being the right. And yet despite all this, monolithically society seemed determined to see Brexit as the opposite of what it really was. Naturally there will be many who say that, no, it is I who have things the wrong way round. So how should an independent reasonable person choose between us? I would say by maximising empiricism, by looking <u>out</u> to the experiences of many countries over many years rather than by looking inwards at beliefs and values. After all, if you base your argument on belief how are we to know whether your statement of beliefs is sincere? Or even if it is sincere, that it is not mistaken?

2.12 Brex-cellent Style
Before closing this section out I just want to make a few points about the manner in which I wrote the last few chapters.

1, I tried to write as clearly as possible and didn't try to bamboozle you with obscure technical arguments about things like trade contracts.
2, The graphs tended to use the maximum possible time frame to avoid being misled by a specific incident.
3, The geographical areas I looked at were as broad as possible for the same reason.
4, I tried to say what I thought <u>and</u> why I thought it.
5, I championed a system not because it would benefit me specifically but everyone generally.
6, The reader may have been impressed by some arguments and unimpressed by others, but all of them were empirical and checkable so any amateur could see if I was making it up. There were no predictions and no attempts to compare what could be observed with what could only be speculated about. I tried to avoid statements of belief.
7, It wasn't a sneer-a-thon.
8, At no point did I appeal to patriotism or national pride.
9, I tried to avoid appealing to the reader's sentiment/values.
10, My arguments flowed from the outside to the inside. I looked at what worked and what hasn't worked in lots of countries over several decades and was persuaded by that.
11, I didn't accuse people who disagree with me of being sub-human racists.
12, I didn't prove anything conclusively because I argued using patterns, and however consistent a pattern is, there is always a chance it could be a coincidence. So, I aimed to provide high probability rather than absolute certainty. This type of approach was formalised by Francis Bacon (the scientist not the painter) and it's called 'inductive reasoning' but to minimise academic jargon I'll call it 'patterns'.

2.13 Patterns
In the mini-essays above I've gone through the main arguments, but of course there were others I could have mentioned such as 'Russia rigged it'.

Note: This was a particularly fanciful argument. On the flimsiest evidence imaginable, Remain conspiracy theorists claimed Putin was the puppet master and that the Kremlin had brainwashed us. This could have been humoured were it not for the fact that the EU were openly doing everything Remainers claimed Russia was doing covertly. An external power had seized control of our society, placed its stooges in every conceivable position of political power, seized control of our money and state broadcaster, bought off its critics, and was employing psychological abuse on a national scale to consolidate its control. Remainers refused to see foreign interference that was staring them in the face but imagined it where it did not exist.

Anyway, obviously I am always going to argue that I am right, and the other side are going to do the same, but I want to pause and take an overview here because I think there is something deeper and more profound going on. In each of the previous chapters I identified a pattern, but now I want to step back and look to see if there is a pattern <u>of the patterns themselves,</u> and I think there is. In each of the previous chapters we see that the accusation being levelled by the Remainers was actually true of themselves. They said membership made us prosperous, but it was the other way round. They said the EU gave us rights, but it was the other way round. They said we were the far-right but it was the other way round. Their claim that we were racist was itself based on prejudices. They claimed Brexit was an emotional spasm when the really big emotional spasm was their own! We were simply advocating a system that had been proven to work across the world for decades. They claimed their war on democracy was a 'People's Vote'. And so on. Again and again when I looked at the empirical reality I found it was the opposite of the narrative being presented. The arguments against Brexiteers consistently involved inverting adjectives.

Why the consistent pattern of antithetical arguments? Why was it that again and again the adjectives used were precisely the opposite of the empirical reality? At this point any genuine enquirer must feel suspicious that something more is going on here. Why is it that throughout the whole affair EU supporters utilised a manner of speaking that portrayed things as exactly the opposite of what they really were?

The short answer is that in the modern world, with Twitter and Facebook it is no longer possible to control <u>what</u> people see, so instead the battle is to control <u>how</u> people see. So if you want to flog a failed, insanely right-wing, democracy-crushing, unemployment-generating, cult, then you say black is white for precisely the same reason why adverts for unhealthy food feature healthy people. But the long answer is more complex and to answer it I'm afraid I'm going to have to psychoanalyse the modern world; and that is what I will attempt to do in the next section, which is the core of this book.

There are heaps of Brexit books out there that will trace the origins of the EU to Richard von Coudenhove-Kalergi or Jean Monnet but I want to look at things a little deeper, and to do that there is nothing for it but to familiarise ourselves with the great Immanuel Kant.

Section 3. Our Kantian World

Now we come to the core of the book, where I'll try to outline some general points about the condition of the modern world. And it's impossible to do that without first familiarising ourselves with Kant's theory of knowledge, his ethics and political writing. But before writing anything about the great man there is a perfunctory disclaimer that needs to be trotted out: Kant was a philosophical genius but a difficult writer, consequently his work is hard to understand and easy to misunderstand. Many people (and you know who you are!) spend their lives studying single aspects of his work and arguing about what he really meant, whereas I am just a curious amateur making passing observations that seem sensible to me. I have taken care not to misrepresent him, but if I have erred then I am happy to defer to the professional Kant scholars.

OK, Aristotle and Socrates criticised the earlier philosopher Anaxagoras, saying that, having made the great advance of introducing the concept of 'mind' into philosophy, he didn't make much use of it. Well if you are looking for someone who made full use of it then Kant is your man. Let's set the scene…

Rene Descartes founded modern philosophy with his famous cogito ergo sum - 'I think therefore I am.' A good illustration of Descartes' Cogito can be found in this passage from Winnie-the-Pooh by A.A.Milne in which Pooh visits Rabbit:

'So he bent down, put his head into the hole and called out:
"Is anybody at home?"
"No!" said a voice; and then added, "You needn't shout so loud"
"Bother!" Said Pooh. "Isn't there anybody here at all?"
"Nobody."
Winnie-the-Pooh took his head out of the hole, and thought to himself, "There must be somebody there, because somebody must have said 'nobody.'"

Here Winnie-the-pooh is correctly applying Descartes' cogito. If there is a question and an answer, then whatever we may doubt, we can at least be certain there is something answering. Rationalist philosophy takes this as its starting point, building intellectual arguments on inner certainties. Where did Descartes come to think of the Cogito? He climbed inside an old stove, so he thought of it whilst isolating himself from the maximum amount of empirical sense perception. He wrote: "I was locked up alone in a stove, where I had the pleasure to be alone with my thoughts".

The next important development (so far as we are concerned) was John Locke stating that the mind is at birth a 'tabula rasa' (clean sheet) and that there is nothing in the mind except what is first in the senses. (This is partly Leibniz's description of Locke's position, but it is fair). Locke therefore seemed to leave us in a materialist universe in which what we experience determines our minds rather than the other way round. But then Bishop George Berkeley entered the fray claiming that, if there is nothing in the mind that was not first in our senses, then my knowledge of a tree is just my perceptions of a tree; so matter does not exist except as a form of thought.

As if that wasn't confusing enough David Hume then delivered the coup de grâce, claiming that we perceive the mind empirically (albeit internally) thus abolishing 'mind' as effectively as Berkeley had abolished matter! Could things become any less certain? Yes! Hume also disposed of the Cosmological argument, the Teleological argument and the 'Argument from Design' for the existence of God. But hey, at least we still had some old certainties about things like causation, right? Like for example, when one billiard ball knocks into another and *causes* it to move? Actually, no. Hume's Treatise on Human Nature contained the devastating argument that what we assumed to be causation was merely the association of commonly conjoined events. What a mess! If the world around us was just a jumble of ideas … and the mind was made up of those … then what was being perceived? … and what was perceiving? Those pesky British empiricists (Locke, Berkeley and Hume) seemed to have dumped us in a world where there was no matter, no mind, no God and no causation! Will Durant observed that Hume's arguments had left philosophy 'in ruins of its own making' - they were so devastating in fact, that they called into serious question our claims to have knowledge about anything at all:

"Since the rise of metaphysics so far as the history of it reaches, no event has occurred that could have been more decisive with respect to the fate of this science than the attack made on it by David Hume" – Kant (Prolegomena).

Hume had filed knowledge under 'probability' and if we don't know anything then how can we know what is right or wrong? This was the challenge Kant took up.

Note: Although having said that, the question of 'What was Kant's project?' is itself contested. Another way of putting it is this: Scientists were forging ahead explaining things that had previously seemed incomprehensible, whereas the profession of philosophy (to which Kant had dedicated his life) seemed a bit of a joke in comparison. Whilst Newton had explained how the solar system worked, philosophy seemed stuck at groundhog day; despite two millennia of speculation, metaphysics was apparently still at year zero with philosophers unable to agree on even basic issues. In the Prolegomena Kant writes: "It seems almost ridiculous, while every other science is continually advancing, that this [philosophy] which pretends to be wisdom incarnate ... should constantly move around on the same spot without gaining a single step". But if somehow philosophy could be put on a firm footing then future metaphysicians would be able to accrue a body of solid knowledge in the same manner as scientists. This is another way to look at Kant's project - to look at the way we think itself, and to use that as a basis for progress. To me the whole idea of giving philosophy a firm basis is problematic. Philosophy is the questions business, so by its very nature it will appear unknowing, but that is another subject.

3.1 Kant's Theory of Knowledge
Kant saw Hume's philosophy as a problem to be solved. How could we prove 'knowledge' wasn't simply probability? Kant thought the only way to answer Hume was to prove the existence of something called 'synthetic a priori knowledge'. This is a classic example of intimidating Kantian terminology, hopefully I can explain it with simple language…

'A priori' knowledge is the opposite of 'a posteriori' knowledge. When you see a flash of lightning, that is a prior warning there is about to be a big clap of thunder, right? When you drink you have prior knowledge you will piss, when you eat a pizza you have prior knowledge you will dump, and so on. When you have prior warning about something you are getting a tip-off. So 'a priori' knowledge is knowledge you have BEFORE experience. A posteriori is the opposite. Your posterior is your bum right? So when you walk into a room your face enters the room first and your bum enters afterwards. A posteriori knowledge is knowledge you have after you've checked the empirical evidence. For example:

The sun will rise tomorrow (a priori)
The heart pumps blood around the body (a posteriori)
Prime numbers go on forever (a priori)
Saturn has moons (a posteriori)

These are contested terms but I'm just giving an outline here. Anyway, 'synthetic' knowledge is the opposite of 'analytic' knowledge. Synthetic and analytic statements both have two parts - a first part and a second part. Analytic statements are definitely true because the second part confirms what we know already from the first part. Synthetic statements add to our knowledge because the second part tells us something that the first part doesn't. For example:

All bachelors are unmarried (analytic)
Triangles have three sides (analytic)
Smoking is bad for you (synthetic)

E=MC squared (synthetic)

An even easier way of explaining analytic judgements is this. Things to do with the bum are called 'anal' right? So we have common phrases like 'anal sex' or 'anally retentive'. Well 'analytic' does not contain the word 'anal' by accident. If we look at these analytic statements:

1, People who run move their bodies.
2, If John killed Fred then Fred is dead.

The second part of the sentence must be true, because it has already been confirmed by the first part of the sentence. The fancy way of saying this is that 'the predicate is contained in the subject'. Imagine that the 'predicate' is the poo and the 'subject' is the food. The poo is contained in the food, and the act of pooing is the necessary consequences of eating, so in an <u>anal</u>ytic judgement the second bit necessarily issues forth from the first.

Because analytic and a priori statements are definitely true, people tended to lump them together. And because synthetic and a posteriori statements require checking to validate them, they got lumped together too. So when Kant set out to prove synthetic a priori knowledge existed, he seemed to be mixing up apples and pears. Why was this type of knowledge so important for him?

Kant said of knowledge "its very concept implies that it cannot be empirical. Its principles must never be derived from experience. It must not be physical but <u>metaphysical</u> knowledge." So his proof had to be a priori - completely independent of sense perception. And his proof had to be synthetic, because it had to tell us something we didn't know already; it couldn't just be an analytic statement of the obvious. So if he could prove that synthetic a priori knowledge existed then that would prove the existence of certain knowledge, which would answer Hume.

Kant proposed a solution which he called 'Transcendental Idealism', academics call this 'epistemology' but to avoid jargon I will just call it 'Kant's theory of knowledge'. It was set out in his Critique of Pure Reason (AKA the First Critique). In it Kant accepted (from Hume) that mere sensations cannot give us certainty, but he maintained there was another type of knowledge whose truth was certain, but which was independent of experience. But where could this knowledge be found? What is the one thing we have direct knowledge of? The one thing we do not experience via our senses? Our own minds.

Kant rejected Locke's argument that the mind was mere 'passive wax' upon which experience and sensation impose themselves, and instead argued that it is an active organ which organises sensations into ordered thought. But how does the mind do this?

Let's say I sense a tree. Maybe I see it with my eyes, maybe I hear the leaves rustling, maybe I touch its bark with my fingers, smell its blossom or taste its fruit, but basically I experience the tree in some way. Let's go for one of the senses and say I am looking at a tree. So far so simple. Kant says that when I see the tree a flowing sequence takes place from it (the object) to me (the subject). So where does this flow begin? Kant says it begins with the 'thing in itself' of the tree.

The phrase 'the thing in itself' is a really awkward phrase to use in an essay, not just because it's an unwieldy term to put in a sentence, but because it's nature is contested. Kant also called it the 'noumenon' which isn't any clearer. Leibniz called it a 'Monad' which is an even worse name. Schopenhauer (who was a better writer than Kant) simply renamed it 'the Will', and described 'the Will' as 'unconscious' (a phrase Schopenhauer invented). Eduard von Hartmann translated Schopenhauer's 'Will' as 'Unconscious' which obviously leads us to Freud. But basically, the 'thing in itself' of the tree is not its leaves, trunk, branches or roots, or any physical part of the tree, it's the phenomenon of nature that arranges minerals and forces (rain, sun, soil, carbon dioxide etc) into the physical object of the tree. For Kant the 'thing in itself' does not exist in time or space, instead it generates what is in time and space. For our purposes the easiest way to conceptualise it is to say Kant's 'thing in itself' is the philosophical equivalent of what spiritual people call the 'soul'.

So the 'thing in itself' organises rain, sunlight and minerals from the soil into a tree, light then bounces off the tree into my eye. I sense the tree, my eye gets visual information from the tree, then (according to Kant) this sensory information flows through a thousand 'afferent nerves' to the brain. Ok we've got to the brain.

These 'sensations' are then 'perceived' by my mind. 'Perception' is what happens when the mind organises sensations in space and time. We sense loads of stuff all the time but only a small number of the things we sense are perceived. For example, right now all my senses are working normally but my mind is choosing to ignore what I'm feeling with my toes or hearing with my ears and instead I'm prioritising the sensations from my eyes and fingers so I can write this. The purpose of the mind orders the perceptions.

Note: Woody Allen said that in his next life he wanted to come back as Warren Beatty's fingertips but according to Kant's theory of knowledge the fingertips themselves don't feel anything, they simply provide sensations for the mind to organise.

Anyway my 'perception' of the tree is not the end of the process. The mind reproduces the external world in our imagination according to rules. These perceptions are organised according to various 'categories'. What are categories? They are the rules for organising the perceptions. For Kant, categories are a bit like the operating system on a computer or the constitution in a country. When we experience what's happening we are not immediately aware of them, but beneath the surface they determine how everything proceeds. What do the categories organise the perceptions into? Concepts. What are concepts? They are the means by which we understand experience. So to quote Will Durant 'sensation is unorganised stimulus, perception is organised sensation, and conception is organised perception'.

As the tree sways in the breeze, as I blink or move my head, my sensation of the tree changes. How do I relate what I perceive now with what I perceived a moment ago? I can do this (so Kant maintains) because my mind has categorised the perceptions into a concept. The sensations don't just flow into my brain willy-nilly; my mind actively meets them and arranges them into knowledge of the tree. For Kant, the core essence of my mind isn't determined by what I experience - it's the other way round - the mind imposes order on our experiences of the outer world. This leads us to his astonishing statement that 'the mind is the law-giver of nature'.

"It sounds no doubt very strange and absurd that nature should have to conform to our subjective ground and be dependent on it with respect to her laws. But if we consider that nature is nothing but the whole of phenomena not a thing in itself but a number of representations in the mind then we will no longer be surprised that we only see her through the fundamental faculty of our knowledge, the transcendental perception".

This can seem bamboozling but the point here is that there is not a simple flow from the outer world to the inner mind. There is no direct relationship between the 'thing in itself' of the tree and the 'thing in itself' of me. Outer 'things in themselves' are unknown and unknowable. They are not substances, they can't be directly experienced and they don't exist in space or time. We can know nothing of external things except our manner of perceiving them.

Yikes! Well if we have no certainty about those things then we would appear to be nonplussed! But hold on. Kant is clear that he is not a Berkeley-ian idealist doubting the existence of everything outside the perceiving subject. Sure we don't know about external things in themselves but we do at least know something was perceived so we do know external 'things in themselves' exist, even though we don't know what they were before (deep breath) our minds transformed the sensations of them into concepts. To put it in the language of Descartes: 'I perceive, therefore external things exist'. What sort of statement is this? It's a synthetic statement because the bit after the word 'therefore' is not contained in the bit before it. And it's a priori because it's based on an analysis of the mind.

Another (hopefully simpler) way of explaining it is this, Locke and Boyle had accustomed philosophy to the idea of primary and secondary qualities. So the sweetness of an apple would be a secondary quality, because the sweetness is not inherent within the apple, but exists only in our experience of the apple. Kant's development was to say that this was applicable not only to the secondary qualities but the primary qualities as well. Indeed to everything in the universe.

I know that asserting 'external things in themselves exist' may not seem like a big deal but at least Kant seemed to have salvaged a bit of certainty from the troublesome Brits; and crucially he based this on an analysis of how the mind works.

Anyway, what about space and time? Can they also be salvaged from Hume's scepticism? Kant thought they could because our minds organise perceptions in space and time. We know time exists because we think, and thought is a sequence of events. And we know space exists because we perceive, so information, sensations and thoughts must be moving from one place to another. And we don't just do this every now and again, every second of our lives, awake or asleep the mind is incapable of ceasing to think. Everything we think is organised in space and time, indeed (Kant maintains) it's impossible to not organise everything we ever think in space and time. Therefore although Kant maintained space and time were forms of perception, to think is to accept they are real because they are inherent in the act of thinking. So space and time can be held to truly exist a priori. Again, see how with Kant's system we know things about the world around us based on analysis of our own thoughts?

What about maths and geometry could they also be saved from Hume? Kant thought they could. He held that geometry related to space and maths related to time. Geometry was the study of the three dimensional universe because it dealt with shapes, distances and angles etc; space had been proven to exist, geometry was the study of that, so it was valid. Similarly, we know time exists, time is a sequence of events, numbers are also sequential, so maths was valid too.

Could science also be salvaged from the sceptics? Yes said Kant - but with a caveat. We have seen Kant drew a distinction between the phenomenon and 'the thing in itself'. If we accept that science is simply a study of phenomena (surface effects we perceive) and not a study of the things in themselves (that we can never know) then its findings can be accepted.

So Kant had established (so he claimed) that external 'things in themselves' existed, that time and space existed, that maths and geometry were valid, and science was valid within a certain remit. What sort of statements are these? Synthetic a priori statements. Bingo! But what about morality? Could the same method be used to establish something as ambiguous as morality?

3.2 Kant's Ethics
If Hume posed a problem for Kant's metaphysical project. It was another pesky Brit, Newton, who posed a problem for ethical philosophy. Newton had explained for the first time how the solar system operated. And when the solar system was observed with telescopes it was impossible to refute his formulation. Why was this a problem for the study of ethics? Because we appeared to exist in a mechanistic universe, and if the 'heavens' could be explained mechanically then how could we be sure that everything was not mechanical? How could there be free will in a Newtonian universe? Maybe what we thought of as moral choices were just mechanical choices dressed up? And if we are not free to choose one path over another then how can we be good or evil? or even know good or evil exist? Additionally, Newton's third law of motion stated that "for every action there is an equal and opposite

reaction". This seemed to relegate God to the position of a cosmic clockmaker, who set everything up and then left it to continue. If all the movements of the heavens could be explained as reactions to previous events then God did not intervene, so even if God ever had existed, how could we know he/she/it was still alive?

Just as Hume had cast serious doubt on whether metaphysics was an ongoing project, Newton's mechanistic universe called into serious question whether morality existed. So we see, before Kant the British could claim to have pretty much shut down philosophy as an ongoing project. I hope I am conveying the scale of the task Kant took on.

How did Kant meet the Newtonian problem? Again by categorising. We have already seen Kant distinguished between the phenomena and 'the thing in itself'. Well, imagine there are two boxes, one called 'phenomena' and one called 'things in themselves'.

We have seen already that Kant put science in the 'Phenomena' box, so ethics, naturally, went into the other box marked 'things in themselves'. How did this work?

Kant sought a completely isolated, absolute moral system not corrupted with anything questionable like sense experience. After all, the outside world may be misunderstood. Religious doctrine may have been written by interested parties. The testimony of people claiming to see miracles could be unreliable. A rich person might be altruistic, but out of self-interest. A law-abiding man might disobey his conscience in abiding by unjust laws. Another example would be the Utilitarians who held that a good act is one that generates the most good, for the most people. But by that reasoning a cruel act could conceivably be ok if it accidentally resulted in good consequences; so Utilitarians could not say whether any act was good or bad until they had first evaluated its ramifications. No, none of the above would count as virtuous in Kant's system as they all sought validation from something external to the person making the moral choice. They didn't count as good because they existed in the phenomenal world.

54

Kant sought to derive an absolute universal necessary ethic from the inner self. How? When we think about how we think, the most astonishing reality is the inescapable moral calling. We can resist temptation or yield to it, but the moral calling is always there anyway. Irrespective of the circumstances, there always is, always has, and always will be, the pain of regret and the gnawing of guilt - the call to moral duty. This is true independent of all experience. It is from this that we arrive at Kant's famous 'Categorical Imperative' which is: "Act as if the maxim of your action were to become (through your will) a general natural law."

That's it. That's Kant's ethic. It's amazing that someone who took 800 pages to set out their theory of knowledge could set out a moral system in one sentence, but there it is. To ask yourself the question we all heard as children: "what if everyone did that?" - You will notice it isn't a list of dos and don'ts, so what should we do or not do? Kant says we decide solely on the basis of whether we follow the moral law within.

A good example of the Categorical Imperative can be found in Charlie and the Chocolate Factory by Roald Dahl. Charlie has been given an everlasting gobstopper by Willy Wonka. Charlie knows that rival sweet makers will pay him handsomely for it – enough to lift his whole family out of poverty! Willy Wonka has just double-crossed him and thrown him out of the chocolate factory without giving him the lifetime supply of sweets that had been promised. Does Charlie do what is best for his family? Does he give Wonka his comeuppance by cheating him back? No. He follows the moral law within irrespective of the consequences and gives the everlasting gobstopper back. Yes, he is ultimately rewarded for this, but he was unaware there would be any reward when he made the moral decision.

How would we describe the categorical imperative? Simple, it's a synthetic a priori judgement. It's synthetic because it tells us something (for example, lying is wrong) and it's a priori because it is derived from our core being, not from the external phenomenal world.

We've got to remember that this is a vast and complex subject and that I'm just giving a layman's summary of something cleverer people than me spend their lives studying. The main take-home point here is that for Kant what is innermost is uppermost. The thing in itself, the noumena, the inner mind, determines all knowledge and morality. It does not exist in time or space but it is the ultimate reality. The world around us that we empirically observe only gives us fallible sense perception. All morality and knowledge is internally generated. Can you see where this is going?

3.3 Copernicus
"The Copernican revolution brought about by Kant was the most important single turning point in the history of philosophy."— Bryan Magee

It is often said that Kant effected a 'Copernican revolution' in philosophy, but there are two problems with this. Firstly, the quote seems apocryphal (the phrase does not actually appear in the First Critique or the Prolegomena). Secondly it seems to me that Kant did precisely the opposite of Copernicus. Copernicus shifted mankind from a 'geocentric' to a 'heliocentric' view of the universe. So before Copernicus, mankind and the Earth were central to God's creation and everything revolved around us. Copernicus flipped this around, placing the Sun at the centre, and us in the Sun's orbit. So in the Copernican system mankind suddenly became peripheral and fairly insignificant in the universal scheme of things. Kant flipped this back again, putting us right back in the centre of things. Sure we were no longer central in the physical, phenomenal realm, but we were in the noumenal moral realm.

"We may make the same experiment [as Copernicus] with regard to the intuition of objects. If the intuition must conform to the nature of the objects, I do not see how we can know anything of them a priori. If, on the other hand, the object conforms to the nature of our faculty of intuition, I can then easily conceive the possibility of such an a priori knowledge." – Kant

3.4 How do we know there is a 'thing in itself'?
Incidentally, is it possible to prove the existence of Kant's 'thing in itself'? I think it is. This is how: When I am asleep and dreaming, things happen in my dream that surprise me. So in my dream I may see the back of someone's head and think, it's such-and-such a person, but when they turn around to reveal their face I am surprised to see it is someone I hadn't expected. How could my mind surprise itself? When I play with the children and jump out from behind a curtain I can surprise them because my mind is independent of theirs. But for my mind to surprise itself there must be something behind my consciousness; some essence of myself that exists beneath the surface of my thoughts. Could my surprise be based on questionable empirical observation? No because none of my senses are involved. There is something behind our thoughts, call it 'noumena' call it 'will', call it 'the unconscious' call it 'monad', call it whatever you like. It doesn't matter what name we give it, what matters is whether it determines knowledge and morality (as Kant maintained) or whether it does not.

3.5 Quick recap
Basically Kant's big idea was that he separated phenomena from noumena and awarded pre-eminence to the noumena. So the phenomenal realm is this world of sights and sounds and buildings and trains and trees, but the noumenal realm is the realm of 'things in themselves' or the 'will', or 'essence' or whatever you want to call it. And having made this distinction Kant awarded the noumenal primary status, and the phenomenal physical world secondary status. The 'thing in itself' is the ultimate source of all knowledge and morality whereas the phenomenal sensory world is just the stuff scientists measure. And so at last metaphysicians could bask in their superiority to the scientists, the status of their profession having been redeemed!

Noumenal	Phenomenal
Primary.	Secondary.
Deep inside you.	Outside you.
Metaphysics.	Physics.
Ethics.	Science.
Freedom.	Determinism.
Things in themselves.	Elements and forces.
Determines knowledge and morality	Provides sensation.

So to summarise, this is Ptolemy:

… he produced a model of the universe where we were the centre. It was called 'geocentricism' and looked like this:

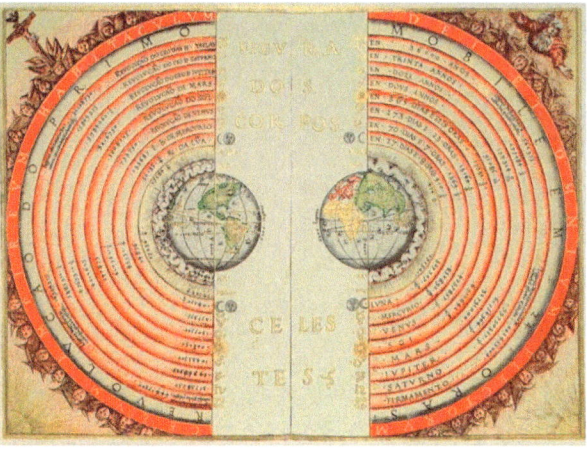

Ptolemy's model was then overturned by Copernicus…

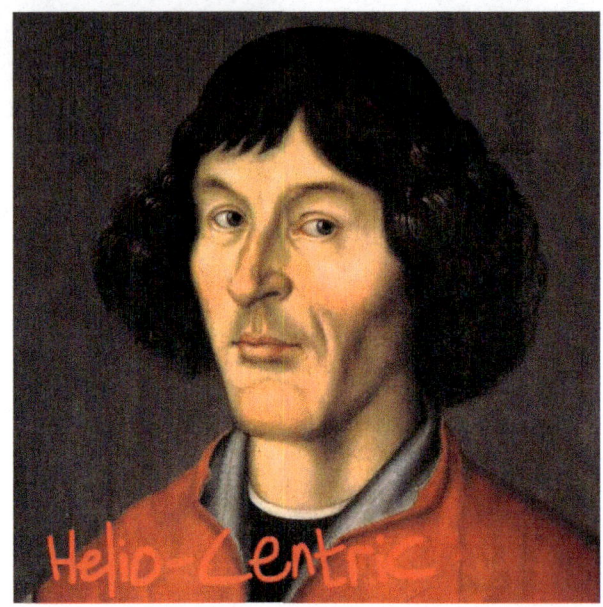

Copernicus' 'heliocentric' model flipped geocentricism around, placing the Sun at the centre and us at the periphery. Like this:

Then came Kant.

Kant accepted from Copernicus that the Sun was central, but insisted that it was only in the centre of the crappy phenomenal realm. In the higher, supreme noumenal realm it was the core of the mind that was the central. Things had flipped back, once again everything substantive revolved around us.

3.6 After Kant
As you might expect, Kant's books weren't exactly top sellers. One commentator described reading the critique as 'a disagreeable task because the work is dry, obscure, opposed to all ordinary notions and long winded as well'. Who said those cruel words? Kant himself! And where he contradicted the orthodox Lutheran Protestantism of the day he was for a long time spared censure because – as one royal advisor said – 'only a few people read him, and these did not understand him'.

Kant was a man of such regular habits that neighbours set their clocks by when he left his house. He worked for years in a lowly academic job that was far beneath him. It is thought he left the small town of Konigsberg just twice in his life. He never married or had children. His life passed virtually without event. He was shy, timid and very small (less than 5' 2"). He wrote and published, but he was a dull writer who usually chose academic terminology over rhetorical flourish – even his famous Categorical Imperative doesn't exactly trip off the tongue! He was not an antagonist. The people he disagreed with were worth disagreeing with so he did so carefully, and never with the blistering scorn of say Heraclitus, Schopenhauer or Nietzsche. He did not seek notoriety, or attempt to ingratiate himself with the influential, or bother in any way with self-promotion. In short there was nothing about Kant's outer appearance to make anyone think he would leave the tiniest ripple in his wake. So why are we even discussing him? What on earth could this incomprehensible little eighteenth century philosopher have to do with contemporary politics anyway? We are discussing Kant because just like his philosophy, the outer appearance was unimportant. His idea that the mind determines reality was about to take over the world.

In his book The Story of Philosophy, Will Durant describes how Kant's critical philosophy dominated the subsequent epoch: 'The philosophy of Schopenhauer rose to brief power on the romantic wave ... Nietzsche won the centre of the philosophic stage as the century came to a close, but these were secondary and surface developments; underneath the strong and steady current of the Kantian movement flowed on, always wider and deeper; until today its essential theorems are the axioms of all mature philosophy"

This brings us to Schopenhauer, who is important here for three reasons:
1, He wasn't just technically brilliant, he was also a very original philosopher who came to define the Romantic age between the Enlightenment and the 20th Century.
2, He understood and admired Kant and took Kant's system as his starting point.
3, He was a master of language in a way Kant simply was not. Schopenhauer's father was a businessman noted for his blunt manner, his mother was a celebrated author, and he was friends with Goethe. He could speak German, French, Latin and English. Basically unlike Kant, Schopenhauer really knew how to get a point across. So it's no surprise that great writers like Will Durant and contemporary commentators like Seth Paskin recommend reading Schopenhauer to learn Kant! For example, what in the First Critique Kant spent 800 pages explaining with laborious terminology Schopenhauer said in six words: "The world is will and idea". What Kant had described with the pedantic term 'the thing in itself' Schopenhauer simply renamed 'will'. What Kant called 'transcendental idealism' Schopenhauer abbreviated to 'idea'. What is will and idea? Everything. We get it.

In 1813 Schopenhauer published his doctoral dissertation 'On the Principle of Sufficient Reason'. His aim in this book was to complete the parts of Kant's theory of knowledge he felt Kant had left insufficiently concluded. Here is a quote from that book that will be important as we continue: "By the preceding explanations of the process of seeing and feeling, I have incontestably shown that empirical perception is essentially the work of the understanding, for which the material is only supplied by the senses in sensation and a poor material it is, on the whole; so that the Understanding is, in fact the artist, while the senses are but the under-workmen who hand it the materials." And in 'The World as Will and Idea' he states: "We must without reserve, regard all presented objects, even our own bodies, merely as ideas."

This isn't how you write when addressing academics; it's how you write when addressing lay people who are philosophical. His blunt honesty and disdain for jargon saw his ideas slowly taken up, not in the universities by professors, but in the salons by artists. Here are four paintings:

Rembrandt. Self portrait 1606.

Van Gogh. Room 1889

Picasso. Violin and Grapes 1912

No14, Mark Rothko 1960

It should be obvious to the reader that I have shown these pictures in chronological order. The first is a good starting point because Rembrandt was always honest. He was technically good enough to have immortalised himself as a handsome hero, but instead he always told the truth about what he saw. In the second we see Van Gogh's state of mind starting to challenge previous concerns to accurately portray objects. With the third Picasso is using subject matter merely as a starting point, but he is also seriously questioning how he sees it. (He left simple representation to the cameras that had just been invented). And finally with the fourth painting we see Mark Rothko disregard using an external subject matter altogether.

I accept that Rembrandt's inner self was in his work and that Rothko made decisions about his painting whilst observing it, but the point is these paintings show a pattern – increasingly artists were painting what was inside of themselves rather than what was in front of them. Before Manet paintings were empirical observations; after Manet the interior began to take over. The classical notion that the picture plane was a window looking at the world started breaking down. As the importance of empiricism declined, what was not empirical came to the fore. How we see became more important than what we saw. Increasingly artists were painting the 'thing in itself' rather than mere surface appearance. In a sense it could even be argued that abstract expressionism isn't 'abstract' at all but a depiction of Kant's noumenal realm! Within the human condition the unconscious, the will, the thing-in-itself, was going from latent to dominant. Can you see where this is going?

Here are some paintings by Mondrian. Once again I have placed them in chronological order. In particular look at the branches.

Mondrian 1898

63

Mondrian 1908

Mondrian 1911

Mondrian 1912

Mondrian 1912

Mondrian 1913

Mondrian 1917

Mondrian 1919

Mondrian 1923

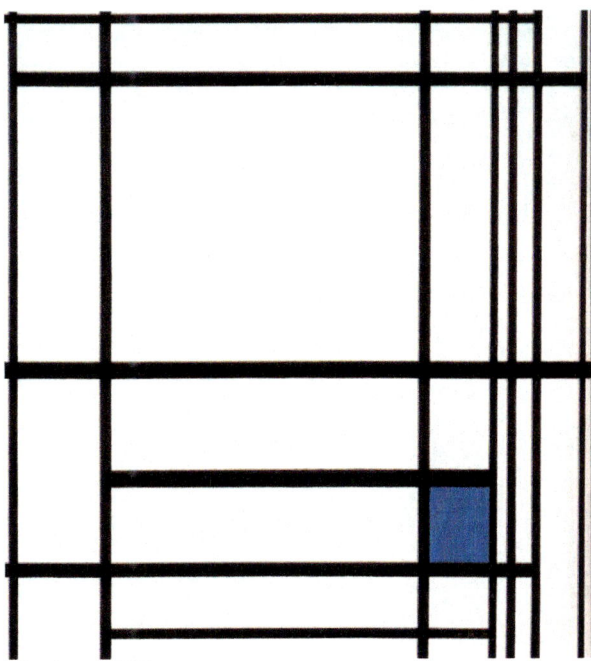
Mondrian 1937

Excuse the pun, but, can you see the pattern? Mondrian started out painting the phenomenal realm but ended up painting the noumenal realm. Obviously one swallow doesn't make a summer, but I think Mondrian's work is indicative of a broader trend in art and by extension humanity itself. Now let's look at it another way. Here are another four paintings:

The Blue Boy. Gainsborough. 1770.

The Druids Bringing the Mistletoe. George Henry and Edward Hornel. 1890

The Red Room. Matisse. 1908

Number 31, Jackson Pollock 1950

Again it should be obvious these pictures are shown in chronological order. Maybe I'm looking for patterns here, but let's for a moment take Clement Greenberg's 'picture plain' as a metaphor for the mind. (The 'picture plain' is about the relationship between foreground and background in a painting). Kant had accustomed us to the idea that 'the thing in itself' *behind* all our conscious thoughts was of primary importance and that what is at the *forefront* of our mind is questionable sense perception. Now look again at the changing relationship between foreground and background in the above four paintings. The 'picture plane' was becoming flatter and flatter. More and more the background challenges the foreground for dominance, to the point where the foreground disappears altogether! Can you see where this is going? What had been in the foreground was drifting into the background, whilst what had previously been in the background was taking over. The 'thing in itself' was becoming dominant within painting and within humanity.

Let's stick for a moment with Kant's influence on painters, because they didn't all flatten the picture plane and reject empiricism. For other painters Kant's influence took a different form. Let's look at the fixation with dreaming in the work of various Victorian painters like Frederic Leighton or Edward Burne-Jones or later artists like Dali and Ernst…

The Garden Court – Edward Burne-Jones. (1894)

Flaming June – Frederic Leighton 1895

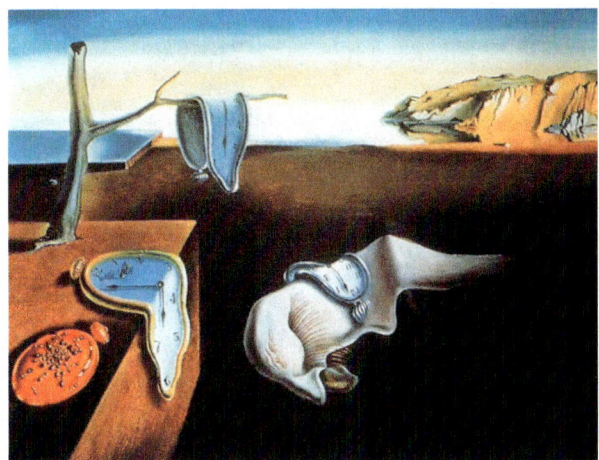

The Persistence of Memory – Dali 1931

Dreams are about the inherent nature of the mind, we don't see them with our fallible eyes or hear them with our fallible ears. But if we remember Kant's claim that ultimately we cannot know any objective truths about any external reality then it's hardly surprising artists would come to see dreams as having a greater authenticity than 'realism'. Dreams and the unconscious became important in art precisely because they bypassed Kant's 'transcendental aesthetic'.

For Marcel Duchamp the viewer completes the experience of art. In a 1957 lecture, he described how "The creative act is not performed by the artist alone; the spectator brings the work in contact with the external world by deciphering and interpreting its inner qualifications and thus adds his contribution to the creative act." It is often said that Duchamp's ideas were revolutionary and that he is the most influential artist of the 20th Century, but here he is simply writing footnotes to Kant, because he is saying that the spectator is an active agent, and that the object (art) is simply handing the spectator the raw materials with which to form a judgement. Duchamp shifted the profound event *from* the creation of the object *towards* the judgement of the spectator. Kant set out what he considered to be the relationship between humans and the universe, centuries later Duchamp said there was a similar relationship between spectators and paintings. So we see it was the quiet reclusive little professor who was the true revolutionary, not the controversial artist!

For Andy Warhol, the subject matter could not be more mundane, but the profundity of his work lies not in the subject matter, or execution of it, but in what the mind has brought to it. The banality of the empirical observations only served to emphasise the increasing importance of the 'thing in itself'. Or if we look at the work of say Keith Haring, it is not the painting as an object that is important but the idea it represents. So we see Kant's influence on art has become so pervasive it is hard to think of work that owes nothing to him.

Extended note: I have given examples of art to show how humanity gradually assimilated Kant's ideas. A critic might reasonably ask why I have focused on the influence upon art of the first two critiques and not the third Critique of Judgement which is specifically concerned with aesthetics. Again I'm anxious not to let this get too long-winded by pre-emptively answering every hypothetical objection. So, as briefly as possible, my reasons are as follows:

1, The first critique identifies two faculties: understanding and reason. The third critique introduces another 'faculty of judgement' which seems remarkably like an appeal to common sense (Reid & Beaty) that the first two critiques have already ruled out.

2, In the third critique Kant claims that true beauty is universally so for everyone everywhere. This is a straight contradiction of his big idea in the first critique, that we can know nothing of anything except our manner of perceiving it.

3, Kant only left Konigsberg twice briefly in his life and he didn't go to shows. The chances are he never saw a great painting or entered a great work of architecture in his life. His idea of the sublime is the starry heavens above; his idea of beauty is Emile by Rousseau. So when he discusses 'art' he means something rather different to what we would understand by the term.

4, Kant famously claimed that art should give us 'disinterested pleasure'. By disinterested he doesn't mean boring, he means something that we like even though none of our personal emotional baggage gives us a motive to like it. But great art does not give us disinterested pleasure, it gives us interested pain. The truly great songs upset us. Think of Citizen Kane by Orson Welles. Kane, has everything, but what does he cry out for? Rosebud - the little wooden sleigh he played on as a child. Not because it gives him disinterested pleasure but because it tears him apart. Because it is the embodiment of the path not taken, of every hypothetical happiness that might have been. Kane has an interest in Rosebud, to anyone else it would be worthless. Every great work of art is your rosebud. Rosebud is your first love, the unfulfilled dream. It is your longing. So when Kant advocates disinterested pleasure it is hard not to see this as the self-justification of one who spurned human relationships to be a lover of metaphysics. See for yourself. Write down your 8 desert island disks. Look at the list. Have you picked disinterested pleasure? No you have picked interested pain.

5, Kant categorised art (from Burke) into the beautiful and the sublime. But what do we do when we have say, a beautiful Ansel Adams photograph of an awe-inspiring mountain? As John David Ebert has convincingly shown, Kant's aesthetic system starts to break down when we apply it to specific works of art.

6, Kant's big idea was to categorise everything into phenomenal or noumenal, to make the phenomenal secondary and to make the noumenal the supreme determinant of all knowledge and morality. I would say artists themselves did a better job of incorporating this big Kantian idea into aesthetics than he managed himself.

7, Having finished this book I stumbled across an essay called Modernist Painting by Clement Greenberg and was fascinated to see he had reached some similar conclusions to myself. Principally that the first two critiques influenced art far more than the opinions expressed in the third critique. Kant's method was similar to his conclusion. It was an internalised method, he used reason to critique itself. In doing so he removed a lot from the remit of reason, but that which remained was more secure as a result. This self-critiquing method ultimately advocated self-critique – following the moral law within. The method became the conclusion. Modernism replicated this method. Art sought to justify its existence by emphasising what was unique to itself and absent from everything else. And this was not just the case with art generally but with its various genres specifically. Naturally as this self-criticism progressed modern art fragmented, categorising itself into a plethora of 'isms' each of which became increasingly pure. So with classical painting we see the picture then remember it is a painting, whereas with modernism we automatically see a painting as a painting. As Kant used logic to critique logic so modernist painting advanced through self-critique.

(End of extended note)

Now let's look at some trends in literature. Here is Schopenhauer talking about a new form of literature that had just been invented called the novel:

"Tristram Shandy, to be sure, has as good as no action whatsoever; but how very little action there is in Nouvelle Heloise [Rousseau] *and Wilhelm Meister!* [Goethe] *Even Don Quixote has relatively little, and what there is is relatively trivial, amounting to no more than a series of jokes. And these four novels are the crown of the genre. Consider further, the marvellous novels of Jean Paul and see how much inner life is set in motion on the narrowest of external foundations. Even the novels of Walter Scott have a significant preponderance of inner over outer life, and the latter appears only with a view to setting the former in motion; while in bad novels the outer action is there for its own sake. The art lies in setting the inner life into the most violent motion with the smallest possible expenditure of outer life: for it is the inner life which is the real object of our interest. The task of the novelist is not to narrate great events but to make the small ones interesting."*

Kant's emphasis on subjectivity and the creative resources that we bring to experience was the starting point for Coleridge and the early romantics who emphasised the creativity of the inner self. For them strong emotion was valued, this led to a toleration of passions (for example Byron's heroes do not exhibit exemplary behaviour). This then leads to nationalism - a romanticised view of the nation. From 'transcendental philosophy' it's a short step to the nineteenth century 'transcendentalism' of Emerson. How did Ezra Pound edit T.S.Eliot's The Wasteland? by removing the sections which anchored the poem in empirical reality. The culmination of James Joyce's Ulysses is an internal monologue. And the importance of dreams and the unconscious were just as pervasive in literature as they were in painting, not just with Freud and the symbolism of Jung, but with writers like Lewis Carroll and Kafka.

Here is Fichte writing footnotes to Kant: "Turn your eye away from all that surrounds you and in towards your inner self". Like Schopenhauer (and unlike Kant) he is writing in a direct way we instantly understand.

Neo Kantian - Max Weber (1864-1920) saw Kant's categories as learned cultural experiences which change over time. This relativised the structures of thought, which made it much harder to maintain there was any objective truth at all. From this you get moral relativism and the various types of subjectivism of the 20th Century, one of which was obviously existentialism. Jean-Paul Sartre held that, we live in a bare meaningless world and we have to create our own values, our own meanings and even our own selves! Not only is the 'I' creating the external world but the 'I' is creating itself! Sartre was able to say this because Kant gave him the tools to do so.

Now let's look at the built environment because Kant can lay serious claim to being the architect of the modern world in more ways than one. Kant's theory of aesthetics held that art and utility were distinct and separate (he categorised them). This led us to Adolf Loos and the abandonment of ornament in modern architecture (see Colin St John Wilson, The Other Tradition). Prior to this structural elements were decorated, but after Kant ornament and utility gradually became separated (categorised) requiring architects to justify their whims with appeals to practicality.

Villa Müller – Adolf Loos

Then when modernist town planners set about rebuilding after the Second World War they took Kant's method of categorising and simply applied it to maps. So there would be an industrial zone in one place, a commercial district in another place, and a housing zone somewhere else.

Note: This was generally considered to have been a disaster. Where it was not done (eg Cologne) it was generally considered successful (see Civic Ground by Patrick Lynch)

Here is a picture of Le Corbusier's hugely influential Voisin Scheme. Could any image more clearly represent the contrast between the old towns and the new zoning?

Now let's look at the plans of the towers directly from above…

74

Maybe I'm being obsessed with patterns here, but see how the block plans bear an astonishing similarity to Kant's famous table of categories? Each is arranged into a cruciform of four groups of three:

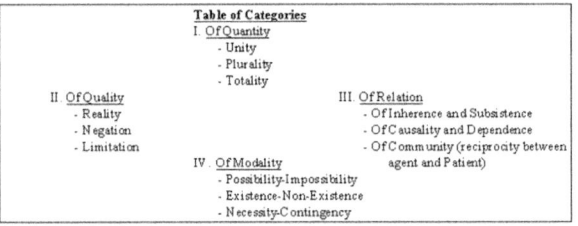

Corb even designed in a Kantian way, by categorising. So he would break problems down into distinct sub-problems to generate his aesthetic.

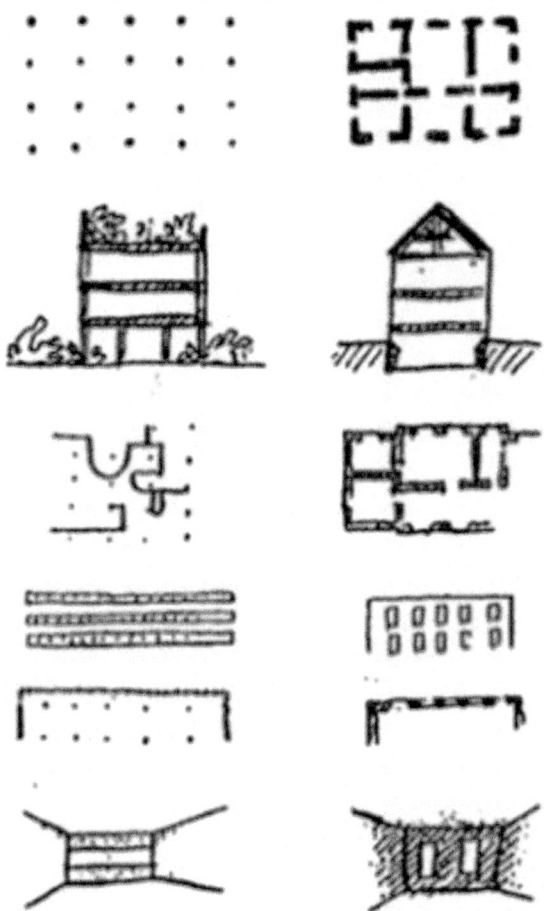

75

Above are the famous sketches from his book *The Five Points of New Architecture*. This is probably the most influential page of architectural drawings of the 20th Century.

His five points are:
1, Columns.
2, Roof Garden.
3, Free plan.
4, Ribbon Windows.
5. Free façade.

On the right we see the bad old way, on the left, Corb's new proposed vision. On the right the walls structure and windows are *fused* into an *ensemble*, on the left they are *categorised* into distinct and separate elements. On the right the building is conjoined with the landscape, on the left it is raised above nature on columns.

So this wasn't just the case with town planning – buildings and even individual rooms were also 'categorised' and arranged according to use. Architects categorised space! Kant admitted to a 'mania' for systems, in which things are separated into clear and distinct categories. It's easy to see a similar method at work with Louis Kahn's concept of 'serving' and 'served' spaces.

Here with Kahn's Richards Laboratories the services are given separate distinct zones (towers) so that the 'served' laboratory spaces are clear and unobstructed. Louis Kahn is categorising - it was a mania for him too! Eventually glass disappeared altogether from the external elevations of Kahn's buildings because he felt uncomfortable with the material ambiguity of something that was both physical and translucent. His elevations became categorised into solid and void.

Anyway the service towers of Kahn's Richards Laboratories provided the prototype for the 'High-tech' architecture of Richard Rogers:

Modernist architecture is about domination by the 'thing in itself'. Maybe the 'thing in itself' is about purity of form (Corb, Villa Savoye):

Maybe it's about the free flowing continuum from internal to external space (Richard Nuetra – Kaufmann House):

Maybe it's about structural rigour (Schindler - Lovell Beach House):

Maybe it's about an uncompromising handling of materials (Sigurd Lewerentz – Church of St Peters):

Maybe it's about breaking the building envelope (Mies, Brick Country House):

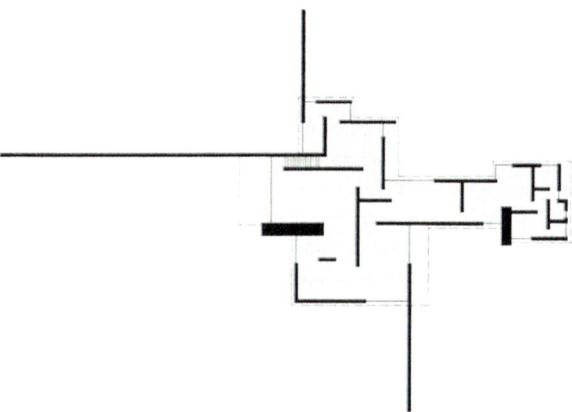

Maybe it's about prefabrication (Eames House):

…But every great modernist building elevates one core idea to supremacy and organises everything else around that. Where does this come from? I would say it comes from Viollet le Duc's theory of the 'key generating idea'. Where does le Duc's 'key generating idea' come from? Le Duc's 'key generating idea' is the Kantian 'thing in itself' of the building. The modernists *categorised*. Their priorities were clearly and distinctly articulated.

Now if we were to look at, say a gothic cathedral or this picture of Specchi and De Sanctis (the Spanish Steps) in Rome, we see the pre-Kantian way. Here structure and ornament are fused together, the geometry is generated partly by the site and partly introduced by the architect, there is no imposition of simple geometry, it is a public space made of private spaces. You go <u>to</u> it and <u>through</u> it, it is a performance space *and* a corridor. It doesn't clearly differentiate between 'serving' corridors and 'served' places the way Louis Kahn would. The design is not about categorising – it is a <u>fusion</u> of many design considerations.

This is my misgiving about Post Modern architecture - it dispenses with le Duc's core governing principle, which is a really useful tool for organising a design, but it doesn't give us in return the unified glory of classical or gothic architecture, in which structure and ornament are fused into a compelling ensemble. This is Asplund's summer house.

Look at the way the stair and fire place crash into one another, he is not categorising, he is de-categorising! For me this doesn't make him a Post-Modernist - it makes him a Pre-Modernist. Ditto Aalto.

Anyway, back to Kant…Here is a diagram from Part B of the UK building regs which (like the first critique) is dry, technical and hugely influential:

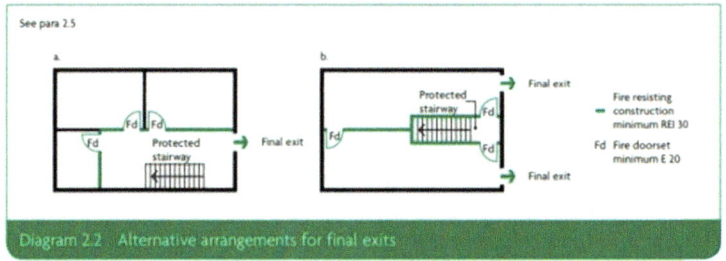

How does it require buildings to be arranged? By categorising space. People will laugh at me for saying it, but in a sense building regs documents are Kantian – they *categorise* the various aspects of a building, they are a technical labyrinth, and although we are unaware of them in our daily lives, beneath the surface they determine the world around us.

Imagine if there was something like Kant's 'synthesis' (that we are not immediately aware of, but which behind the scenes organises how we see the world) but that, instead of it being internal within my mind, it is the organising structure of the collective consciousness for all society? Well Foucault did precisely that. He basically got Kant's epistemology and plugged it into sociology, and called it 'episteme'. More on Foucault later.

If we consider the film *The Wizard of Oz*, the parts of the film set in the 'real world' are downgraded to the black and white sections of the film, whereas the substantive part of the film takes place in Dorothy's technicolour dream. There are loads of other examples I could give, but I don't want to write a history of the modern world, so here are just a few more instances showing how Kant's theory of knowledge steadily seeped into popular culture … In 1963 an up-and-coming band called the Beatles released their first album. On it there is a song called *'There's a Place'*. It's played in the same jaunty uplifting way most of their early material is played, but the interesting thing is that the lyrics seem to anticipate their later psychedelic work that would come to define the decade:

*'There is a place,
Where I can go,
When I feel low,
When I feel blue,
And it's my mind.'*

Here is another example. In Star Wars, Obi-Wan Kenobi is teaching Luke Skywalker how to use a light sabre. Luke is trying to defend himself against a small robot that flies around trying to zap him.

The robot zaps Luke's bum. Obi-Wan then says Luke should wear a helmet with the blast shield down:

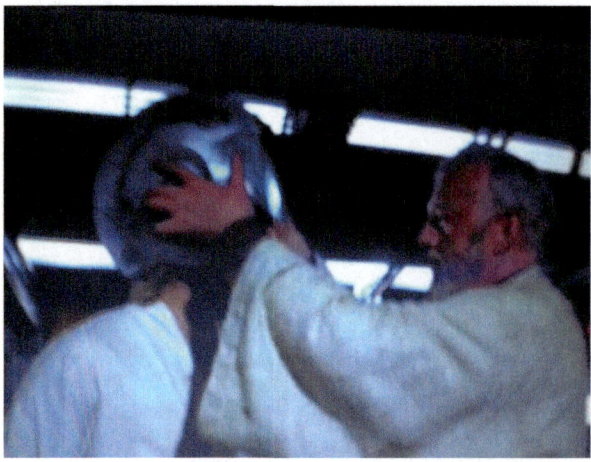

Obi: "I suggest you try it again Luke but this time let go of your conscious self and act on instinct".
Luke: "With the blast shield down I can't even see – how am I supposed to fight?"

Obi: "Your eyes can deceive you. Don't trust them. Stretch out with your feelings"

Luke then having deprived himself of visual sense perception uses 'the Force' and straight away has more success against the zapping robot. And when preparing to fire the shot that blows up the Death Star, does Luke appraise his speed or proximity of target the way any professional marksman would? No. Instead he switches off his tracking computer and uses the 'Force' which he feels flowing through him. The rejection of empiricism was catching on.

This is Martina Big, she was born a white, German woman but identifies as black. She has now been 'baptised' as an African woman and is learning Swahili. Along with her boyfriend Michael Eurwen, she is undergoing tanning injections to make her skin darker. They are among a growing number of 'transracial' people who believe the race they outwardly appear differs from the one they feel affinity with, and seek to change it.

Some readers might be hoping I have introduced Martina as a figure of fun, to sneer at her. Not at all! I mention her because she provides a great example of what happens when Kantian ideas permeate society. Remember the Schopenhauer's Kantian quote? "We must … regard all presented objects, even our own bodies, merely as ideas". When growing up she saw she was white, but that was merely sense perception obtained from the study of surface appearances. She dispensed with that knowledge to make room for belief, and her belief, derived from her understanding of herself, was that ultimately she was a woman of colour. That trumped the empirical evidence she saw in the mirror. Like Kant she saw the mind as 'the lawgiver of nature' so she projected her belief on her world. So although some may find this peculiar, in terms of Kantian philosophy it is easy to explain. And who are we to disagree? Can we espouse liberty and deny her right to identify as whatever she likes? Do we claim to understand her better than she understands herself?

We have seen that Kant advanced a method called 'categorising' which involves breaking complex problems into seperate clear distinct groups. Although not critical for my argument, it's worth noting that this method became hugely influential, and today categorising and ordering are often assumed to be the same thing (whereas in the Classical age the opposite was the case). Modern art categorised itself into numerous pure 'isms'. The state has been categorised - in the premodern age the head of the state was the head of the church and the army, and their word was law, whereas in the modern world the functions of the state are <u>categorised</u> into separate entities: executive, judiciary, monarchy clergy etc. For a blacksmith their employment, exercise and skill were the same thing; now we go to the gym to keep fit, we do jobs we hate for money and educate ourselves at evening classes. Space has been categorised - cities are categorised into zones: industrial, brownfield, green-field, conservation area etc. Rooms in houses are categorised as per their use, as are elements of buildings. Ford categorised manufacturing, intellectual disciplines have been categorised, and so on. But there is one important area where we have de-categorised – gender. But could this also be explicable in terms of Kant? Could there be a link between 'transcendental idealism' and 'trans' in the contemporary debate about gender? I think there is. Kant said: "I call all knowledge transcendental if it is occupied, not with objects, but with the way that we can possibly know objects". If the 'thing in itself' is female, but the empirical object is male (or visa verse) Kantian philosophy allows us to say that the thing in itself gets the last word, and that the physical form of the body is mere surface appearance!

Or if we look at an influential contemporary thinker like Noam Chomsky we see his system is clearly Kantian. Chomsky holds that the mind is <u>pre-formed</u> to assimilate language, that the <u>inherent nature of the mind</u> synthesises language as the mind synthesises sense data in Kant's system. Chomsky simply took Kant's theory of knowledge and plugged it into the modern philosophy of language.

And this isn't just a counter-cultural thing. Kant's influence on the way we think has become so pervasive we see it cropping up in the most unlikely places. The great man would be spinning in his grave to hear me say it but in some ways Donald Trump can be seen as a Kantian phenomenon: The hero of his own story, Trump creates his own reality, for him empirical facts are simply material to arrange as he sees fit. They don't change him, he changes them. He is right because he believes he is right.

Now let's consider economics. In the mercantilist age we bought and sold physical stuff, commodities were king. Then in the industrial age we bought and sold labour, and now in the information age what do we buy and sell? Our intellectual property. Thought has been monetised. Apple can sell a handful of minerals for £1000 why? Because of the thought that has gone into it. Why do Facebook, Google and Twitter harvest your personal information? Because their capital is your mind. Who are the new gods? The influencers.

This is business consultant, influencer and life coach Simon Sinek arguing in a Kantian way without even realising it. In his lecture 'Start With Why' he employs a Venn diagram of concentric circles. The outer one represents WHAT a business does, the middle circle represents HOW the business does what it does, and finally the central circle represents WHY the business does what it does. Sinek argues that successful businesses start from the centre and work to the periphery, constantly repeating his mantra "People don't buy what you do, they buy why you do it". I'm not attacking Sinek who is obviously intelligent and perfectly nice, I'm simply observing that Kant is behind a lot of what he says: that core beliefs are supreme and that it is good to work from those to the outside world.

But this is just one example of Kant's influence on the 'influencers'. Generally every advert targets your 'thing in itself', appealing to your conscience and presenting you with a fait accompli: to invest and be at peace or to not invest and be cursed. Some choice! Kant's 'thing in itself' has been monetised! And as the 'thing in itself' has been monetised, so it has become the new battleground - territory to be contested. As our computer screens fill up with infinitely subtle psychological nudges the mental health epidemic escalates accordingly. When we look at social media we feel like we are being attacked because we are. We have become more depressed and anxious even though - as a species we became more healthy and comfortable.

In the 1956 sci-fi film Forbidden Planet, the United Planets starship C-57D lands on Altair IV on which a race called the Krell perished overnight 200,000 years previously. But before perishing the Krell had created an infinitely powerful machine that could create anything by thought alone. Invisible monsters that seem to defy the laws of physics keep attacking the crew. We eventually learn that the Krell died out because they abandoned physical existence and instead 'uploaded' their minds onto the 'metaverse' of the machine, the monsters are of course the nightmares the Krell's minds are having inside the machine. They've gone mad. It was science fiction, now its social realism.

Even money itself has become Kantian. When Nixon took the dollar from the gold standard in 1971 financial transactions became decoupled from empirical reality. Our currencies are fiat currencies meaning they are not backed by anything. The value of money resides only in how you see it. This has reached its apotheosis with Bitcoin – the world is moving to a financial system in which we are literally buying and selling an idea and the value of everything else is denominated in that! Over the last 300 years across various fields of human endeavour there has been a decoupling of value from empirical reality.

So to sum up so far. Kant proposed a theory of knowledge in an 800 page book that was virtually unreadable to anyone but a few professional philosophers. In it he used a method called categorising to develop a labyrinthine philosophy in which everything was either secondary (in a physical/phenomenal world) that we empirically observe, or primary (in a moral/noumenal realm) felt with the conscience. Then Schopenhauer (like Hegel and most post-Kantian philosophers) adopted and elaborated on Kant's system, but crucially he wrote in a way that was completely accessible to the new middle classes and amateur philosophers. Then for some fringe artists, how we see came to be more important than what we see. The way the mind conceptualised the sensory information it received became increasingly important. Artists started to paint how they felt rather than what they saw. This became 'Modern Art' which in turn moulded popular culture, and today in many ways we find ourselves living in a Kantian world. Empiricism is secondary, what is innermost has primacy. Art need not be about the profundity of the subject matter but the profundity with which mundane objects are considered. Right and wrong are no longer derived from ten external commandments but our examination of our own consciences. In law we don't simply judge consequences but also the intended consequences. Police have transitioned into clerics; prosecuting misdemeanours in the noumenal realm like 'hate' and pronouns, whilst attacks in the phenomenal realm like theft are ignored. And within politics, 'values' have become as important as policies. More and more we are urged to 'get in touch with our feelings'. How far has this gone? In the modern world someone with a penis can say 'I am a woman'. I have absolutely no problem with the trans community and I'm not making a criticism here, I'm simply opining that if there is one thing in the world humans should be able to make confident empirical observations about, it is our own bodies, so if a person with a penis can consider themselves as a woman then that must surely represent the ultimate triumph of the noumenal over the phenomenal.

I have argued that Kant's influence resulted in painting transitioning from empirical to noumenal, and that something very similar also happened with gender, money, ethics and literature. Later when we discuss Foucault we will see this is also the case with sex, violence, and power. Every reality TV program and film culminates in an outpouring of emotion from deep inside that determines the physical reality. It is impossible to buy a packet of biscuits from the supermarket without hearing nervous breakdown music. Everywhere empiricism is in retreat, the noumenal is triumphant.

If the dominant philosophy is a Kantian one in which the mind is the ultimate law giver, and sense perception is regarded as untrustworthy and truth is derived from an analysis of mind, then the following things are likely to emerge in society: People will tend to argue, not about what they see but how they see it, empirical evidence will be secondary, the way we feel about things will be primary, and when two people are in disagreement it will be impossible to choose between them if one of them is basing their position on their core values, so each will try to settle the disagreement by claiming their core values are more virtuous than their opponent's. Can you see where this is going?

Societies tend to be in the image of their philosophies, and philosophies tend to be in the image of their authors. I would describe modern western societies as technically labyrinthine, pedantically categorised, subjectivist, morally relative, excessively sceptical of empiricism and insufficiently sceptical of belief. Remind you of anyone? Maybe I'm guilty of looking for patterns, but I think Kant's influence is far more pervasive that people realise. Kant never married or had a family, but in many ways we are all his children. His epistemology has gone from being an incomprehensible philosophy to a social movement. Tech geeks think this is all to do with the internet, but all the internet has done is super-charge a set of ideas that already existed. Kant's idea that knowledge and morality are internally generated created the episteme that we call 'Modern'. Today people in categorised buildings search their feelings and try to change our minds. We are living in a Kantian world.

Note: Those who think philosophy is pointless speculation need to think again. There is a serious argument that the world is defined by philosophers.

3.7 Objections

I think the influence of Kant has been partly good and partly bad. But, as with all systems, there are problems. Here I'm going to respectfully go through my misgivings. First some pedantic pot shots:

1, Kant claims the mind reproduces sensations in imagination according to a rule. But how can anything dependent on something as ambiguous as imagination yield a priori knowledge? How do we know we are doing it according to a rule?

2, If the mind recreates in imagination then it is sensing itself which is surely just another form of empiricism, and as fallible as any other type of sense perception.

3, When I want to sleep I darken the room and turn off the music, when I want to wake up I wash my face. Every day the exterior influences the interior. It's not simply one-way-traffic of the mind determining what is outside itself.

4, Are the claims of Hume and Newton not mutually exclusive? If the Universe is mechanistic causation is analytic. If causation isn't analytic then the universe can't be mechanistic.

5, If we should follow the moral law within, then why are our biggest regrets our impulses rather than the things we discussed? And, how do we later appraise whether the correct decision has been made? - If we can't then there is no guilt or morality!

6, Kant thought that women should not participate in democracy for 'natural reasons'. Let's be more than generous and excuse this error on the grounds that he was unmarried and was writing before the success of universal suffrage. In fact, let's be *excessively* generous, and pretend that his position here is actually correct. If he thinks that women's minds are inherently different to men's then surely we require two versions of transcendental idealism? One for each gender! And if we entertain the contemporary view that gender is non-binary, our difficulties increase accordingly. And if we admit exceptions based on gender then why not admit others too? Is Kant's system a description of how he thinks? how we all think? or just how good people think when they think correctly? If transcendental idealism describes just how Kant thinks then what use is it to the rest of us? If it describes how we all think then what if someone's age, mood, alcohol intake, cultural background or genetic code alters their purpose of mind? And if transcendental idealism just describes how good people think when they think correctly, then how do we decide who is enlightened, when they are enlightened, or what the unenlightened should do?

7, Are we really to suppose that observations of causality made by chemists and physicists should be regarded as second-tier knowledge, but that fallible observations of fallible minds by fallible psychologists should be regarded as a priori true? With the best will in the world Kant seems to have given pre-eminence to the least deserving.

8,1 Remember Schopenhauer's Kantian quote that perception is the work of the understanding. What if there is a problem with the understanding?

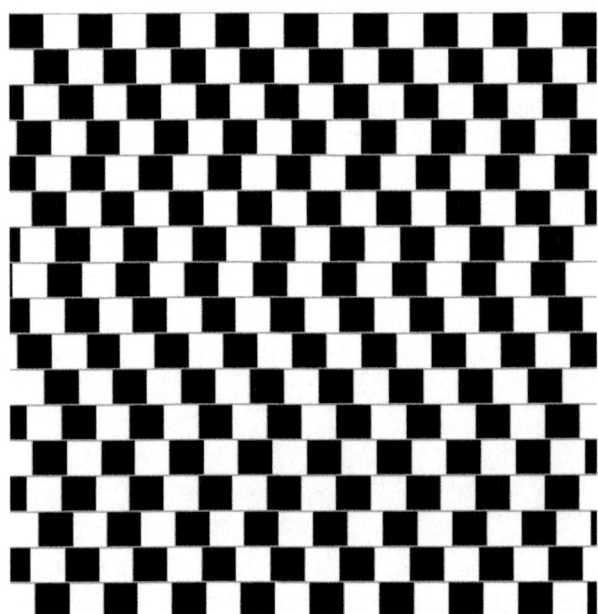

Here is a simple optical illusion. The black and white squares (yes squares) are in horizontal rows but appear to be sloping. There is no problem with your empirical perception; it is your understanding that is making the mistake. Your mind is not ordering the sense perception, it is disordering it! Virtually all 'magic' tricks involve the audience having belief about something that is not true. Your senses give your mind information, your mind perceives the sensations and arranges the perceptions into an idea, which in the case of the magic trick is completely wrong.

8.2 You look at the clock. It's four o'clock. But it isn't. The batteries ran out an hour ago. You <u>believe</u> it's four, but it's five. Your belief is wrong. How do you correct the error? By searching your feelings? No. By cross-checking.

8.3 Shower farts smell different. Now of course every fart is slightly different in its own way, but shower farts smell very different. Because they *are* different? No. Because your nose senses differently at higher temperatures.

8.4 Old people tend to put too much salt on their food. This is because as we get older our taste buds become less sensitive so we think food is increasingly bland, so we add more and more salt.

8.5 Here is Malvolio (Stephen Fry) trying to charm an unimpressed Olivia (Mark Rylance) in Shakespeare's Twelfth Night. He thinks Olivia loves him and wants him to wear yellow stockings cross-gartered. Only it's not true - too much imagination, too little empirical investigation!

8.6 Let's take the statement VX=L. A Kant scholar might look at 'VX=L' and immediately see it to be a synthetic a posteriori judgement. It's 'synthetic' because the second part isn't in the first part, and it's a posteriori because we will only know if it's true after checking the values. But it's not. VX=L isn't an equation, it's a sum, only I played a mean trick by writing it using Roman numerals. Today we would say 'Five times ten equals fifty'. VX=L is analytic and a priori true. It is an analytic judgement because it consists of two parts in which the second part must be true because it's contained in the first part. And it's a priori because it is true independent of experience. Why am I playing these silly games? Because this is precisely the opposite of what is supposed to happen in Kant's system. According to Kant the purpose of the mind orders a jumble of sense perception into the unity of knowledge. Maybe it does, but it can also do the opposite and mistake an analytic a priori judgment for a synthetic a posteriori judgement.

A Kantian might protest that these examples merely show the importance of having certain knowledge independent of sense perception but with the above examples it's not the empirical bit that's the problem, but how our minds organise the perceptions.

9, Between the ages of 25 and 50 Kant wrote several scientific papers, and though it wouldn't be fair to call him a failed scientist, these works are regarded as curiosities, nowhere near as important as his philosophical writing. Could it possibly be that he was slightly jealous of the endless triumphs ratcheted up by the scientists? Is it sheer coincidence that he created a philosophy in which what he was good at was the most important thing, and what other people were good at was secondary?

Anyway, the above are just some quibbles I'm chucking out there, a bit of throat clearing. Here are my serious objections:

3.7.1 Serious Objections

How do we know when we are wrong? It's a practical question.

If knowledge and morality are derived from an analysis of the mind, and empirical evidence has been discounted as a method of proof, then what do we do when people disagree? We all misunderstand things from time to time but what does a misunderstanding Kantian do? How is misunderstanding rectified if the mind is the rule giver for everything outside itself? Cross-checking involves sense perception so that's out, what does that leave? Nothing really, other than to look deeper and deeper inside ourselves until we find a kernel of truth so pure that to disagree would feel like an attack on our character. For example, let's look at the Categorical Imperative. If we are to 'act as if the maxim of our actions were to be a general rule' then what do we do when the general rule I think is good differs from the one you think is good? If a third party adjudicates then I am not following my innate moral sense but theirs. So we end up in a world of moral relativism in which there are a large number of subjective truths and a small number of objective truths. Our obsession with beliefs has rendered us incapable of discussing the simplest disagreements.

3.7.2 Necessary Knowledge
Kant wanted to establish knowledge that wasn't just a priori true but *necessarily* true. But 'necessary' knowledge is a very particular, rarefied type of knowledge. Necessary knowledge is knowledge that could not possibly be false (eg squares are rectangles). But in the modern world it is no longer certain that such a thing exists. In Kant's day Newtonian physics and Euclidian Geometry were considered necessarily true, now we know they are not. (And some Philosophers like Quine even question whether maths is necessarily true!) Because Hume had undermined causality Kant based his philosophy on the fundamental nature of the mind because that was the one thing we have direct access to independent of questionable sense experience. This led him to relegate a posteriori knowledge to a lower class of knowledge, which for him was just the study of mere surface appearances (the study of phenomena not noumena). So his quest for necessary knowledge led him to a very extreme form of subjectivism.

3.7.3 Unifying opposites
Kant's great genius was in unifying things that seemed mutually exclusive, for example his philosophy gives us morality without organised religion, a secular belief system, determinism <u>with</u> free will, and a reasonable argument for following our inner conscience.

The 'continental rationalists' (Descartes, Spinoza, Leibniz) held that knowledge should be built on a small number of inner certainties, whereas the 'British empiricists' (Locke, Berkeley and Hume) held that the exterior formed the interior. Kant sought to marry these two schools together with his famous phrase 'precepts without concepts are blind, concepts without precepts are empty'. But this is not some yin and yang type meeting of equals, Kant maintains perceptions are <u>met</u> by our minds. For him the mind was the active agent that ordered the raw material of sensation into knowledge. Because he was interested in unifying the philosophies of the Continental Rationalists and the British Empiricists it's surprising to see him ultimately come down on the side of subjectivism here. Why not say (as Freud would later on) that there is a reciprocal arrangement in which the core of the mind both forms and is formed? He could have held that position and still refuted Locke's claim that 'there is nothing in the mind that was not first in the senses', but he was so anxious to refute Hume he downgraded empiricism altogether and sided with Leibniz that 'there is nothing in the mind that was not first in the senses – except the intellect'. But this took us to the opposite extreme – a philosophy in which what is innermost is uppermost, the interior dominates the exterior, solipsisms run riot and there no objective check on what we believe.

3.7.4 Arthur Holmes
Doctor Arthur Holmes says: "Kant in effect tells us, the most I can say at this stage of the analysis, is that I am a transcendental unity of my perception, I am the unified totality of all my thought. Well, that's a bit better than what old David Hume did, when he said 'I am a bundle of perceptions' but didn't have anything to bundle them together with."

This is a terrific argument but surely I'm entitled to flip it around and ask 'from whence cometh the thing that bundles the perceptions together?' It must be an assemblage of things that were formerly external. What do our minds form themselves with? If the mind learned how to do it then that shows a reliance on outside influence. And if the mind is preformed to do it then that sounds like precisely the sort of 'common sense' argument of Beattie and Reid that Kant had already rejected. (That's James Beattie the Scottish philosopher, not Warren 'yo-yo pants' Beatty with the fingertips). So we end up with Sartre's idea that somehow we create ourselves. If 'precepts without concepts are blind' then from whence cometh the concepts? If concepts can organise perception, but what we perceive can't influence how we conceptualise then Kant hasn't really succeeded in marrying the rationalist and empiricist traditions.

3.7.5 Psychology

Recall the famous scene in King Lear where Lear, his fool, Edgar and Kent are in a storm outside a hovel. There is Lear himself who is going senile. There is the fool who is a simpleton but in many ways is the most knowing. Edgar 'poor tom' is feigning madness, and Kent is sane to provide dramatic contrast to the others. The scene is set within a storm to symbolise humans in their most basic form. Here Shakespeare is anticipating what would later be called psychoanalysis. He observed different mental conditions, attributed them to different characters and bundled the characters together in one scene for dramatic effect. In Kant's time this is what passed for what today we would call an examination of madness.

The word 'psychology' already existed in Kant's day (indeed he was one of its pioneers) but whilst artists have always observed the human condition, in the 1780's the formal scientific study of the mind was in its infancy - it would be another century before Freud. Kant was happy to found his philosophy on an analysis of the mind because for him, man was the rational animal. For him a melee of sensations cascade into the mind where they are organised. For him the mind was the thing that orders, not something that disorders. For him empiricism was the problem not the solution. For him the mind provides solutions not problems. For him answers are inside not outside. For him the shadows are outside not inside. But what if it's the other way round? What if we are mad and our inner conscience is not a check on our outward excesses but a generator of them? What if we are not mad but so emotionally invested in something that our mind becomes an unsuitable thing on which to base our knowledge? What if the shadows of the mind overwhelm our faculty of reason and we become selectively sceptical, outwardly appearing to be rational whilst adopting positions based on emotional baggage? What if someone has a personality disorder and they feel no inner moral call to duty? Can you see where this is going? Not only does Kant's system not seem to acknowledge the existence of madness, but if nothing can be known of any external 'thing in itself' then his system would seem to make any diagnosis of madness impossible! If cross-checking is ruled out then what is to prevent us from going mad? And here I'm not just talking about you or me, I'm talking about the human species generally. With the best will in the world, the great man seems to have abolished objective knowledge and objective morality. This has deprived us of our most useful tool of refutation and opened the door to a dictatorship of spasms.

3.7.6 The shadows are far more powerful than we would like to admit.
This is a problem Schopenhauer foresaw. Later on in The Fourfold Root he says "What is properly called thinking, in its narrowest sense, is the occupation of the intellect with conceptions … Conceptions must not be confounded with pictures of the imagination … Even when used to represent a conception, a picture of the imagination (phantasm) ought to be distinguished from a conception". But how do we know when we are confounding conceptions with phantasms? Once Kant has awarded supremacy to the mind and applied infinite scepticism only to empiricism, what is there to stop our imaginations running away with us? Nothing. And this is a serious problem because our imaginations are far more powerful than we would like to admit.

Above is a picture called Hand in Doorway by Ralph Gibson. Let's contrast it with these anatomical studies by Leonardo.

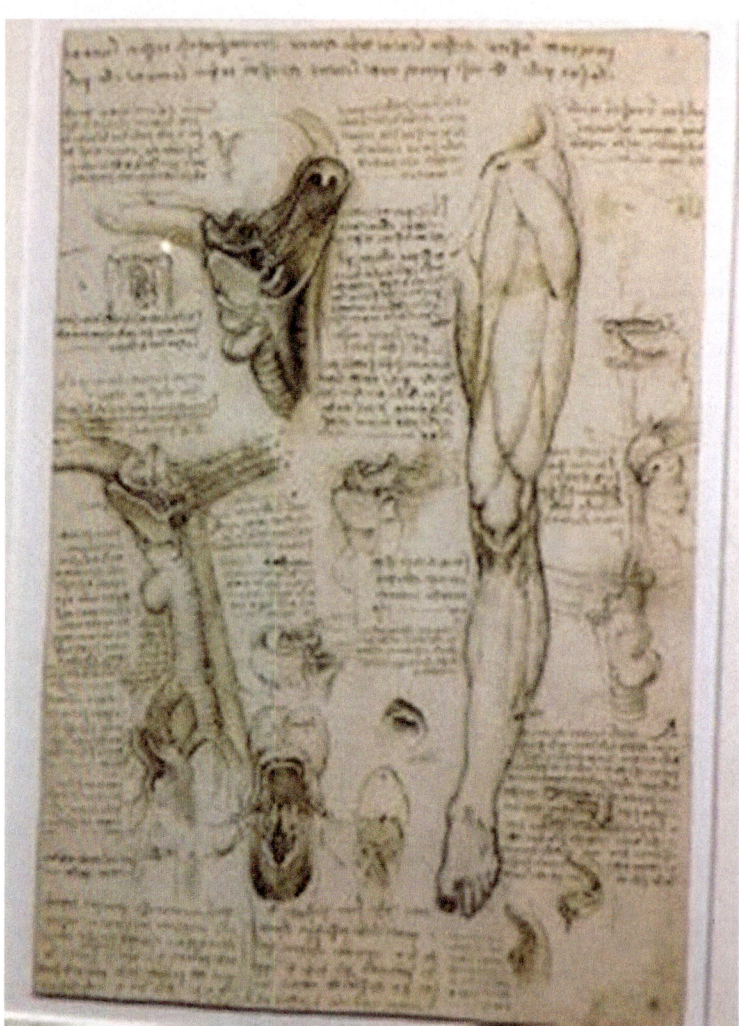

The Gibson is implicit whereas the Leonardo is explicit. The Gibson is about imagination whereas the Leonardo is about observation. The Gibson could not be less graphic, the Leonardo could not be more graphic. The Gibson deliberately restricts what we see so our minds fill in the blanks, whereas Leonardo does the opposite, showing us the actuality from various angles. Which image is about sex and violence? The one with naked dead body parts? Actually no. It is the Gibson that is about heavenly pleasures or nightmarish suffering, because *Hand in Doorway* is a repository for our imagination whereas with his sketches, Leonardo is concerned to leave nothing to the imagination. So whereas the Leonardo brings knowledge to our minds, with the Gibson, it is all about what our minds bring to the image. I'm using these as examples to show how the imagination can take us over. If we are given a small amount of information, everything we don't know can become the repository or infinite fears, hopes or desires. As Gibson has restricted what we see, so the emotional hold his work has over us increases, whereas for all its graphic dismembered gore, the Leonardo sketches actually enlighten.

Another example. In Othello, Othello and Desdemona have everything going for them. There is no reason at all why they should not be happy together for the rest of their lives. But Iago manages to destroy their love and their lives. He does this with the most miniscule amount of empirical evidence –

one little handkerchief. But once Iago had planted the seed of doubt, Othello sees reasons for doubt everywhere. It is Othello's own imagination that does Iago's work for him. So the more virtuous Desdemona is, the more subtle her deceit appears to Othello. How was this great man laid low? Not by force of arms, but by his own imagination, because our imaginations control even the greatest of us much more than we or Kant would like to admit.

Now ask yourself, what if the value of empiricism is undermined altogether? What prevents Schopenhauer's 'phantasms' from completely taking over? The everyday reality around us is mundane and finite, whereas what we can imagine is fantastic and infinite. The people here are partly good partly bad, the people there are superheroes or monsters. If the dominant philosophy is one where the mind imposes itself on what is around it, we can easily find ourselves overwhelmed by the gulf between what is and what we imagine. Given that our minds are full of shadows, how can a study of the mind yield more dependable knowledge than cross-checking patterns? I would argue it can't.

(Note, this is why religions often seek to prohibit certain images or restrict certain views – to maximise irrational hysteria.)

3.7.6.1 To sleep perchance to dream
It is well documented that Kant rose early, and some commentators think his self-imposed lack of sleep may have contributed to his senility in old age. When the mind goes from unconscious to conscious the rational side returns to dominance. So every day Kant sought to maximise the time spent in the rational state. Obviously I am speculating here but could it possibly be that whist he awarded supremacy to the noumenal realm, Kant was not fully prepared to accept its true nature? That the thing-in-itself of a human being is not divine, but a churning drive of desires and fears? Obviously the Romantics who came later would have no qualms about this.

3.7.7 Belief is the problem not the solution
Belief is the problem. In the modern world we frequently hear people say "Yes – but that is what I really believe". And they actually say this as if it were some sort of serious explanation, when a weaker argument is difficult to imagine! Belief is thinking something true despite the evidence. Knowledge is accepting evidence despite the belief. What societies are the cruellest? The ones based on belief. Which societies prosper? The ones where people can speculate. Where is there war? Where theists give answers. Where is there peace? Where people can ask questions. Do you get married because you *believe* in it? Hopefully not! Hopefully your marriage is based on knowledge of what someone is really like!

In all three of Kant's critiques (the critiques of Pure Reason, Practical Reason and Judgement) he makes clear there is no possibility of metaphysical knowledge in the traditional sense that involves logical certainty and objectivity, but that there is a basis for metaphysical beliefs. Maybe he is right, I don't know, the problem is that belief tends to generate decline, cruelty and insoluble conflict.

3.7.8 Empiricism is valid
What if I watch a play, say Oedipus by Sophocles. The journey from the 'thing in itself' of Sophocles to the 'thing in itself' of me could hardly be more convoluted. The play was written 2500 years ago, translated (at least once), directed by someone concerned it should be conveyed in a certain way, and acted by people, every one of whom will bring their own experience to their interpretations. Again and again, at every stage along the geographical and historical chain from Sophocles to me, empiricism has played a part. Is the knowledge we derive from it a lower class of knowledge? Does it somehow not count as *proper* knowledge? Not at all! Despite the tenuousness of the relationship between object and subject there is an emphatic connection between the two. Sophocles has looked into our souls and we have looked into his. If what we gain from watching Oedipus, or listening to Beethoven cannot be called knowledge then I don't know what can!

3.7.9 Surprise!
If the external is determined by the internal then why is life full of surprises? Seriously. What is a surprise? It's when our expectations are confronted by an external reality. And here I'm not just talking about winning the lottery. Think of someone you know really well, say your best friend. You have a picture of them and what they are like, but when you meet them for a pint, the external reality of them will push against your idea of them and the conversation will be different to the conversation you expected, which is, I suppose precisely why you meet for a pint! But here I'm not just talking about surprises in our daily lives but our dreams too. Kant assumes that when we think about how we think, that act is independent of sensory experience so we can call it a pure a priori form of intuition, but dreams are full of surprises. And for a surprise there has to be one who surprises and another who is surprised. So the mind cannot be a singular entity. For a dream to be surprising the mind must consist of at least two active parts. And if a mind is multi-conscious, then that would seem to dispose of the Cogito, Rationalist philosophy, and the whole idea of gaining a priori knowledge from epistemology. If the mind is a singular thing, why do we struggle with ourselves?

3.7.10 Where is the love?
Why is love apparently absent from Kant's system? Does that reality somehow not count? And here I'm not being philosophy-light. This is a serious objection. In the whole 800 pages of the first critique love doesn't get a mention. But surely love is painful precisely because it involves the thing in itself ceasing to be a thing in itself and starting to be part of a greater unity. The mind is created by an interaction between a man and woman in which a sperm enters an egg and they fuse into a greater unity. If that is how the mind begins, why should it not continue in a similar manner? With a reciprocal enrichment between the external and internal? in which that entering and that receiving both form and are formed? The categories do not organise the perceptions any more than the egg organises the sperm - they fuse into a greater unity.

And if I might intrude an argument as vulgar as procreation, is desire to live and make life, not a categorical inner law, synthetic and a priori? Not only can this (morally ambiguous) act yield pleasure (which is a type of goodness) but it can also result in the greater (greatest?) good of parenthood. The desire to procreate and the joy of parenthood are as innate and universal as any call to moral duty. Which innate call do we heed if the argument for one could just as easily be made for the other?

3.7.11 Knowledge comes from interaction not introspection

Kant's system is obviously of monumental importance, but it is founded on the notion that knowledge and morality come from introspection rather than interaction. When I am doing my job drawing a building, and I think there is something wrong, do I search my feelings? Do I look inside myself to establish a priori knowledge? No. I do the opposite. I cross-check external information to try to work out where I erred. I establish knowledge by looking outwards not inwards. Who would you prefer to fly the plane – someone who goes with their feelings or someone who cross-checks? Which chair is the best? The one where a genius built their dream? Or the one where an experienced carpenter learned from several prototypes? If in a moment of moral crisis we trust our inner feelings, then how do we later decide whether the correct decision was made? Decisions based on feelings are easier to live with than decisions based on discussion because they don't have to be explained, but that doesn't make them exempt from being wrong, indeed someone whose life is defined by obeying their inner calling is very likely to lead a catastrophic life.

Now imagine that this isn't just a misunderstanding for Basil Fawlty or Malvolio but a broad social movement in which there is a wholesale denial of empiricism on a national, even continental scale. Well, I ask you to imagine it, but the problem is, it doesn't require any imagination at all. Humanity is involved in a collective struggle for sanity.

Note: These are obviously hugely contested issues regarding a very complex person, who was important for both the enlightenment, romanticism, modernism and post modernism. But I don't want to bog things down too much by pre-emptively answering every hypothetical objection. I apologise if it seems I am thrashing about against a sea of troubles, trying to address everything at once, but I don't see how else I can discuss general trends in many places over many years. How other than by generalising can the big picture be established?

3.8 The EU is a Kantian Project

Now let's bring this back to Brexit. Here is a Venn diagram, with synthetic judgements on the left and a priori judgements on the right. We have seen already that Kant was interested in synthetic a priori judgements, so where these two circles overlap I have put a 'K' for Kant.

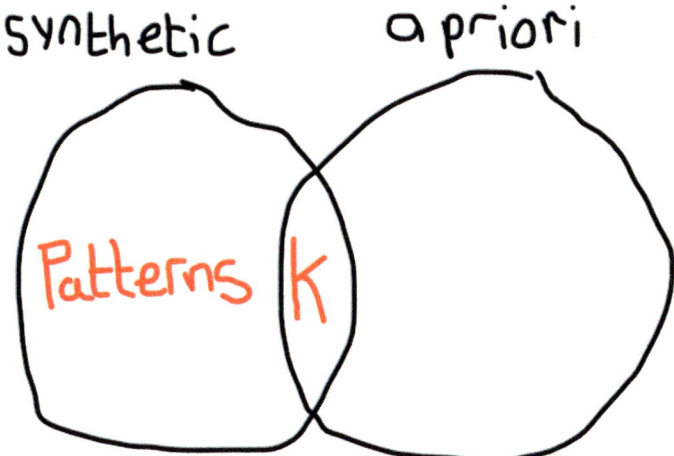

Earlier on in this book I made various arguments where I tried to identify general, approximate patterns from empirical observations. What if I wanted to plonk my arguments onto this Venn diagram? Well my arguments were synthetic a posteriori so that's why I've written 'patterns' inside the synthetic set, but outside the a priori set. Basically a Kantian looking at my arguments would be perfectly happy to dismiss them altogether; after all, in Kant's philosophy a posteriori judgements don't even count as knowledge at all!

Remain arguments never ever consisted of factual explanations about why us democratically governing ourselves was a bad thing, they never gave *examples* of laws we couldn't write for ourselves, they never gave *examples* of countries that made the mistake of becoming independent democracies. Ultimately Remainers would not recognise my arguments precisely because my arguments pertain to the phenomenal realm.

What sort of arguments did the EU supporters make? Arguments based on inner values rather than observations. I have shown already that if we look at the empirical evidence there is no reason to associate the EU with peace, prosperity or human rights. Indeed being an independent democracy was far more likely to achieve those things. But nonetheless EU supporters associated the EU with peace, prosperity and human rights, and because they considered those things to be morally good, for them supporting the EU and being ethical were one and the same. Even when the empirical evidence showed the EU generating unemployment, driving down wages, enriching the elite and crushing human rights in Greece and Catalonia, Remainers' core values overwhelmed those observations allowing them to disregard a mountain of empirical evidence. How would we describe Remain's arguments? Once they had fused together morality and EU membership it was simplicity itself for Remainers to trot out synthetic a priori arguments for membership. Their arguments were a priori because they rejected empiricism and synthetic because they weren't analytic. Remain's arguments were Kantian. They considered themselves noumenally good and ourselves noumenally bad, nothing else mattered. Their 'thing in itself' was moral so they were right, ours was immoral so we were wrong.

Not only were Remain's arguments for membership Kantian, but their arguments against Leavers were as well. Apparently we were bad, mad, stupid or racist. (I've given examples of this already) These were attacks on our character. Overwhelmingly Remainers targeted the 'thing in itself' of me and my fellow Brexiteers. Kantian.

We fought our campaign in Kant's phenomenal realm. Remainers fought theirs in Kant's noumenal realm. Arguments for leave were empirical observations. Arguments for remain were belief-based. Remainers attacked leavers by accusing us of having a bad moral core.

The EU is a Kantian project
1, The EU and Transcendental Idealism were both set up with the best will in the world by decent people.

2, Kant proposed a federation of nation states.

3, Kant and the EU advocate democracy in theory but not in practice. Kant was by nature of liberal temperament and greeted the French revolution with joy. He maintained that we should treat every man as an end in himself. If we take this to mean that every man should count equally in determining actions by which many are affected, then yes, Kant was a democrat; but as usual with Kant it is more complex than that. He advocated states being republican, but by 'republican' he simply meant that the people who write the laws and the people who implement them should be separate. He does not mean there should be no king, indeed he says it would be easiest to get a perfect government under a monarchy. Writing during the French 'reign of terror' he was suspicious of how democracy establishes executive power, as majority rule was a threat to individual liberty:

"The 'whole people' so called … are not really all but only a majority: So that here the universal will is in contradiction with itself and with the principle of freedom."

We have already seen that Kant thought women should be excluded from democracy for 'natural reasons', he also thought men who did not own property should be excluded too. So we see he introduces qualifications to curtail what he sees as the excesses of democracy, when it is surely better to introduce democracy to curtail the excesses of the unelected. "only a majority"? … Only? Better a majority than a minority – or a monarchy! I have discussed the EU's anti-democratic nature in an earlier section.

4, How are misunderstandings acknowledged and rectified? If the Commission, bureaucrats and five EU 'presidents' don't have to face the electorate then they are as independent of appraisal as Kant's 'thing in itself' is from empirical observation!

5, The EU is a belief-based system. (See section 2.5) Who said 'We have to do away with knowledge to make room for belief'? Kant. (See also bit about belief in section 3.4)

6, The EU and Kantian philosophy are both labyrinthine in nature. There are two types of people: Those who understand the labyrinth and those who don't. Those who don't are reluctant to criticise something they don't fully understand, and even if they do make a valid criticism they can always be dismissed by someone claiming to truly understand it (even if the person claiming to understand it is a charlatan!) And what about those who genuinely do understand the labyrinth? Well, they probably understand it because they have spent years immersed in it; and why spend years immersed in something you disapprove of? It has become part of their life so now they hope to profit somehow from their specialist knowledge of the labyrinth. Thus complexity becomes a source of comfort for them, preventing their specialist knowledge from being devalued; it becomes seductive, a shield from awkward questions and a hill to defend. They come to view complexity as sophistication, and its shortcomings as foibles. So who will stand against a labyrinth? Those who can explain it have an interest in it, and those who can't have no interest in it. Who does that leave? Just a couple of pedantic misfits arguing the toss when they could be doing something more fun with their lives like reading to the kids, going down the pub or smacking one out. This isn't to say complex systems can't be good, just that they're better at insulating bad arguments from scrutiny than simple systems.

7, Arguments for the EU and the Transcendental Analytic both consist of incomprehensible gobbledygook. In them there is none of the blunt cogency of the American Constitution (inspired by Tom Paine and John Locke).

8, Laymen like myself are reticent to air reasonable objections, as we are constantly told the apparent absurdities of the system are down to our ignorance rather than the system's imperfections.

No surprise then, that it was the British with our history of empiricism who dramatically rejected EU membership, and that the continentals should find this so incomprehensible.

3.9 There Is A Name To My Pain.
Between 2016 and 2020 there was clearly something going on in British society, a cultural and social phenomenon in which a mind-set and a consistent pattern of behaviour emerged, not in one or two people but in an entire section of society. I want to write about that, and to make it easy to write about, I want to give it a name.

Initially I thought of calling it 'EU Syndrome' or 'Remain Syndrome' but quickly decided against that, partly because it felt like I was just accusing people who disagree with me of being crazy, but mainly because I could see the errors made by EU supporters being replicated by lots of other groups around the world. So then I thought of calling it 'Antithesis Syndrome'.

Everything about Brexit was antithetical. (See section 2.11) The real far-right condemned democrats for being the 'far-right'. Theresa May sought to keep us under EU rule with her 'Withdrawal Agreement'. Remainers mounted a coup whilst shouting 'Stop the Coup'. Self-proclaimed socialists staunchly defended a neo-liberal entity. The Liberal Democrat party campaigned against liberal values and democracy. The Labour Party ('For the many not the few') sided with the elite and condemned the proletariat as bigots. Young 'activists' defended the existing system while a bunch of middle-aged has-beens effected a revolution. Nothing was as it seemed. At every turn the adjective which most totally misrepresented the reality was employed. This was no accident, but a campaign of mass psychological abuse and disinformation on a continental scale designed to achieve the maximum power over the maximum number of people, by the minimum number of people, constrained by the minimum amount of democracy.

But then when I looked at various other major issues I saw 'Antithesis Syndrome' cropping up all over the place. There is the Thatcherite who embraces neoliberalism because they advocate high growth, when neoliberalism has delivered crappy growth levels, globally for decades. There are the climate change deniers who reject a mountain of empirical evidence and attack nature in the name of liberty when nothing could curtail our liberty more than the destruction of nature. There are the capitalists who destroy the environment to 'create wealth' when nothing could destroy wealth more effectively than destroying the environment. There are the apologists for Islam who masquerade as liberals and who condemn the critics of Islam as illiberal. There are those who claim Islam to be a religion of peace when, from its inception, it has been primarily concerned with the domination of territory. Then there are those who try to outlaw free speech in the name of decency. Also we see Antithesis Syndrome in several ways with the supporters of Donald Trump. Firstly, some like the way Trump is seen to be tough on Islamists when nothing could reduce the power of Islamic states more than ending dependence on oil and investing in renewable energy, strategies which Trump wholly rejects. Then there are the Trump supporters who like him because they feel he embodies 'Christian values' when a less Christian person is difficult to imagine. (Spiteful, vengeful, unforgiving, craven, covetous, belligerent, greedy, cruel and dishonest!) There are the holocaust deniers who refuse to accept one of the most exhaustively documented events in history. Then there are the flat-earthers (Seriously!) Theists, creationists, anti-Darwinists, the 'Conservatives' opposed to conservation, the list goes on but all the above are exhibiting symptoms of the same syndrome to a greater or lesser extent. I came to this from my particular background as a Brexiteer, but saw there was a pattern in which many other groups were making similar basic mistakes to the Remainers.

The above are serious problems for the world and the human race, in each above instance a mountain of empirical evidence is being disregarded by people apparently in the grip of a type of emotional spasm. There is overwhelming empirical evidence that something is real, which for emotive reasons they can't bring themselves to accept, so they scorn evidence that confronts them and embrace evidence that comforts them. Their minds impose their inherent values on the information they receive. And because the mind is the law-giver scepticism is applied selectively depending on belief. In short, the above are examples of the sort of bullshit you have to wade through if people under-rate empiricism and over-rate belief (Kantian).

Then I had another rethink about the name. As a phrase 'Antithesis Syndrome' was a bit pretentious and academic. So what to call it? Finally, I thought of a name I felt happy with: 'Othello Syndrome'.

Othello Syndrome is when people describe things as their opposite, attack what they should defend and defend what they should attack. Othello Syndrome is when people do this because their imagination has overwhelmed their reason. Othello Syndrome affects clever people as much as silly people because however intelligent we are, our knowledge is only finite whereas what we can imagine is infinite. (for all of us the path not taken will always be more fantastic than the path taken, because the path not taken is the repository of our imaginations). Othello Syndrome sees the worst in the unknown. Othello Syndrome tends towards extremity. As we exclude people who challenge us from our social circle and befriend those with whom we share common interests, so we find ourselves more and more in a world which confirms our world view. This creates a vicious circle. Evidence that confronts is scorned, evidence that confirms is embraced. Opinions become more hysterical, the imagined depravity of those with different opinions becomes more extreme. We stop seeing them as real human beings. 'Our lot' are heroes 'their lot' are monsters.

I wonder what my hero Karl Popper would make of 'Othello Syndrome'? I think he would be concerned that I was simply seeing it everywhere in the same way Adler saw 'inferiority complex' everywhere. But prioritising how we see over what we see is indeed widespread. And I think 'Othello Syndrome' is falsifiable: If lots of observations in lots of places confirm a clear pattern then that isn't a 'phantasm'.

What do the following have in common? Donald Trump, Remainers, flat-earthers, climate change deniers, the neoliberal who desires economic growth, the person who pollutes because they desire prosperity, Darwin sceptics, the person who associates Islam with peace and multiculturalism? All the above reject empirical observation as a method of proof. They are guided by an inner voice which selectively applies excessive scepticism to empiricism and insufficient scepticism to gut feelings. Their core beliefs are so powerful as to overwhelm the empirical evidence they perceive. This I call Othello Syndrome.

With the best will in the world Kantian philosophy can lead to Othello Syndrome in which empiricism is sacrificed for beliefs, and because this is derived from the inherent nature of our minds there is no mitigating check we can make to get us off the road to extremity. Worst of all Othello Syndrome is not simply one person's misunderstanding – it has become a social phenomenon.

3.10 Have I got any better ideas?
Well If I am going to criticise the great man's system I suppose I am required to propose an alternative so here goes:

3.10.1 Thinking and Believing
The ears are for hearing, the nose is for smelling, the eyes are for seeing and the mind is for … thinking. Religions (belief systems) use repetition, psychological abuse and cultural coercion to try to get your mind to do the opposite of what it is supposed to do. Religions seek to de-rationalise, to train your mind to make spasmodic, unthinking decisions. And sure enough when we look around the world where belief systems prevail we see the destruction of humanity and nature. The believers (the thoughtless people) generate problems whereas the questioners (the thoughtful people) generate solutions.

3.10.2. Knowledge Belief Definitions
So I want to say belief and knowledge are different, and that belief is bad and knowledge is good. But if I want knowledge and belief definitions that are binary, and I lump everything that isn't necessary knowledge under 'belief' then that isn't going to give us much usable knowledge to work with. So how about we define knowledge as that which is supported by evidence, and belief as that which is not? This will give us some approximate, rough-hewn knowledge to work with. Kantians may protest but it seems to me that obsessing about a priori 'knowledge' is the problem, not the solution. To stop ourselves, our societies and our planet from being destroyed by madness we need a knowledge that is proportional to evidence, a knowledge that is mutually agreed, a knowledge founded on observations of the exterior rather than the interior, a knowledge that accepts the validity of patterns. We need synthetic a posteriori knowledge.

So let's say knowledge isn't that which is proved but that which isn't disproved. Something for which there is some evidence for and none against. I am sitting on chair. Maybe I can't prove I'm sitting on a chair, but the salient point is that you can't prove I'm not. If there is some evidence I'm sitting on a chair and none that I'm not, then we 'know' I'm sitting on a chair pending refutation. The onus is on those doubting what appears to be real, to produce an argument.

Surely we don't require an analysis of the workings of the mind to accept that maths, geometry and science are valid? Surely the important thing is not that we can prove them sound but that we can't prove them unsound? So why not simply accept as correct ideas that have withstood attempts to prove they are incorrect? Or accept them as correct given certain assumptions?

So if I ask you what the above is a drawing of, and I agree with your answer, then we can say something true about the drawing, correct? Why not derive knowledge from cross-checking rather than introspection? I'll summarise the above with a simple phrase: Knowledge requires no belief. Belief requires no knowledge.

I'm sure there are people much cleverer than me who will immediately see problems, but my definitions allow me to say "we know Beethoven was a great composer", Kant's does not. With my definitions Newtonian physics is an objective reality, with Kant's, time and space are just subjective forms of sensibility. For someone who accepts Kant's answer to Hume, any pattern, however consistent cannot give knowledge. But what is more absurd, saying we can know things from patterns, or that we can't? Kant was clear that his interior-based system cannot give objective knowledge, so why not make do with the virtually-objective 'knowledge' given to us by external cross-checking and dialogue?

It seems to me any thought must involve some degree of empiricism, so we must either accept empirical evidence has some merit or leave the last word to Hume, accept there is no such thing as knowledge, and fall off the edge of the world. To base knowledge on introspection leads to the madness of hermits, irresolvable belief wars, mass mental health issues and computer screens filled with psychological abuse.

Traditional philosophy holds that pure, necessary knowledge is virtually non-existent; but if, instead of assuming ignorance pending proof we agree knowledge pending refutation, we can say we know all sorts of useful things. I know my left from right, and the rules of chess, how to tie shoe laces etc. Relational knowledge, involving cross-checking gives us the jury system, peer review, love, football and all manner of perfectly usable knowledge to live by.

Belief is internally generated pseudo knowledge. Knowledge must be independent of belief, because if it wasn't then it wouldn't be knowledge. "I believe" precedes irrelevant statements. Saying that you believe something is not an argument. We should not fear a lack of belief but an excess of it.

The great errors of history are belief based. We need to stop talking about belief as if it were somehow a valid basis for proceeding. And certainly we should not accord belief some rarefied status whereby it is exempt from criticism. So don't think there is nothing pernicious about all these silly children's programs where the heroes win because they believe in their dream. Believing is a recipe for disaster and nothing to be proud of.

Thoughtless people make problems, thoughtful people make solutions. If I were to ask a carpenter about how their chair works they would talk about the materials, the way the joints work and the task it had to fulfil - they would explain with recourse to something *external* to themselves. Similarly, if I were to ask a structural engineer why a building stands up or a doctor why a medicine works. They would explain, not by referring to internal beliefs but external tests. Gangsters do the opposite, their explanations amount to little more than *"because that's what I think"*. We can call this *'the dictator's prerogative'* or we can call this *'the divine right of kings'* but what we can't call it is an argument. Something is the case because that's what you believe? Call that an argument? If it's true because you *believe* it's true, then how do we know your belief isn't:

A, Insincere
B, Mistaken
C, Insincere *and* mistaken

Note: If I say the 'ruling elite' are collectively wrong, then obviously by the same argument, the lower classes can be too. However, I would argue that the lower classes are always less likely to be collectively wrong, because their lives tend to involve a greater degree of interaction and cross-checking with other social groups.

Thinkers: submit ideas to people (best ideas prevail).
Believers: people submit to ideas (most coercive prevail).

Necessary Knowledge or Belief?
Kant is clear his system does not provide objective knowledge about the external world. So why not flip it around and make do with the approximate knowledge we get from cross checking? It's not an either/or choice between necessary knowledge and belief. For example 'Pi = 3.14' or 'winter is colder than summer' may not be *necessarily* true, but that doesn't make them belief, that makes them approximate knowledge. Traditionally approximate knowledge is under-valued by philosophers and highly valued by everyone else.

Basically
The TLDR is this. According to Kant's system, "but that's what I believe" is an argument that has validity; according to mine it is not.

3.10.3 Relational Knowledge

Let's consider the statement "I walk in Brighton". Traditional philosophy has been fixated with nouns and verbs; and in that sentence there are two nouns and one verb. But what word in that sentence is permanent? I may not always exist, walking may not always exist, Brighton may not always exist, but there will always be relationships, there will always be things inside other things. The one thing in that sentence we will always need a word for is not the verb or the nouns but the little relational word 'in'. Heraclitus and Parmenides inaugurated a science concerned with verbs and nouns (respectively). Though useful, maybe this has led us to overlook the value of relational knowledge. (See also Russell, Problems of Philosophy. Chapter 9).

3.10.4 Abolish the 'I'

I've already said I think we should base knowledge on interaction more and introspection less. So, if Berkeley can abolish 'matter' and Hume can abolish 'mind' then how about if we abolish the 'I'? Abolishing the 'I' is not as crazy as it may first appear. After all, some argue that society doesn't exist, some argue that countries and borders shouldn't exist, so why should the assumption that individuals exist go unchallenged? Could it be that Descartes' Cogito was wrong from the first word?

1, The act of creating life itself is one of interaction, not introspection, so why not say the same of knowledge? If the mind is formed by sexual interaction then it is not absurd to suggest that it continues in a similar manner - that it develops via interaction between inside and outside. The mind does not organise sense perception any more than the egg organises the sperm. What if the ultimate reality is not the 'I' but the 'we'? What if 'I' am not an 'I' at all? but a semi-autonomous part of 'us'? Knowledge is the unity of sense perception with the 'thing in itself'.

2, The 'I' cannot be autonomous because our dreams are full of surprises, and for a surprise there has to be one that surprises and another that is surprised. So if dreams have surprises, the mind must have at least two active parts. There is nothing more human than to be in conflict with ourselves. So if knowledge must be relational (even when it is internal) all knowledge must be relational. The cross-checking required to establish things doesn't just take place between us but within us as well. (If different parts of the mind are in conflict with one another, the whole notion of mind-generated knowledge seems to be out the window.)

3, I have already mentioned that love is painful precisely because it involves the 'thing in itself' ceasing to be a 'thing in itself' and starting to be part of a greater unity. Surely love has as valid a claim to reality as Kant's noumena?

4, 'Every time we say goodbye I die a little'. When someone close to us dies, or when our children are born, or when we make love or marry or split up there is an overwhelming feeling that something within ourselves has fundamentally changed too; we are moved precisely because they are a part of us. Schopenhauer said Kant's chief merit was the distinction of the phenomenon from the 'thing in itself'. But things in themselves are not autonomous. They are interconnected. By what? Phenomena.

5, What are the most important moments of our lives? Not when we are alone (like Descartes in the stove) but when we are alone *together*.

6, We share a joke, we read a book, we look at a painting, we listen to a song, we remember or look forward to a meeting. Meaning is relational, and that is an ultimate reality I am prepared to set against anything Kant has to offer. I'm not saying that art should be created by teams of people but that art is never simply about the artist, it is always about their relationship with us.

7, Newton conceded that 'if I have seen further it is because I stood on the shoulders of giants'. He gladly acknowledged that his work built upon previous work by Copernicus, Kepler and Galileo. What if there is no invention or inventors, only synthesis, and that knowledge is simply something we refine then pass like a baton to the next generation?

8, Minerals constantly enter and leave my body so why regard myself as a singular autonomous entity? The blood cells in my body seem to have a life of their own, there are various organisms/bacteria/mites living in or around me, my hair grows through its own will not mine. The extent of my mind's control over my body is limited, for example if I decide to not sleep or go to the toilet it will eventually happen anyway. An octopus has nine brains, leeches have 32! The Portuguese man o'war looks like a jelly fish, but it is not a single creature – it is a colony of smaller units called zooids. And I am part of a family that is constantly growing, dying and being born. All life depends on interrelationships so it seems an error to see the mind as an autonomous isolated thing. 'I' am an us.

9, Here are two bits of architecture:

The first is a design for the House of Agricultural Guards by Claude Nicholas Ledoux (1785) the other is Bibury in the Cotswolds.

One is the perfect unbuilt dream of a genius; the other was incrementally developed in situ by builders. Which offers us a design for life? The one where the design and construction are *integrated*, where the object and subject form a feedback loop constantly informing and enriching one another. When I design furniture, however much knowledge I have of tools and materials, I always find myself having to adapt the theory to the reality. The great compositions are by those who set up a feedback loop so the theory and practice inform each other.

10, And there is an ethical basis for abolishing the 'I' – after all, which people do the most to enhance the world? The ones who consider others. Additionally the goodness seems proportional to the consideration. So, the bad person considers only themselves. The good person considers others. The very good person considers every person and animal. And the best person of all always considers the entire glory of nature, that ever has been or that ever will be.

Note: Kant's ethical system is obviously of monumental importance, but there are difficulties. The main one being that there are acts which Kant would certainly disapprove of which are difficult to condemn using the categorical imperative. For example, a suicide bomber will consider themselves to be making a moral sacrifice, and their wish will be that everyone else also gives their lives to the same cause. So whilst you and I and Kant would be appalled by such an act, the problem is it becomes difficult to condemn using Kant's system. If however we say goodness is proportional to consideration of everyone and everything else, then denouncing suicide bombers becomes a formality. So instead of searching our conscience in a moment of moral crisis, we should constantly maximise consideration of everyone and everything else. Additionally if we follow this line of thinking through, I politely disagree with Islamic ideas not because I dislike Muslims but because I *don't* dislike Muslims. Overwhelmingly they are decent intelligent human beings so I do my best to help as much as I am able.

11, Philosophy is mostly about ontology (What is there?) and ethics (What should we do?). What is real and good? Well the most real and good thing I have experienced is when a woman said "Yes" to me. This obviously involves something external to myself. It is not knowledge derived from the mind's examination of itself, it is relational. Knowledge and morality are not derived from <u>within</u> but <u>between</u> us. It is the conjoining of the exterior and interior that matters. I maintain this is valid empiricism. Here again I am not making any particularly radical claim, I am simply restating what everyone who has been in love has known. The mind is relational, not autonomous.

Note: It is worth noting here that the three philosophers most preoccupied with the will/thing in itself (Kant, Schopenhauer and Nietzsche) never had families. In their lives they practised extreme autonomy. Sure enough where Kantian philosophy predominates there are low birth rates.

12, Kant was obviously much more intelligent than myself, but for all his genius, what I think he missed is that the most important moments of our lives are when 'things in themselves' conjoin or separate. The key events are the changing relationships between people (at birth procreation or death, saying 'hello' or 'goodbye' or 'I love you' or reading a book, looking at a painting or play etc). If meaning is relational then why shouldn't ethics, metaphysics, and ontology be so as well?

13, Everything is affected by what is adjacent (in space and time). Everything is simultaneously entering and leaving. Nothing is permanent except transition. What if the same was true of knowledge, but that instead of relativising knowledge, this made it approximately objective?

14, For Marx, Hegel and Spinoza the individual is virtually an irrelevance. For Nietzsche, Sartre and Kierkegaard society is virtually an irrelevance. The former proceed from the outside to the inside, the latter from the inside to the outside. But for me what is salient is the relationship between the two. 'I' am not an I, but part of us. Sartre's play 'No Exit' concludes with the words "Hell is other people". I think heaven is other people. Hell is what happens when beliefs are unchecked and unencumbered by considerations of others.

15, Now let's flip this around and ask ourselves, what do bad people want the least? Discussion. Every tyrant, sex offender, gangster, bully, thief, abusive partner, etc all say the same thing: "Don't talk". Even if you dispute what I propose you still have to accept I am advocating what bad people want least. Whenever you visit relations and you are warned in advance that there is something you should not mention, the very fact that there is pressure to be silent demonstrates there is something bad that needs to be discussed. The silence doesn't just confirm the problem – it becomes the problem.

16, I have produced my best work when I surrounded myself with people with people I admired and listened a lot - generally if I am the cleverest person in the room then I am in the wrong room! (Fortunately that doesn't happen very often) This is probably true of people generally - we have become too enamoured by the idea of the lone romantic genius. Interaction is underrated and will is overrated.

17, If the natural state of the mind is to be in conflict with itself, then it is an unsuitable thing on which to build rationalist axioms.

18, Which decisions do we most regret? The ones we didn't discuss.

19, Our minds are changed by interactions so knowledge (like sex or love) must be interaction-centric.

20, The apple is not sweet in itself; some species may consider it bitter. It has to potential to be sweet for humans. The sweetness only exists when the external (apple) interfaces with the internal (our sense perceptions) fusing into a unity we call 'sweetness'.

So my argument is that 'I' is just a semantic term of convenience that involves all sorts of assumptions. Because all right-wing politics is predicated on the notion of the individual, if the 'I' does not exist then the ramifications for right-wing politics are considerable.

The Rashomon Objection
In the film Rashomon by Akira Kurosawa the same events are retold by various protagonists, each of whom prove themselves to be unreliable witnesses. So does this undermine my idea that knowledge should be collectively cross-checked? I admit it does pose a problem for my theory, but however great the problem it poses for me, it poses an even greater problem for those claiming that knowledge and morality should be centralised.

Other objections
Obviously I'm reluctant to argue against myself but there are a couple of objections I'm obliged to acknowledge. Firstly I have argued that Kant is the architect of the modern world, but Bach's Well-Tempered Clavier meets every description of modernist music and predates the first critique by 59 years. This is significant because it is one of the few truly great works of art we can be confident Kant experienced first-hand. So possibly the idea of extreme distillation is something that Kant adapted rather than invented. Secondly, in 1776 (five years before the First Critique) Adam Smith published *Wealth of Nations*, giving the famous description of the manufacture of pins. This is an industrial process called the 'division of labour'. Previously one craftsman would have manufactured the pins but this task has now been categorised into a series of elemental acts. So it might be argued that the industrial process influenced the epistemological theory and not vice versa.

Conclusion
Could it be that the whole of existence is simply changing relationships between semi-autonomous 'things'? And that physics and chemistry are simply the coupling and decoupling elements and forces? The reader is welcome to forget everything I've written except the following: The 'I' is not autonomous.

Abolishing the 'I' gives us a useful form of knowledge based on cross-checking patterns and shared experience. Additionally abolishing the 'I' helps us to understand how we are enriched by sacrifice - how we get by giving. Also it helps us understand why some people in history have worked on projects like gothic cathedrals which they knew they would never see completed. They did it not for themselves but for a greater good.

3.10.5 Cluster Fuck-Yeah!
I would say, not only is the 'I' not autonomous but all knowledge is the relationship <u>between</u> minds. This would also help explain why greatness seems to happen in clusters. The great work of Mozart, Beethoven and Schubert all happened in Vienna within just 48 years. The great work of Socrates, Plato and Aristotle all took place in Athens in less than 50 years. Leonardo and Michelangelo knew one another, Leibniz was in direct contact with Locke and Spinoza. Hume knew Adam Smith, Rousseau and Boswell. Porter, Berlin and Gershwin knew one another. Ditto Warhol, Reed and Basquiat. Before instant global communication it was rare for someone to reach the heights of intellectual achievement in isolation.

3.11 Recap.
Ok here is a summary of where we are so far. In the earlier section of the book I demonstrated (as best I was able) that arguments for EU membership and against Brexit were consistently antithetical. The adjectives used, again and again were chosen to mislead and misrepresent the empirical reality rather than describe it. In this section of this book I attempted to explain why this was.

Hume carried his scepticism to such extremes that he could not say he knew the sun would rise tomorrow. This is a desperate situation. He had to be answered. Kant answered Hume brilliantly, but he did so with an epistemological argument that created as many problems as it solved. Kant's system relegated time and space to 'mere appearance' and abolished objective knowledge and morality with a system in which knowledge and morality are internally generated. The problem with Kant's system is not that it is strewn with errors or poorly thought through but that it dispenses with the method of cross-checking patterns to establish knowledge so there is no mitigating check to prevent our imaginations running away with us.

Although Kant remains an obscure figure, the influence of his ideas is far more pervasive than is commonly thought, to the extent that his ideas have become a social movement. People with similar beliefs cluster together to form a feedback loop, excluding what confronts, and embracing what confirms. Entire sections of our society have turned their faces against a mountain of empirical evidence. I came to this from my background as a Brexiteer but I see similar things happening with climate change deniers, holocaust deniers, Donald Trump, and people who embrace neo-liberalism because they want to be better off etc. How absurd has this become? The capacity of our planet to support life is being undermined and yet people carry on as normal! An inter-generational, inter-continental religious war is being waged across the world and entire sections of our society are refusing to even discuss its existence! One wonders how much empirical evidence is required, or how consistent the patterns have to be, before the beliefs are reappraised. But then again, the whole point of beliefs is that they are immune from precisely this type of correction. This I have given the name Othello Syndrome. I'm not a neuroscientist; this is just my pejorative term of convenience.

Humans became the dominant species because we looked up. But as the mind came to determine <u>how</u> we saw, our domination became a rotten thing. We imagined gods and monsters but somehow failed to see the destruction of plants, animals and humans.

Regarding Brexit, Othello Syndrome caused Remainers' imaginations to overwhelm their empirical observations causing them to attack everything they claimed to support and defend everything they claimed to reject.

My Brexit arguments tended to be inductive (I worked from the general to the particular). So I observed that countries where more people had more democratic control over more power were more good than countries where a small number of appointees decided things in secret. Remainers would not recognise my arguments because Remainers tended to operate on the basis of core beliefs that reject empiricism as a method of proof. I answered this in two ways. Firstly I argued that to base knowledge and morality on our core beliefs can lead to a dictatorship of spasms that no amount of proof can overturn. Secondly I proposed a way in which inductive reason can be held valid. If we define knowledge as that which isn't disproved (as opposed to that which can be proved) then empiricism gives us lots of perfectly sound information to live by. Then finally in this third section I proposed a possible solution: to abolish the 'I' and to see our minds as multi conscious and ourselves as part of social groups. Knowledge is trans-intellectual it is the relationship <u>between</u> minds.

So if you think Brexit is old hat think again because Othello Syndrome is heading for a news bulletin near you! And if you are worried that the world is going mad then that is my proposed solution – to brush aside all propositions founded on internal values and beliefs and to instead cross-check lots of information from lots of people in lots of places over a long period of time. Talk to people you disagree with!

So that's my basic argument – life on Earth is imperilled by humanity's belief-based collective neurological disorder and the solution is to cross-check synthetic a posteriori knowledge. I hope the reader will not see this as a diatribe of self-justification, but a serious attempt to work through what I think and why I think it. My motivation for writing this book was not fame or fortune (I expect neither) but to minimise suffering of all humans and animals by maximising the public scrutiny of power.

Section 4. Odds and Ends

Below are a few rants to supplement what has already been said. Sorry if it's a bit of an ideas boot fair.

Mark Steyn
In his 2006 book America Alone, Mark Steyn correctly identifies the dwindling demographics of Western societies. Steyn is terrific but brings a lot of his own baggage to the issue and attributes this to left-wing issues like tax and welfare. But I think there could be another explanation. In terms of the 'I' having children makes no sense at all; it means less sleep, money, sex, time and socialising. To have children is to sacrifice the 'I' for the 'we'. It is individualism not collectivism that has stopped us seeing the greater happiness of parenthood. This might explain why, where Kantian philosophy has become a social movement birth rates have declined. Indeed if we look at the philosophers whose work is centred upon the individual, Kant, Schopenhauer, Nietzsche, Kierkegaard, and even to an extent Sartre, we see a general inability to form committed human relationships.

American Psycho
I don't intend to read the Bret Easton Ellis book as it seems a bit gory for me, but it is important for introducing the idea of the unreliable narrator. Going back to Rousseau's Confessions, we have grown accustomed to the idea of the narrator as a datum, an internalised version of Hamlet's Horatio. But what if the internal voice is not a confession or datum? What if we are mistaken, imagining or mad? What if the narrator confuses rather than enlightens? Clearly looking ever deeper inside is not going to get us very far, we need to cross-check.

Not I
We see something similar with Samuel Beckett's 'Not I'. The regret we have for our mistakes generates an almost irresistible incentive to self-create a false history that makes the passing of time easier to accept. What motive do we have to not lie to ourselves, and to live in a self-created reality where nothing is our fault? And, what if this isn't simply an issue to discuss with a therapist but a social movement? Our refusal to cross-check and to be persuaded by whatever unsavoury conclusions emerge, is damaging us collectively.

Je Regrette?
Kant was hugely influenced by Rousseau's idea that feeling is superior to intellect. So what are best - head decisions or heart decisions? The brilliant thing about heart decisions is that there is no way we can subsequently appraise them. The most idiotic, petulant spasm can always be explained with the words. 'I believed it was right at the time'. And how are we supposed to critique that? With feelings? Heart decisions allow us to go through life without regret or guilt. And if our emotions tell us our previous emotions were mistaken, on what basis do we decide which emotions were right? This has led us to the current pre-eminence of un-contestable spasms.

The consequences of the choices we make and the paths we take are enormous, not just for ourselves but also for those around us. So it's easy to see why so many gravitate to the idea of heart-based decisions, where the mind is side-lined, and emotions at particular moments determine our lives. Thus allowing us to grow old without regrets – it's hard to think of anything more seductive. So what do we do? We must grow up as a species and admit our spasmodic heart decisions were often wrong and accept the burden of regret this entails like adults.

Trans
Do my objections to transcendental idealism oblige me to reject the trans community? No, so I don't. I happily accept that they are not obliged to see themselves as I see them. Similarly it would be wrong of them to insist I see things their way. After all, to insist I see things their way exactly replicates against me the outrageous abuse that was inflicted upon gays and trans people in the past. Neither side can demand the other sees things their way. We have agreement!

If gender is non-binary then phrases like 'man' and 'woman' must be ambiguous in which case there is little point in being pedantic about how we use them. If gender is binary then using such words is a formality. Either way arguing about terminology seems an exhausting way of achieving little. Those who get het up about such things are just another bunch of clerics insisting we should have a pure soul, like them.

What is wealth?
Fiat money is just the proxy for an asset. What is an asset? Gold? Ultimately no, because gold depends on something external to itself to enrich us. Ultimately capital is that which lets us live, think, heal and love. This is the surface of the Earth given to nature. So the capital of the human race is:

$N (4\pi r^2)$

$4\pi r^2$ is the formula for the area of a sphere. N (Nature) is a variable, it is high where there is biodiversity and low where there is desert, and r (radius) is 6378km. We may choose to factor in sunlight, or the distance from the Earth's crust to the stratosphere, but that would be an amusement rather than a labour. The crucial point is that we were raised to think that those who create waste create wealth. Again, it's the other way round. The real wealth creators are the gardeners, thinkers, doctors, teachers, artists and lovers because they generate that which generates everything else. E.F Schumacher was right, the problem is not capitalism per se but the misattribution of its terms, our ecosystem is the ultimate asset and pollution the most uneconomic liability.

Sanctions Work
In just five years (late eighties to early nineties) sanctions brought about peaceful revolutions in South Africa, East Germany, Poland, Czechoslovakia, Estonia, Lithuania, Latvia, Azerbaijan, Georgia, Moldova, Ukraine, Belarus, Armenia, Yugoslavia and several other countries in Eastern Europe. Conversely failing to impose sanctions against Russia, China, Saudi Arabia, Qatar, Kuwait, the UAE and Iran has failed by every conceivable measure. Our continued engagement with these dictatorships has resulted in a human and environmental catastrophe so enormous as to be almost beyond comprehension. The onus is on those opposing sanctions to produce a credible argument.

Collective Action and Class
Let's say you are part of an environmental group and you want to do a bit of collective action, you will find it's bloody hard work! There are people to organise, posters, stickers and badges to make, leaflets to write, check and print and venues to book. It takes time and sacrifice. But for the people at the pinnacle of society, forming a union is not work - it's play. They go to the same parties and conferences, they hang out, they holiday together, they meet at Davos and frequent the same institutions, they marry one another and their children marry one another. For the people at the top, forming a mutually supportive network is not work but a leisure activity. Their differences of opinions are superficial, the default setting is to conserve the system in which they have prospered, which they see as benign. They do this by mutual promotion. The obvious threat to this is democracy because it hands control of their world to outsiders. This is why among the wealthy there are superficial acts of altruism intended to conceal their substantive acts against democracy.

Additionally it should be pointed out that the time I spent fighting for Brexit is time I could have spent with my family or earning money, or pursuing my career. When Remainer appointees fought Brexit in the Lords, the Supreme Court, the civil service or at the BBC they were being *paid* to do so, campaigning for Remain was their day job. Brexit was a sacrifice I made. It damaged my family, my career, my marriage, my reputation, my health and my finances. This was a huge advantage for Remain and a huge disadvantage for us.

Do Yourself a Favour
Think I'm talking rubbish? Suit yourself, but there is also considerable evidence that Othello Syndrome makes you poorer. Do I have your attention now? The great investors tend to be quant-driven. They are analytical, they cross-check, and look for patterns. They ask questions and are persuaded by the evidence. They look for what confronts rather than what confirms. They keep their feelings in check. They are 'thinkers' as opposed to 'feelers'. They prioritise sense perception over intuition. They may say they 'believe' in a project, but that is just a semantic error, their methods emphatically evidence-based.

No Deal is Ideal
The democracy haters were endlessly inventive in concealing their disdain for the judgement of the people. Sometimes apparently democracy was wrong because its advocates were uncultured, unintelligent or unfashionable; sometimes because its advocates had some mental illness, phobia or prejudice, and very often because us being an independent democracy was apparently incompatible with achieving a trade deal. We were told nothing was more important than getting a deal, so it necessarily followed that 'no deal' was the fantasy of people who were bad, mad or stupid, to be dismissed with a wave of the hand, a laugh and the shake of the head. Always the assumption was that the judgement of the people be subject to the approval of some higher authority (which seemed to include themselves). It was incomprehensible to them that in 2016 the truly supreme authority had handed down its judgement and that the trade deal had to accommodate the democracy rather than the other way round.

Imagine you are head of a society that has just voted to become an independent democracy. History provides us with lots of perfectly functional examples of exit strategies. Why not simply copy those? It's a practical question. Why not just replicate what worked perfectly well for the USA, India, Canada, Australia, New Zealand, Switzerland, Greenland, Iceland, Georgia, Costa Rica or any of the other normal independent democracies? Why not just copy how Poland or Czechoslovakia seceded from the Soviet bloc? Why not become a normal independent democracy and *then* sign whatever trade deals are consistent with that? I'm going to give this a name: the 'Jefferson/Gandhi Method'.

The Colonies 'crashed out' of the biggest trading bloc the world had ever seen, illegally, without a deal, with a war thrown in to the mix. They changed their name to the USA and became the most prosperous nation in history. India 'crashed out' of the largest empire the world had ever seen with no deal, a shattered nation, racked by poverty and besieged by religious conflict. Did India collapse? No, they increased their agricultural production and eradicated whole classes of childhood diseases. Now they have a space program and three times as many billionaires as the UK.

The Jefferson/Gandhi method is simple to explain. First you declare independence, then you organise the minor issues (like trade negotiations) around that. So ... the declaration that your country democratically determines all its own laws determines the scope of trade deal, not vice versa.

Now imagine that you wanted to go about your exit strategy in the most idiotic way possible. This is how you might do it. You would enter into labyrinthine trade negotiations with the body from whom you were seceding, you would place people sympathetic to the other side in charge of your negotiating team, you would place an obligation upon yourself to strike a deal, handing a de-facto veto to the other side, and finally you would have that trade deal determine what you are allowed to vote about. We can call this the 'May/Johnson Method'. I'm struggling to think of any society in history that pursued an exit strategy more idiotic than the one the Tories adopted post-referendum. And of course, I am being too kind to even describe it as idiotic, because that implies that they sought to implement the referendum result but due to incompetence, went about it the wrong way; when obviously what really happened, is that they deliberately chose an 'exit' method hard-wired to prevent democracy from flourishing. How else can we explain the decision to not use the Jefferson/Gandhi Method with its proven track record of success?

So, let's run through a comparison:

1, With the Jefferson/Gandhi method the declaration of independence determines the trade deal, whereas with the May/Johnson method the trade deal determines what we can vote about.

2, The Jefferson/Gandhi method works from the general to the particular, first the form of the constitution is established, then the details follow, whereas with the May/Johnson method the generalities are contingent on the technicalities.

3, The Jefferson/Gandhi method sees exit as an event, whereas the May/Johnson method sees it as a process. Heath took us into the EEC with a stroke of the pen; he didn't even bother with a referendum! We left the ERM in a single day, Greenland implemented a referendum to leave the EEC without any fuss. There is no reason why secession should be any more convoluted than accession.

4, You negotiate how to join a club, not how to leave. The Jefferson/Gandhi method (rightly) saw negotiations as a path to calamity, whereas the May/Johnson method assumed (wrongly) that it would be a calamity to *not* negotiate.

5, Those who agreed with the Jefferson/Gandhi method demanded "No Deal", whereas those who agreed with the May/Johnson method said "We *must* get a deal".

6, The Jefferson/Gandhi method had an observable track record of success, whereas the May/Johnson method had an observable track record of disaster. So when I say the Jefferson/Gandhi method is superior to the May/Johnson method that is as close to an invincible argument as you are ever likely to read.

To make it ultra-clear I've taken the above and summarised it into these two columns:

Jefferson/Gandhi Method	May/Johnson Method
Exit is an event.	Exit is a process.
Works from general to particular - declaration of independence determines scope of trade deal.	Works from particular to general - trade details determine what can be voted about.
Established independent democracy before trade deal.	Trade deal came first.
No negotiations.	Negotiations.
Did not seek approval of former rulers.	Sought approval of former rulers.
Insisted on 100% democratic control of laws.	Traded democratic control for market access.
Success.	Failure.

The three main Remain errors were:
1, Produced no argument against left column.
2, Wrongly assumed Brexiteers were required to defend right column.
3, Wrongly assumed a critique of right column invalidated left column.

(99% of all Remain arguments are invalidated by this).

Those who disagree with me will probably base their disagreement on the technical process of leaving, but because the May/Johnson method is obviously *inferior* to the Jefferson/Gandhi method, the whole idea of a leaving *process* is wrong *in principle*, so I wouldn't recognise the very basis of their argument. 'Process of leaving' is an oxymoron, there can be no *process* of leaving. To even think of exit as a 'process' is to *not* leave.

What I am saying is completely unremarkable. 100 years ago there were 100 countries, now there are 200. Generally countries are becoming greater in number and smaller in size. Secession happens all the time. There is no reason why our becoming an independent democracy should have been any more problematic than the experience of numerous other countries.

Within a democracy the supreme act is the vote, so the 2016 referendum *was* our declaration of independence, and Parliament, Cameron and the Queen failed in not automatically recognising it as such. They had no authority to interpret or approve it or oversee its manner of implementation. On 24th June 2016 Cameron should have acknowledged that the supreme authority had handed down its judgement, and that henceforth our laws were generated only by our votes and that external 'laws' and courts no longer had any authority. He could have triggered Article 50 as a box ticking exercise, and if they wanted they could have negotiated whatever trade deals they liked with the EU (or any other country for that matter) but our Declaration of Independence was supreme and the trade deal only secondary, so it was for the trade deal to dance a waltz around the Declaration of Independence and not vice versa. And if anyone disagrees then I would be curious to know from whence their authority emanates.

In a democracy votes generate laws, so to refuse to acknowledge our vote to leave as law is to be anti-democratic. Not on the statute? So correct the statute. Problem solved. Is there anything else I can help you with today?

Because the Brexit talks were about trading our capacity to democratically determine our own affairs in exchange for access to their market, the negotiations and the war against democracy were the same thing. You cannot negotiate independence. To negotiate is to *not* be independent. The negotiation and the failure were the same thing.

So it was always easy to spot the democracy haters because they would witter on about the necessity for an EU deal. They didn't seem to care that we had no trade deal with the USA, but pissed their pants that we have one with the EU. Why? Because that was their best hope of separating votes from power. They were opposed to democracy in principle, but didn't have the courage to publicly campaign for it, so they obsessed about trade negotiations because that allowed them to stealthily conceal their war on democracy behind labyrinthine trade details.

If the 2016 referendum had gone the other way the result would have been implemented in a heartbeat. EU supporters selectively saw things as either events or processes in order to conceal their contempt for democracy. Besides, what were the EU supposed to offer us? Nothing they could put on the table was more desirable than us having full democratic control over all our laws. Because us becoming an independent democracy would make us better off (as we have seen from all the precedents) and any deal with the EU would involve following their rules, it necessarily followed that seeking a deal with the EU was an act of self-harm.

Never in British history was a better outcome easier to achieve. All we had to do was nothing and under the Article 50 process all bilateral deals with the EU would have simply expired. But no, that was too simple, too functional, too obvious for the Tories. So the Tories didn't fuck up Brexit by accident, it was a deliberate choice. They were never interested in a political system that could allow voters to confront plutocracy. They partially and reluctantly embraced Brexit only because it was that or lose power. It's no more complex than that. The real curiosity is why the Labour Party seemed to think there was political mileage in trying to out-crap the Tories! Buy hey, people like Brendan Chilton, Fawzi Ibrahim or Will Podmore are much better placed to answer that than myself.

Foucault
Francis Bacon famously said 'knowledge is power'. Foucault flipped this around, for him power determined knowledge. Foucault observed that those with power tended to define what knowledge was as a means of social control.

In *Madness and Civilisation*, Foucault explains how in the 18th century the word 'madness' was used to categorise not just the mentally ill, but the poor, sick, homeless, eccentric, in fact, anyone whose display of individuality was unwelcome. 'Madness' was ascribed promiscuously, not from ignorance of psychology but from knowledge of its effectiveness as a means of social control.

In *Discipline and Punish*, Foucault looks at the establishment of prisons in France, and notes how, as prisons were introduced, punishments involving violence against the body (like floggings and executions) were phased out. Because France was becoming more civilised and decent? Not at all says Foucault, it was actually because the authorities realised that controlling the mind was a more effective means of social control than punishing the body.

Then in his last book *The History of Sexuality*, Foucault observes that after Freud we came to look on sex as a function of the mind rather than the body. Psychoanalysis encourages us to discuss sex openly, but this involves revealing our innermost desires. This confession therefore places us completely at the mercy of others, its usefulness as a method of control is therefore hard to overstate.

For Foucault there were two types of power: 'repressive power' and 'normalising power'. Repressive power is about guns, bullets, guillotines and punching, it is about governors, police and soldiers. It's obvious physical power, but it's also a second-rate type of power because it is about forcing you to do something you don't want to do. Normalising power however, is much more subtle and takes the form of a myriad nudges and lessons that are barely perceptible, but normalising power is a first-rate type of power because it moulds us into the sort of people that society wants us to be.

Obviously it is nailed on that Foucault is a Kantian. Schopenhauer observed that Kant's chief merit was the distinction between appearances and things in themselves (WWR 1,444) and we have seen that Kant awarded primary status to the noumenal realm of the 'things in themselves' and secondary status to the phenomenal realm of appearances. Well that's exactly what Foucault did. Repressive power targets our bodies, it is about physical pain, punches, and bullets; and sense perception. Its obvious power, but it's also a lower order of power because it's in the phenomenal realm. Normalising power however targets the inner mind, it's almost imperceptible in everyday life, but it is a higher order of power because it targets the will - the thing in itself. So Foucault basically took Kant's system and plugged in his pet subject of power.

What does all this have to do with us? Because the Remain campaign can be seen as a textbook illustration of Foucault's ideas. Foucault observes that true power targets our minds, not our bodies. Remain simply substituted the word 'madness' for 'racism'. The word 'racism' would do just as well because it's similarly difficult to define, unfalsifiable, and easy to ascribe promiscuously. Was the Remain side genuinely concerned about racism? Sometimes, but on the whole I found their protestations insincere. As a means of social control obviously, the usefulness of the 'R' word is difficult to overstate because it pre-emptively silences legitimate protest with an unfalsifiable accusation. And because the accusation of racism is so devastating, if I am having an argument with someone about, say representation, if I can fuse the argument together with an argument about racism then I get to automatically win! Trying to defend a shit system? Got no empirical evidence? Losing the argument? Want the people with power to continue to have power? Want voters to be powerless? No problem, just stick the 'R' word on your opponents.

So EU supporters weaponised the state broadcaster (the BBC) and relentlessly disseminated the conflation that maintaining EU rule was the same as being decent, and rejecting racism, and that to be for the EU was the same as being for peace prosperity and human rights. The media controlled by the rich and powerful relentlessly pumped a monolithic wall of Foucaultian normalising power, it was psychological abuse on a national scale. Then as soon as the establishment lost the Brexit vote they placed their agent Nick Clegg in charge of Facebook where he promptly started shutting down pro-

Brexit pages. We see this again now, with the BBC's monolithic pro-vaccination propaganda in the Covid pandemic.

So to see Brexit in the context of Foucault, the EU regards the UK and Switzerland in a similar way to how China views Hong Kong and Taiwan, the principal difference being that China places a greater emphasis on 'repressive power' whereas the EU opts for 'normalising power'.

Another example of Foucault's ideas can be gained from the contemporary debate about free speech. In pre-modern times the state was violent and we had no right of free speech. Today the state is less violent and we supposedly have a human right of free speech. But people are as fearful of expressing themselves as they ever were. Why? According to Foucault it is because the coercion never actually stopped, it simply transitioned from repressive power (in the physical world) to normalising power (in the noumenal realm). Violence didn't decline, it metamorphosed into an information war.

So in Foucault's system, 'normalising power' can be just as coercive as 'repressive power'. This obviously raises an enormous question: should free speech be punishable as if it were a violent attack? This would merit a whole book in itself, but for me the TLDR is that free speech should be sacrosanct for two reasons:

1, If we prosecute free speech as if it were a violent attack then that would create a dictatorship by those claiming to be offended.
2, To prohibit offense creates a legalistic absurdity because some people find censorship offensive; consequently those prosecuting offense, automatically become criminals by their own arguments.

But it is a problem that Foucault's philosophy makes it very easy to selectively see mental violence only when it is convenient to do so. So we see our arguments as legitimate concerns and the arguments of others as an attack. How do we differentiate? As with all offshoots of Kantianism it's difficult to see how we can. I think Foucault is right where he identifies that we are engaged in a mental conflict. For example, Islam is advancing not because it has great weapons or arguments but because its critics have been collectively, psychologically abused into silence. But if I am to make such a statement I am also required to examine my own behaviour and to invite the critique of my fellow human beings who are Muslim.

Note: My misgivings about Foucault are twofold. Firstly coercive power and normalising power overlap and are not distinct and separate. Secondly coercive power was not simply abandoned because targeting the mind is better, but because the powerful don't like getting their hands dirty.

Pinker V Sullivan
Foucault gives us a useful perspective on the recent disagreement between Andrew Sullivan and Stephen Pinker. Pinker is drawing our attention to the decline of violence in the phenomenal world whereas Sullivan is drawing our attention to the increase of violence in the Kantian, noumenal realm. So initially the positions of these two fascinating writers seem diametrically opposed, but actually they are entirely compatible. The violence didn't decline – it transitioned.

Paul's Rule
On 31st January 2020 I was in a pub with Michael Lightfoot and Paul Perin, wondering aloud about how we might differentiate between our Remain supporting friends who were decent and the democracy haters. Paul brushed aside my pontifications with the immortal words "Do they want power over me?" My question was answered in six words.

And who knows, maybe Paul's Rule is useful in other applications too! How about if we try using it to differentiate between hate speech and inconvenient arguments? So if I say that anyone should be able to question and vote about anything, then that can't be hate speech because I am not seeking privileges for any particular person, group, race or religion. But if someone is demanding a transfer of power from 'us' to 'them' then yes, that would count as mental violence. Who do I mean by 'us'? Humans generally. Who do I mean by 'them'? Appointees - those who didn't get votes but who did get power. The religious leaders, dictators, trade negotiators, lords, chairmen, judges, royals, commissioners, the acronym gang, heads of NGOs and inter-national organisations, community leaders and governors. If it's asserted they should have more power over us and we should have less over them, then by this formula, that would constitute an attack. So seen through the prism of Paul's Rule, suddenly the accusers and accused in the free speech/hate speech debate are inverted! Who knows what other useful applications it will have!

So what is Mental Violence?
As a free speech maximalist I'm obliged to reject the prohibition of hate speech (mental violence) but still it's useful to have a definition of mental violence so we can tell the difference between that and disagreeing. I sugest mental violence meets these three criteria:

1, A person or group seek to consolidate, expand or conserve their power.
2, They urge the rejection of empiricism.
3, They threaten unpleasant consequences.

Strange that when we apply this definition suddenly the accusers and accused swap around!

Good Laws Precluded by EU Membership
I was recently challenged by a friend to name one good law EU membership precluded. I accept the challenge. As an environmentalist I think all packaging should be either biodegradable or modular standardised glass jars with screw-on lids. That way once a jar of, say jam, oil, or shampoo was finished, the container could be washed and reused like an old fashioned milk bottle, or the glass could be recycled if it ever broke. This would obviously fall foul of EU law regarding the free movement of goods which requires that any products sold in one member state should be available in any other member state without additional compliance. So the free movement of goods prevents us from implementing such a law. So there, I was asked to give an example and I gave one. Now I would like to flip around the question and ask EU supporters – which laws should we NOT have democratic control over? Name one. Just one.

Immigration
Immigration has enhanced my life beyond measure. But whatever immigration policy you or I prefer is irrelevant; the important thing is that the policy be democratically agreed, and if free movement is imposed by a treaty then it becomes impossible to improve that policy by voting. EU supporters are concerned that the democratic method would result in a bad policy, whereas I am concerned that laws should be democratically legitimate and improvable. I understand their concerns and I hope they understand mine. As a democrat I am obliged to own the consequences of being a democrat, and accept that I may find myself having to accept a democratically agreed policy I may not agree with.

Why Democracy is Supreme.
Theocracy, plutocracy, aristocracy, autocracy - all the other 'cracies' tend towards extremity. Democracy is the only 'cracy' that doesn't because it's inherent nature is to self-critique. Its judgements flow from the periphery to the centre, not the centre to the periphery - they involve feedback. This is why a bad law passed by a democratic system is preferable to a good law passed by an undemocratic system - a democratic system can critique its errors. So while I am a democracy maximalist, I am incapable of being a democracy extremist because democracy is by its very nature consensual and moderating. Superficially this may appear to be an article of faith but it is merely a pragmatic observation pending refutation.

Why the EU fails
The EU fails because it wants to. At the time of writing (Feb 22) the EU is printing even more money per capita than the US (!) but unlike the US and UK the EU is not even discussing raising interest rates. This is a recipe for Weimar inflation on a continental scale.

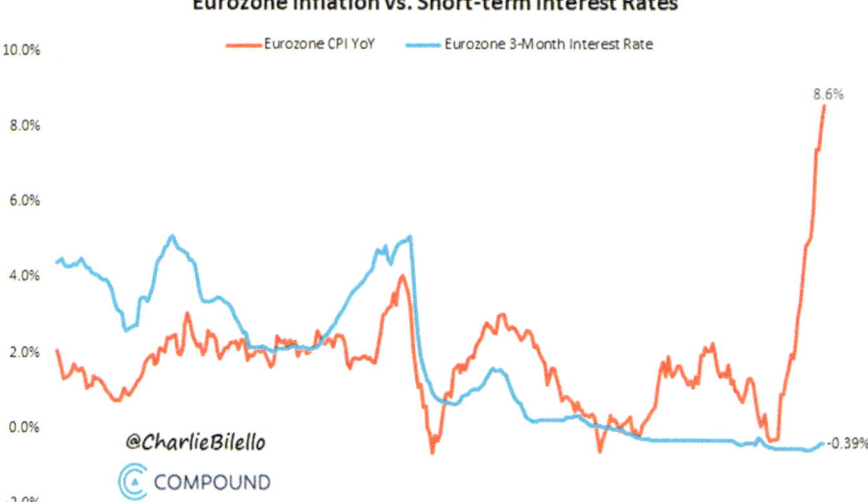

The US and UK have these pesky things called voters who have an annoying habit of not doing what they are supposed to do. The EU doesn't have to worry about mid-term-elections, or council elections or presidential elections, because no one with power in the EU was elected. The only votes it permits are for the European Parliament which is just an amending chamber and which only contains MEPs sympathetic with the project. The EU doesn't care about unemployment or growth or inflation or empirical reality because it doesn't have to, it has only one objective – integration - and everything else can go hang. So paradoxically the EU *likes* crises because they can be used as justification for increased integration. Climate crisis? '*We need to coordinate our response!*' Migration crisis? '*This calls for an inter-governmental conference!*' Unemployment crisis? '*We need a common approach!*' And so on; you can take your pick of whatever bugbear is doing the rounds this week. It doesn't matter what empirical evidence gets fed into the eyes and ears; what comes out the mouth is predetermined: "*the problem is local democracy and the solution is central authority*" Thus a vicious circle is established whereby the centralised undemocratic system generates crises that are seized upon to justify more centralisation and less democracy. Paradoxically they have a motive to fail!

How Free Movement Can Make Us Poorer
The basis of left-wing economics is the 'Keynesian Multiplier'. It's difficult to conceptualise so I would recommend watching a couple of YouTube videos on the subject. But basically it involves governments investing in the economy. That initial investment gets re-spent as it circulates within the economy creating a multiplier effect, such that the wealth generated is actually greater than the initial investment.

Here is why that isn't working in the EU. Say the Italian government wants to stimulate the economy so they 'invest' 10 billion Euros building a train line. The bosses of the construction company will pay themselves bonuses which they will then move to off-shore tax heavens. But hey, nothing illegal about that when you are constitutionally bound to the free movement of capital right? Then the workers take their wages and send as much as they can to their families in other countries, say Poland. Again, nothing illegal about that when the free movement of labour and capital is constitutionally enshrined right? What do these bosses and workers do with the rest of their money? Spend it on cheap imported goods. Italian goods? Probably not, but hey, nothing illegal about that when you are constitutionally committed to the free movement of goods, right? Do you see what is happening? The initial investment that should be re-circulated in the Italian economy is being smartly removed from that economic area before the beneficial multiplier effect can take place. So we end up with the worst of all possible worlds – Governments getting in debt so they can increase spending on projects that only generate crappy levels of economic growth! The initial 10bn Euro investment is paid for by Italians without actually generating any prosperity for them!

In 2018 I discussed this with Morning Star Editor Ben Chacko and he observed that this would explain why a dreadful outfit like the Chinese government still managed to achieve high levels of economic growth – they didn't allow free movement of capital, so their investment generates much more growth than that of the EU.

Suggested Actions
The frustrating thing is that achieving a better world is so simple, obvious and easy. Some suggestions:
1, Allowing free speech in principle is not enough, we need to actively criminalise the silencing of questions. We must pass (and enforce) a law that makes the censorship of political opinion a criminal offence.
2, No aid trade or sport played with any country that does not allow free speech. (We define this by looking at the Reporters Without Borders, *World Press Freedom Index* and simply blacklist the bottom 50 nations, bankrupting them. This would create a 'race to the top')
3, Prohibit the burning of fuel.
4, Anyone turning vegetation to desert to pay to restate the vegetation.
5, No item may be sold unless it is readily reusable, repairable, recyclable or biodegradable. Single use plastic prohibited.
6, All manufacturers to use the same standardised packaging. Either paper (that can bio degrade) or standard size glass jars (that can be cleaned and reused).
7, Most taxes to be abolished and replaced with a combination of VAT and a land tax of 2% P/A of the price the land was bought at. Land is an asset impossible to hide, but cheap and simple to tax. The sale prices of land are publicly available at Land Registry. This would tax real things that are empirically observable rather than income tax which penalises endeavour. Furthermore people could reduce their tax burden over time by settling, adapting and improving their locality. So someone could have infinite wealth but it would only be taxed at the point it is transformed into a tangible physical reality.
8, We clearly have an excess of people going hither and thither, it is polluting the environment, spreading disease, destroying indigenous cultures and depressing wages. In the information age it is no longer necessary for large numbers of people to be hyper-transient. There should be no more than one airport runway per 25 million people; and a total halt on the creation of new transport infrastructure.
9, Re-wild 1% of brown field sites per annum until sustainable balance between man and nature achieved.
10, All power contingent on votes. Anyone occupying any position of political authority, who receives public money, must be directly elected by the people.

But the above are just ideas I hope will be of interest. Overwhelmingly for me Brexit was about *how* laws were made rather than *what* laws were made. So long as laws are written openly and democratically I'm not hugely fussed what they are because I trust the cross-checking of democracy to function.

It was all lies lies lies!
One Remain argument that did the rounds a lot was the idea that the Brexit campaign was founded on lies. This argument tended to rely on impromptu errors made by characters like Farage, Johnson, Cummings, Rees-Mogg etc during the referendum campaign. As usual it was the other way round. Blair, Brown and Cameron all lied they would give us a referendum on the Lisbon Treaty. Cameron and May lied that they would implement the referendum result. And those were not run-of-the-mill, common-or-garden lies, but manifesto promises on which governments were elected. And going back in history, what about Heath's lie that remaining in the EEC would not affect our sovereignty? And what about the lies that EU membership has given us peace, prosperity, human rights and improved trade? Do those lies somehow not count? Are we not discussing that particular *genre* of falsehood today? Remainers only saw lies that confirmed their own prejudices.

Here is a simple explanation of how the 2017 intake of MPs misled the electorate. Firstly they ran on a manifesto commitment to honour the result of the referendum:

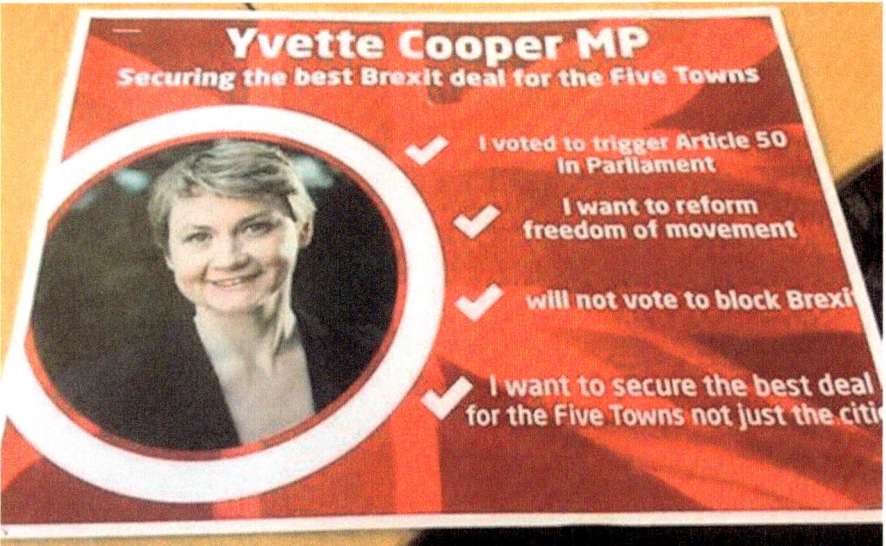

Then once safely elected they did everything humanly possible to preserve EU control. If you say you want to 'leave with a deal', but insist the deal replicates membership, then 'leaving with a deal' becomes an oxymoron: to leave *with* deal is to *not* leave. But … but … but *that's* not lying right?

What if any of us conducted ourselves the way the 2017 Parliamentary intake conducted themselves? What if I sold someone a fridge that made the food warmer? Or ran a removals company that left the furniture where it was? What if any of us little people did precisely the opposite of what we promised in our interview or agreed in our employment contract? There would be an entirely legitimate claim that people had been misled right? And when people are misled in the most public way imaginable, on the largest possible scale, that makes the deception more serious, not less, right? Sorry if I'm testing the readers' patience by explaining what shouldn't need explaining, but clearly it does. Devious people did precisely the opposite of what they promised and attempted to pass it off as some technical anomaly. It's called lying.

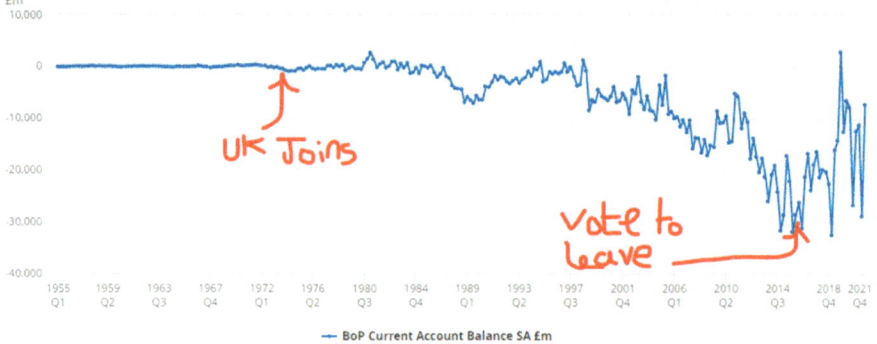

So they accused of us of lying and I'm saying the same about them, but is there a difference between their accusations and mine? How does a reasonable undecided person chose between the two arguments? Well I'm basing my position on maximum empiricism. For example the lie that EU membership improved trade can be debunked by referring to the Office For National Statistics page entitled 'Trade Balance' which provides data covering the last 80 years – maximum empiricism – whereas the Remainers' accusations of lying are founded on subjective opinions of the character of a few select people – minimum empiricism.

Are Borders Evil?
The Remain campaign sought to portray borders as inherently bad. (Never mind that the EU absolutely has a border as well as a fence in Morocco that Donald trump would be proud of!) But I would argue this comes from a conflation of borders with the bad systems they can sometimes define.

Some countries (like North Korea) have definite borders and authoritarian interiors. Some countries (like EU member states) have open borders and increasingly authoritarian interiors. Some countries (like New Zealand, Switzerland or Iceland) have definite borders and democratic interiors. But it is hard to imagine a country with open borders and an increasingly progressive interior. How can a country have a well-designed interior and an undefined perimeter? How can we design a better society if we can't even specify where it is? If you have an open border then how exactly do you apply laws or decide how many hospitals, schools and houses you need? It's a practical question. No border = no plan.

Who hates borders the most? The rich! Open borders allow them to move capital to tax havens, import cheap labour and sell their goods and services whilst complying with the minimum democratic oversight.

So, if borders are not evil then where should they be? And the obvious answer is – where people <u>don't</u> live! Borders should be determined by things like deserts, seas and mountain ranges as people tend to not settle in those places, which minimises the chances of war; whereas politically imposed borders seem to generate conflict. So I am arguing that geography should prescribe the borders to us rather than us projecting our cultural beliefs on geography. (No surprise there given what I have said already).

When I see Britain on a map of the world I notice it has a lot of blue stuff around it. That is not my opinion, it's not what I *think*, it's how I find the world. How fortunate that mother nature should hand us an obvious, functional border on a plate! But what about say the Isle of White or Anglesey should these be independent states too? Well no, because if peace is our objective it makes sense for these minor islands to be governed from the adjacent major area. For example:

-It seems natural that Tasmania be governed from mainland Australia.
-The two islands of New Zealand should share one government because if they didn't they would constantly be in conflict with each another.
-The group of islands that make up Japan should clearly have one government so that they don't endlessly attack each other.
-Chile appears a silly shape, but that is because it is sensibly defined by a sea and a range of mountains.
-Clearly Italy is better off as a unified peninsula rather than the previous warring city states.
-You will see from this map of the world that the four vast nations of Russia, China, Kazakhstan and Mongolia have borders that converge at the same place.

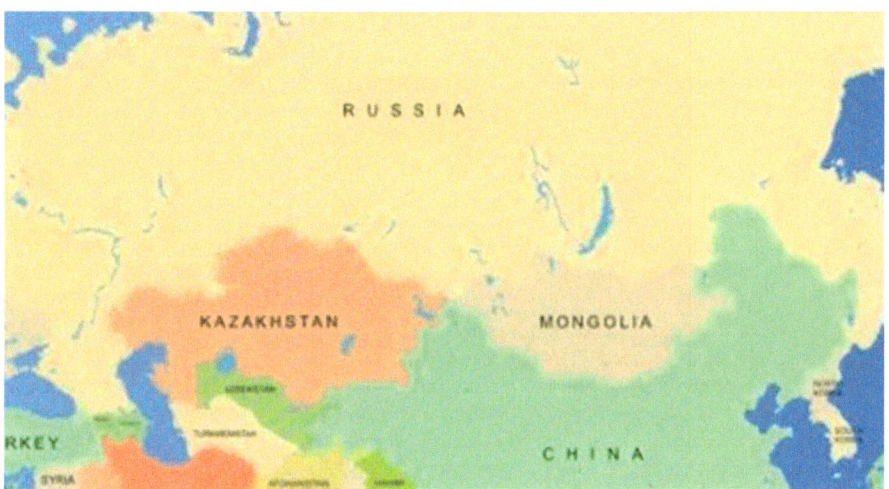

What do you suppose it's like there? Quite sensibly, it's a snow-capped wilderness:

The place where these borders converge is called Friendship Peak.

What happens when this isn't done? Conflict. For example: Sri Lanka, Ireland, Papua New Guinea, Cyprus, Haiti and the Dominican Republic, Checkpoint Charlie etc. Similarly the Korean peninsula should obviously be unified. Having two governments on one piece of land generates conflict. Obviously geography is a complex and subtle thing and there are loads of exceptions that could be endlessly debated. But the point is I take my cue *from* nature rather than projecting my

123

opinion *upon* nature. My ideological position is determined not by beliefs but observations of the world.

Interestingly if I follow this thinking to its logical conclusion I am obliged to reject English, Scottish and Welsh nationalism, and advocate a united Ireland. This is my disagreement with UKIP – they favour the UK rather than Britain which to me seems like replacing one artificial political union with another. So let's shut the Scottish and Welsh assemblies and locate the British Parliament in some poor town in Northern England like Carlisle or Newcastle.

Iberia is a tricky one, I suppose my theory compels me to advocate a general Iberian government with a large degree of autonomy for the Basque region, Portugal, Andalusia etc. Yes some would call that crazy, but the point is, it's no *more* crazy than the Basque region being crushed and the Iberians having austerity foisted on them from Frankfurt! But generally how Europe determines its borders is up to them, for the purposes of the Brexit debate I am simply observing that England Scotland and Wales are just here-today-gone-tomorrow cultural ideas (like Mercia and Northumbria) whereas geography tells me Britain is an empirical reality which provides an eminently more sensible way of organising things. I am sure there are numerous objections that could be raised to my position but I am also sure that any alternative method of delineating nation states would have problems of its own, and at least my position spares us the endless dopey conversations about cultural identity!

'Us'

So when I use the word 'us' I am basically referring to the inhabitants of Britain, the geographical entity nature has so fortuitously handed us as our nation. But am I allowed to use the word 'us' in any meaningful sense? An assumption from the EU side is that if I refer to 'us' then I am being tribal and nationalistic (never mind that they are happy to consider themselves a European family). So how do I win? It seems if I don't defend 'us' then I lose by offering no resistance and if I do use the word 'us' then I am an unspeakable monster. It seems that I am not allowed to use the very words I must use to defend our society. It's win/win for the language police!

Defence

Now there are a large number of small countries, rather than a small number of large countries (as was the case in 1940) there is less military conflict. So having more independent democracies defined by natural geographical borders seems to generate peace. But doesn't that make the smaller countries more susceptible to take over? What happens when a big country attacks a smaller country? At the time of writing (mid 2022) we have seen just such an event with Russia and Ukraine. Before the war many people who frankly should have known better described Putin as a 3D chess player running rings round the dopey western leaders. Farage idiotically advised that *'we should not poke the bear with a stick'* reinforcing many people's opinion of him as a Kremlin patsy. China was watching, if Putin got away with it then they could get away with invading Taiwan and Singapore. So what happened?

Well, Mr. Genius 3D chess player rolled in the tanks and started killing people, and (just like in WW2) all the second-rate western leaders formed an alliance that involved no political union. We imposed sanctions. The Rouble collapsed and Russia's economy was wrecked. When buying my daughter a cycle crash helmet last week I could make an extra donation to Ukraine. People in my street (including us) have Ukrainian flags in the window. We have donated to people in Poland taking in refugees. A very nice Russian student of mine mentioned that her bank account had been frozen. Genius 3D chess player hadn't thought of that had he? Obviously I am not writing with your benefit of hindsight but Putin seems to have already lost more than he could ever hope to win in the conflict.

Yes the western leaders are second rate, but Putin is no great intellect, indeed the strategy of Mr. Genius 3D chess player seems to have been little more than 'Hulk smash!' Strategically he is more George W. Bush than Magnus Carlsen. Putin hasn't remained in power because he is a brilliant strategist but because he destroys the lives of people who challenge him. Within his inner circle there is no one who tells him (as my critics will tell me) that I am wrong and need to rethink. The loneliness of power has addled his brain. But the salient point here is that the mighty centrally controlled army is finding it much harder than anticipated against its decentralised adversaries, and that, when making our donations or boycotting Russian goods no political union was necessary. Paradoxically it was the EU member states (who were involved in political union) that did the most to empower Putin by providing him with a market for Russia's commodity exports. Unsurprisingly Russia had allied themselves with OPEC to form an alliance of democracy-hating pollution-sellers.

Saudi Energy Minister Prince Abdulaziz bin Salman and Russian Energy Minister Alexander Novak attending an OPEC+ meeting.

What effect did Russia's invasion of Ukraine have on the EU's 'Common Defence Policy'? It showed the CDP to be as divorced from empiricism as all the EU's other initiatives. No sooner did the Russian tanks roll in but Sweden and Finland applied to join NATO.

The EU and Islam
Obviously it was absurd that many Brexiteers lazily conflated the EU project with the Islamic project. (If only the Islamic world really was more familiar with Kantian philosophy!) But in some ways it is easy to see why so many Brexiteers got these two things mixed up:

1, For both systems territorial domination and belief work in tandem: the former is achieved by the latter.
2, Both projects are expansionist.
3, Both projects are belief systems that generate social failure.
4, Both systems are administered by an unelected elite.
5, Both systems want ordinary people to shut up and listen. One decries 'fake news' and 'hate speech' the other decries 'blasphemy' but both are about explaining rather than listening.
6, Both systems are obsessed with your submission to the hierarchy.
7, Both systems consider themselves to be superior, and regard non-believers as sub-human. The assumed moral superiority is a pre-requisite for their contempt.
8, Both systems disregard empirical evidence that does not confirm their prejudices.
9, Both systems seek to achieve through threats, psychological abuse or legal technicalities what they cannot achieve through voting.
10, Both projects have their own legal system which sees as good that which expands the project. Both are therefore legal shams – the court simply being a wing of the clergy.

11, The leaders of the EU project and the Islamic project have little reason to fear each other. EU leaders like Islam because it attacks the indigenous cultures that must be destroyed if the EU is to advance. On the other hand, Islamists see the EU has no desire to challenge their ideology.
12, Why are the elite silent about the advance of Islam? Because they agree with it? No. Because Islam has proven itself to be an excellent means of subjugating the proletariat.
13, Both are genuinely far-right ideologies which accuse those who confront them of being the far-right.
14, Both are takeover strategies.

If we consider Brexiteers' position in relation to the above points, generally we would take the opposite position: Brexiteers do not have designs on neighbouring countries but seek only to order our locality. We want the people to tell the leaders what to do rather than the other way round. We favour the functional over the ideological. We favour listening systems to explaining systems. We favour a disinterested legal system etc etc.. The point I am making here is that although the EU project and Islamic project are different things, they are not only compatible but complementary. The advance of one does not require the retreat of the other. So it's understandable to see why many Brexiteers got them mixed up.

Kalergi
The Charlemagne Prize is the most prestigious and best-known prize, awarded for work done in the service of European unification. It comes as no surprise that the EU should name their highest award after an unelected, conquering, religious emperor, obsessed with territorial domination. Who was the first ever recipient of this award? Count Richard Nicolaus Von-Coudenhove Kalergi, an Austrian/Greek/Japanese aristocrat, whose family could be traced to Byzantine royalty via Venetian aristocracy. Count Kalergi served as the founding president of the Pan European Union for 49 years. The European unification movement began with the publishing of his manifesto "Paneuropa" and it was his idea that Beethoven's Ode to Joy was the EU national anthem.

(Note: the Charlemagne Prize is often referred to as the 'Kalergi Award').

Kalergi favoured social democracy as an improvement on "the feudal aristocracy of the sword" but his ambition was to create a conservative society that superseded democracy with "the social aristocracy of the spirit". (Rosamond 2000, pp 21-22). His literary style was Nietzschian, but without the genius:

"Inbreeding strengthens the character but weakens the mind. When inbreeding and race mixing are favourable they result in the highest human type. Where inbreeding and race mixing are unfavourable they result in a degenerate type with weak character and dull mind. The man of the future will be a mixed breed...The Eurasian-Negroid race of the future, similar in its outward appearance to the Ancient Egyptians, will replace the diversity of peoples with a diversity of individuals."

If I were to be charitable, I would describe Kalergi's fixation with skin colour as dubious. If I were to be candid, I would describe it as sinister. I've double checked two different translations of his book Practical Idealism to satisfy myself that he actually said the above and that it isn't a mischievous translator's misrepresentation – he mentions 'inbreeding' 44 times! It's an obsession for him.

It is to Kalergi's enormous credit that Hitler hated him, but what is disturbing are the similarities between the two. Both men reject equality and claim some are superior to others. On what basis? Race. How are things improved? Correct breeding. As is often the case with far-right nutters, both manically assert a correlation between will, intellect and skin colour. Both advocated a united and undemocratic Europe. Their differing views on race are more superficial than they first appear – Hitler thought whites were superior and that Jews should be dispensed with, Kalergi held the same odious view, the only difference being that he flipped the ethnicities the other way round:

"Through unspeakable persecutions throughout a millennium Christian Europe tried to exterminate the Jewish people. The result was that all Jews who were weak-willed, opportunistic or sceptical let themselves be baptised in order to escape the torment of endless persecution ... Thus in the end from all these persecutions arose a small community, shaped by a heroically endured martyrdom for the idea and cleansed of all weak-willed elements and poverty of mind ... Therefore gracious providence provided Europe with a new race of nobility through spiritual grace ... The prominent position held by Jewry these days is owed to its spiritual supremacy which enables it to win the spiritual battle over enormous superior numbers of favoured, hateful, jealous rivals. Modern anti-Semitism is one of the many reactionary phenomena of the mediocre against the supreme ... As a people Jewry experiences the eternal struggle of quantity against quality, inferior groups against high quality individuals, inferior majorities against superior minorities."

Kalergi is clearly right that the persecution of Jews was unspeakable. He is also clearly right that the contribution of Jews to the arts and sciences is magnificent and immeasurable. But to claim a causal link between the persecution and the excellence is questionable to say the least. Does persecution generate excellence? Yes or no? If yes, how do we condemn the persecution? If no, then Kalergi's argument fails. Either way it's hard not to see him as a bargain basement Nietzsche.

He rightly condemns the appalling treatment of the Jews whilst selectively disregarding human suffering that is inconvenient for his argument. The Russians, Chinese and Hindus were killed in their tens of millions. The West Indians didn't suffer? Life was no bed of roses for the Irish or the Scots, but they have contributed immeasurably to humanity. No spiritual supremacy for them then? The word 'slave' comes from the word Slav, presumably they also suffered. As did the indigenous peoples of North and South America and Australasia. No heroic martyrdom for them? The Byzantines and Zoroastrians were subject to ethnic cleansing, and so on. Why does Kalergi champion some ethnic groups but not others? On what basis does he determine which cultures should be conserved and which should be modernised into extinction? The impression I get is of an aristocrat who didn't suffer much, but was happy to romanticise the suffering of some, whilst disregarding the suffering of others altogether.

As a white person I am embarrassed by Hitler's claim that 'we' are somehow superior to other races, and I am sure my Jewish friends and colleagues are similarly uncomfortable about Kalergi's caricature of them. So the horrors inflicted on Jews have somehow benefited them in the long run? I'm sure Jews would much prefer the persecution had not happened in the first place! Kalergi seems to be looking for the positive aspects of discrimination he never had to endure himself.

Obviously the principal difference between Kalergi and Hitler is that Hitler was a psychotic genocidal mass-murderer. But Kalergi did say 'replace the diversity' thus advocating similar ends albeit via different means. Additionally Kalergi was a far-right nutter by virtually every measure: a wealthy, well connected, socially conservative, anti-democratic aristocrat. He did not consider the races to be equal, instead he held that there was a correlation between skin colour, and character. He did not see skin colour, as a consequence of people freely choosing their partners, instead he seems to see skin colour the way a chef might see ingredients, or the way someone might breed dogs - as qualities to be blended in such a way as to achieve the correct mix. Why is 'inbreeding' good for some but not others? We are not told.

Following WW2 western nations set up welfare states and care for the elderly was nationalised. The tacit understanding was that the state rather than families would be the primary provider of care for the elderly. Birth rates plummeted and taxes increased (except for the rich). The state provided pensions and care homes. Adults became lost in a never-ending childhood of sensual pleasure and individualism. Then in 1971 Nixon decoupled fiat money from empirical reality. Now the post war generations are entering retirement. Inflation is causing their fiat pensions to decline in value exponentially. But never mind, their children and grandchildren can support them right? Wrong, they didn't have any! So who *will* provide for our old folk? Imported labour. And what is the most sensible thing the imported workers can do to secure residency and access to healthcare, education and housing? Have children. Thus nations fall. It's almost as if, post WW2, Kalergi's views on 'inbreeding' became social policy. Certainly many conspiracy theorists think so, pointing to the fact that Merkel, Heath and Blair (all of whom also received the Charlemagne award) pursued policies consistent with Kalergi's desire to 'replace the diversity of peoples'. Maybe there is something in this conspiracy theory, but personally I can't be bothered to research it. If westerners are so stupid that they think raising well educated children is a worse pension plan than paying money to the government then I can't muster much sympathy for their plight.

Thanks Will!
Following on from the above, there are a couple of great examples I saw in Will Podmore's excellent book 'Brexit – The Road to Freedom' that I want to quote:

In 2011 the European Commission called for a 'Global Migration Approach' to encourage even more migration into EU countries 'to meet its projected labour needs via targeted immigration of third party nationals' EU unemployment at the time was 20 million.

Next, here is a quote from Lord Kerr of Kinlochard, former UK ambassador to the EU who drafted the EU Constitution / Lisbon Treaty.

"In my view, immigration is the thing that keeps this country running. We native Brits are so bloody stupid that we need an injection of intelligent people, young people from outside who come in and wake us up from time to time."

Let's hope the above quotation was just intended as a joke. For if it were not, then we would have to conclude that 447 million EU citizens are living under a constitution drafted by an unelected far-right loony who thinks that some human beings are inferior to others, and that race-based social engineering should be used to eradicate genetic characteristics he disapproves of. Unsurprisingly Lord Kerr prefers a political system where the people who decide things are like him – unelected, powerful and rich.

Brexit and Football
On 11th February 2019, writing in the Guardian Sean Ingle speculated about the affect Brexit would have on football:

Little Englandism after Brexit could endanger sport's prowess and appeal
Sean Ingle

Elite level athletes and organisations have benefited from unfettered access to Europe; few are fully prepared for the ramifications of whatever happens on 29 March

Somehow, us becoming an independent democracy again would make us worse at football. Eh? So how does Ingle's prediction look now we have some empirical facts to compare it with?

In Euro 2016 (Four days after the referendum) England were knocked out by the mighty Iceland. In the 2018 World Cup England reached the semi-finals. In Euro 2021 England reached the final. And in the last five years (2017-22) the Premiership produced more Champion's League finalists than all the rest of Europe combined. Call that a '*loss of prowess*'?

See the word '*could*' on the top right? His argument is conjectural, not empirical - he's making it up. So why not go the whole hog and have his picture showing him dressed as Professor Marvel gazing into a crystal ball? His argument is fear-based – something BAD could happen! Whose fault would it be? The Little Englanders! Our sin of demanding democratic self-rule would be punished by the judgement of 'elite level athletes and organisations'. And we daren't piss off the elite right? Notice how Ingle assumes quality is imported, not nurtured? He is stuck stuck stuck in a defeatist mind-set, which conflates *here* with inferiority, and *there* with superiority. Apparently the way to a better world is not to nurture our youth, but to allow the elite and their money to come and go as they please.

We can therefore see Ingle's article for what it really is – conjectural nightmarish propaganda, masquerading as authoritative disinterested comment. He is directing psychological abuse at the proletariat, apparently if we refuse to be ruled by unelected appointees then our national sport lose its 'prowess', it will serve us right for being 'Little Englanders', we will be sorry and Ingle will say 'I told you so'. This is one example (I could give many more) of how the real far-right weaponise news outlets to attack the character of those who confront them, to pre-emptively silence our demands to live in a democracy. The fact that Ingle (and Guardian journalists generally) would swear blind that they are against the far-right shows the degree of subtlety with which the advocates of authoritarianism operate.

It's a funny old game
On 26 October 1863 Ebenezer Cobb Morley met some friends at the Freemasons' Tavern, in Covent Garden, and they wrote down one of the most important documents in human history – the rules of Football. Football is a protocol, a set of dos and don'ts. It could exist without this or that player, team, stadium but we could not alter the protocol without altering Football itself. Football is good to play and

watch so its popularity has spread. Now let's consider this extract from David Hume's essay 'Of the Standard of Taste' in which he discusses the Koran.

"The admirers and followers of the Alcoran insist on the excellent moral precepts interspersed throughout that wild and absurd performance ... But would we know whether the pretend prophet had really attained a just sentiment of morals? Let us attend to his narration, and we shall soon find that he bestows praise on such instances of treachery, inhumanity, cruelty, revenge, bigotry, as are utterly incompatible with civilised society. No steady rule of right seems there to be attended to, and every action is blamed or praised so far only as it is beneficial or hurtful to the true believers."

So of the two protocols the sporting protocol appears to opperate in the opposite way to the religious protocol.

The sporting protocol establishes what is right or wrong for the participants, whereas the religious protocol assumes those who accept the protocol are right and those who do not are wrong.

The sporting protocol is not concerned with anything outside the protocol itself, the religious protocol is.

For the sport there is a territorial battle between people acting within the protocol itself, for the religion the territorial struggle is between those who accept the protocol and those who do not.

The sporting protocol completely prohibits violence, the religious protocol does not.

The primary concern of the architects of Football was to achieve an event that is meaningful, in human terms, for participants and spectators. This is because sport is voluntary, so if Football failed to achieve this then it would die out. Because Football does achieve this there is no need for any rule requiring participants to conserve, deepen or expand obedience to the protocol itself. Indeed such a rule would be an absurdity, a de facto admission of a failure of the protocol - that it could not endure without being imposed.

The religion does the opposite – it is primarily designed to maximise submission to the protocol itself. The religious protocol insists that it be conserved, deepened and expanded, thus dispensing with the need to function in human or social terms. By dispensing with the need to function in human social terms it actually becomes an excellent incubator of the dysfunctional. It follows that the greater the social failure of the protocol the more extreme the coercion required to maintain it.

Good ideas don't need to be imposed because they are chosen freely. Bad ideas do need to be imposed or they don't survive. Those who have a good system have little need to be evangelical, they submit it to us and we decide whether or not to participate. But those who prosper from a bad system must manically insist we submit to it – or else they lose power. Thus the imposition becomes inversely proportional to the excellence of the protocol.

Indeed if a protocol states that the imposition of itself is good in itself, then it is more of a military strategy than an ethical guide; which I suppose is precisely what we would expect from a philosophy designed by a warlord. So the sporting protocol is submitted to people for consideration, whereas with the religion, the people submit to the protocol.

The sporting protocol establishes a level playing field (literally!) so small communities can compete against large ones on equal terms. The religious protocol establishes inequality in which the weak submit to the strong.

The sporting protocol generates meaningful events in human terms, the religious protocol establishes meaningless spiritualism.

The sporting protocol brings humanity together - the religious protocol sets humanity at each other's throats.

So, one is voluntary, the other compulsory. One may be freely discussed, the other prohibits discussion. One can be endlessly debated, the other asserts debate is unnecessary because all the answers have already been given. One establishes equality irrespective of culture; the other establishes inequality depending on ideology. One has referees whose performance is critiqued, the other, clerics who are not. One enhances social life, the other destroys it. One establishes meaningful events in human terms; the other (wrongly) asserts meaning to be spiritual. One is a joy, the other a threat.

Which of the two protocols has yielded the most meaningful human experiences for the most people and destroyed the lives of the fewest? The one that is voluntary obviously. Let us raise a glass to Ebenezer Cobb Morley! May the best protocol win!

Kindi's Dilemma
Al-Kindi (801-873) was a great Islamic intellectual who pioneered the translation of Aristotelian texts into Arabic. But Aristotle's god is a very mechanistic god in an eternal universe. As a Muslim, Kindi was obliged to reject the idea of an eternal universe - he *had* to believe in creation. But Kindi sought to reconcile these two schools of thought. It was helpful that, at this time the great intellectual developments were taking place in the salons, rather than the mosques, but still his project was politically sensitive - at one point his library was confiscated! Kindi's great contribution was the revival of Greek philosophy and the preservation of the apparatus of philosophy itself.

Al Farabi (872-950) asserted that the Universe is indeed eternal which was closer to Aristotle's position than Kindi had been. This was a departure from the orthodox line. Additionally he diverged from Islamic doctrine by claiming that creation was necessary and not a gift from a benevolent God. But he was similar to Kindi in that he sustained Islam's engagement with Greek ideas and sought to use the Greek system to make sense of the Islamic faith.

Al-Biruni (973-1050) was an astonishing polymath who, almost singlehandedly, invented anthropology. How did he invent social science? With his book *The India* which was an appreciation of Hindu culture. Previously Islamic intellectuals dismissed Hinduism as polytheistic idol worship. Biruni showed Hinduism to be a far more subtle and complex intellectual construction than the Islamic world had given it credit for. He described the Hindus and Greeks as 'two families in the same house'. He also wrote extensively on the timing of the religions festivals of the Buddhists, Sogdians, Zoroastrians, Christians, Jews and Pagans. His lifelong obsession with time led him to the study of the planetary motion. His proposition that planets moved in ellipses anticipated the work of Kepler. This posed a problem for the religious (and followers of Farabi) who asserted that the heavens must move in perfect circles rather than wobble along in ellipses (as is actually the case). It's no surprise that Biruni flourished in an environment where there was relatively little disparagement of non-Islamic science. His work was largely ignored in the Islamic world.

The most original Islamic philosopher, Avicenna (980-1037) was (justifiably) immodest. He drank a lot and actively pursued worldly sexual pleasures (for which I do not blame him). Perennially controversial Avicenna was a colourful character who travelled from court to court seeking a patron for his genius; sometimes he was in hiding, sometimes in prison! His argument for the existence of God is (Aristotelian) that God is the necessary first cause. Because Avicenna sought an intellectual explanation of God he ended up with a 'god' that is like some concept of theoretical physics not dissimilar to Spinoza's god. This obviously is an altogether different proposition to the intergalactic Dumbledore offered to us by religion. He was a determinist and held that every cause issues an effect in an entirely deterministic way, and since the world turns out to be a necessary emanation from God, if there was another world, then it would be identical to this one in every way. (If I drank a lot and nobbed loads of women then I would probably also be attracted to a philosophy in which everything was necessary). But if everything is necessary then how can we be moral agents choosing between good and evil? Indeed how can moral choices even exist in a deterministic world? Additionally he agreed with Farabi that the Universe was eternal. The theologians were always going to be pissed off.

Al-Ghazali (1058-1111) saw Avicenna as an enemy to be refuted. He felt Avicenna's philosophy (indeed philosophy in general) was incompatible with Islamic faith. His arguments against Avicenna are interesting in that they appear similar to Hume's arguments against causation. Al-Ghazali's concern was that if everything about God is necessary, then it would be a necessary act that God creates us rather than an act of kindness; and that Avicenna therefore posed a challenge to Islam. Al-Ghazali's books tended to have brilliant titles, the most famous of which is *The Incoherence of the Philosophers*, in which he stated that since all truth is in the Koran, there is no need of speculation independent of revelation. But then Al-Ghazali had a mental breakdown which he attributed to a crisis of faith and confessed to only being a Muslim verbally. He then spent several years wandering and meditating. In later life he became a devout Sufi, but still produced interesting work. Like Kant he was interested in critiquing reason itself, albeit to justify his cultural prejudices. (Maybe Kant also sought to critique reason to justify his cultural prejudices but at least he tried to do it dispassionately). It seems to me Al-Ghazali was a prodigiously gifted thinker who made the error of applying infinite scepticism to reason but insufficient scepticism to religion. This is all the more erroneous when we consider that religion relies on an appeal to something higher and external to itself, whereas reason does not.

Averroes (1126-1198) (the great commentator on Aristotle) was a believer, but not rigidly orthodox. He said that philosophers alone were qualified to interpret the Koran, and that holy text which contradicted philosophy should be considered as merely allegorical. He held that the world had not been created, and that after death we don't go to heaven but become part of a type of Hegelian universal intellect. When Averroes came across Al-Ghazali's *The Incoherence of the Philosophers* he responded with the winningly titled *The Incoherence of the Incoherence* in which he referred followers of Al-Ghazali to various commentaries on Aristotle written by … er … Averroes! But Al Mansur had published an edict to the effect that God had decreed hellfire for those who thought that truth could be found by reason. Averroes was accused of cultivating the philosophies of the ancients at the expense of the true faith. He was put on trial, banished and his books were burned.

Do you see the pattern that is emerging? The relationship between the great Islamic philosophers and the clerics is one of permanent conflict not harmony. The further the Islamic geniuses pushed their ideas, the more they came into conflict with the clerics. The intellectual investigation and religious conflict appear directly proportional. Conversely the greatness of the philosophy seems inversely proportional to the religious devotion. Within Islamic history there does not seem to be anyone like Augustine, Kant or Leibniz who simultaneously advanced both philosophy *and* theology. Obviously this is a subject that merits a whole book to itself, but that should not discourage us from observing the general pattern: the 'good' were not great and the great were not 'good'. Similarly the most magnificent Islamic contributions seem to be those least concerned with religious doctrine: <u>algebra</u>, <u>algorithms</u>, Al-Biruni's anticipation of elliptical orbits etc.

The great Islamic philosophers were generally looked upon with suspicion by the theologians, and owed their safety (when they were safe) to enlightened patrons. This should come as no surprise to anyone, a belief system by its very nature must be in conflict with the sort of synthetic a posteriori knowledge we find in Aristotle, because synthetic a posteriori knowledge is about learning from observations, whereas belief systems are about unalterable internal values that determine *how* we see. Philosophy is the questions business, religion is the answers business. Philosophy is about wondering, religion is about explaining. Philosophy looks for errors, religion blocks out doubt. Philosophy is about developing ideas, religion feels threatened by ideas. With philosophy new ideas come to us and change us, with religion internal beliefs are projected from us onto the world. Philosophy is about changing our minds, religion is about not changing our minds. Philosophers submit arguments we can accept or reject, theologians impose belief. Philosophy is a series of unique statements, religion uses repetition to train the mind to act automatically without thinking. Philosophy is about thinking, religion is about not thinking. It is the questions, not the answers that matter most.

Of all the above my least favourite is Al-Ghazali because ultimately he came down on the side of religion. But still Al-Ghazali deserves credit for seeing that he had an either/or choice. Al-Kindi tried to reconcile the philosophy of Aristotle and Islam. Let us call this '*Al-Kindi's Dilemma*' - In pursuing this Al-Kindi was wasting his time and his talent looking for square circles. And today we see millions of decent intelligent Muslims wrestling with their own version of Al-Kindi's Dilemma: the gay Muslims, the Muslim feminists, the Muslim figurative artists, the Muslim socialists, the Muslim philosophers, they are all wasting their time seeking to reconcile two inherently irreconcilable things. When philosophy and religion are in conflict, why not fix the religion? After all religion crushes people, prohibits thought and generates war, whereas philosophy enriches people, cultivates ideas and generates peace.

Note: Additionally the above reading helps explain the magnificent achievements of Islamic scholars in the fields of mathematics and geometry. Within Islam it is possible to excel in these fields without incurring the wrath of the theologians, so if you are an Islamic genius, like Al-Khwarizmi, why choose a career in which you have to live in fear of persecution?

Apparently there is a funny TV show called *We Are Lady Parts* in which some Muslim girls form a punk band. I'm sure it is very good, but why waste our lives wrestling with Kindi's Dilemma? The inherent nature of punk music is to rebel against authority, whereas the inherent nature of Islam is to submit. An Islamic punk band is an oxymoron. Around 1976 in New York three types of music were invented – punk, rap and disco. Today these three music forms dominate the world, but how have they fared in the Islamic world? Punk is out for the reason already stated and disco is tolerated only in specific circumstances so long as its theme of gay liberation is suppressed. But what about rap (hip-hop)? Rap is fine, firstly because it's male dominated, but primarily because rap distils music into just beats and words, so there is nothing inherent in the nature of rap that negates ideas of conquest, submission or territorial domination. It's easy for Rap to be a sermon that completely accords with orthodox doctrine.

Let's say you disagree with my argument. I'm sure many will. To *demonstrate* that my argument is wrong you are required to provide lots of examples of philosophers, figurative painters, campaigners for gay rights, campaigners for women's rights, campaigners for democracy, campaigners for equality, punks, campaigners for multiculturalism and campaigners for free speech who were not persecuted by the clerics.

Viva Civil Rights!
Around 2018 some Kenyan students were massacred by Islamists. I re-tweeted the horrifying news with the message "Black Lives Matter". Black lives matter is a truism. No human life doesn't matter, blacks are humans, therefore black lives matter. QED. Over the next few years BLM became a global movement, and 'taking the knee' became common at sporting events.

I have mixed feelings about taking the knee. For BLM, taking the knee seems to be about rejecting a specific type of racism, they are right to do so because racism is real, it is wrong, it must be rejected, and because yes, black lives *do* matter. My only misgiving is that whilst it is good to reject the racial abuse of black people, it is even better to simply reject *all* racism. The whole point of rejecting racism is that we should not do so selectively. Rejecting racism selectively has the appearance of not really rejecting it at all – in fact it smacks of preferring a particular ethnic group when surely we should prefer no ethnic group.

For the last five years the British working class have been called 'gammon'. Apparently because we had the temerity to vote for an independent democracy that made us sub human bigots. Where were the civil rights protests about that? In March 2019 when the most voted-for thing in British history was cancelled, did the football authorities sanction any protests? When a foreign power seized control of our society which authorities sided *with* us *against* them? When external rule was imposed on us against our will, which institutions (that are supposedly there to ensure fairness) raised objections? We looked on in horror as the ruling elite and connived with foreign powers to prevent us from regaining the democratic independence we had <u>VOTED</u> for. Remain declared thermonuclear war on British democracy. We saw the rich and powerful close ranks against us, and weaponise all the media they could seize to bombard us with Foucaultian normalising propaganda. For years after the vote to leave, every news bulletin put out on the BBC (the state broadcaster) was designed to make us give up hope. The endemic corruption of the British political system became impossible to deny. And after all that, the rich unelected hierarchy in charge of football ask fans to get behind the taking of the knee? Fine, ok, I'm never going to criticise an anti-racism demo, but these authorities (like all the other authorities) appear incapable of recognising the hate campaign directed at *us*. Is taking the knee against <u>all</u> prejudice? Yes or No? If yes then where were these people when we democrats were being subject to the most relentless, comprehensive and best-funded hate campaign in modern British history?

The EU is an expansionist project. It's about accruing power and territory. Every pronouncement by every EU leader is designed to achieve the same thing – our submission to their rule. They might advocate 'harmonisation' or 'dynamic alignment' or a 'level playing field', a 'customs union' or a 'single market', but these are all just code words for the same thing: us being ruled by them. Them controlling our money, laws and borders, and us being told how to live by their judges in their courts according to their interpretation of their rules. EU leaders never said 'the UK has made a democratic decision we should all respect'. Every action and every word of the EU was designed to achieve the maximum transfer of power, territory and money *from* us *to* them. They bought off dissent and promoted their stooges to every conceivable position of political power until their influence was so great that in March 2019 they managed to suspend our exit that had been agreed in international law. I put it to the reader that if anything warranted a civil rights protest it was the blatant, raw naked power grab by the EU. But who took the knee about that?

Similarly every Islamic act appears consistent with the domination of territory. And here I'm not just talking about the obvious examples like the bombings, stabbings, beheadings or driving vehicles into crowds of people. There is the war against free speech, the persecution of intellectuals and comedians, the framing of all criticism as 'hate speech' the selective appeal only to the human rights that expand the project, and the disregard for the human rights of those outside the project. How can we explain the bizarre and barbaric practice of female genital mutilation? Simple, it is easier to force the submission of a woman who has first been mutilated. Women's education is discouraged because uneducated women tend to have more children. Women are subjugated because those who are not have fewer children. Likewise gays are persecuted because those who are not have fewer children, and the ideology producing the most children will eventually have the most territorial domination. The Jizya tax is a tax on *not* being Muslim, it is institutional, financial discrimination. Then there are the nudges which are so subtle they could be passed off as innocuous, for example the prohibition of figurative art. Why investigate the nature of humanity when all the answers have already been given? The very act of thinking about the nature of humanity cannot but threaten an ideology claiming to be the last word. Then there is the fasting which is a basic form of military training. The wailing dissonance of Islamic music is a de-rationalising call to arms. Even the head coverings that the men compel the women to wear can be understood in this context. The head covering is not a stylistic sartorial choice but a partition, a cordoning off, a demarcation of human demographic territory, in a similar way to how a man might put a cover over his things outside the house.

Obviously the way other people dress and the music they listen to is up to them, I'm sure there are plenty of people who think that my clothes and music are dreadful, and often they would be right! But my point is there seems to be no Islamic act inconsistent with the domination of territory. From what point of view do all the above make perfect sense? From the point of view of those seeking to maximise territorial and demographic domination. No Islamic leader ever says "Women should dress how they like" or "I support gay rights!" or "Free speech? Fine by me!" because if they did say those things, then they wouldn't be an *Islamic* leader. Every insistence that one side must accommodate and the other side must be accommodated is a microcosm of the same vast intergenerational, intercontinental conflict.

Islam, from its inception, has been primarily concerned with the domination of territory; so to say or do anything that might reduce territorial domination is to be *not* Islamic. Which I suppose is pretty understandable. After all if Islam and morality are conflated then it necessarily follows that anything that expands Islamic territory cannot be immoral, and that anything which reduces submission to Islam cannot be moral. This is exactly what we would expect from a philosophy designed by a soldier, who dedicated his life to the conquest of hearts, minds and territory.

The point I am getting at here (in an admittedly roundabout way) is that following the vote to leave the British were entirely justified in considering themselves besieged, by not one, but *two* vast geo-political entities: the European Union and the Islamic religion. Both of which were absolutely hell bent on our submission to their rule. Everything, absolutely everything said and done in the name of Islam and the EU was about maximising their power over us; conversely nothing said and done in the name of Islam or the EU is about us democratically determining our own lives as we see fit. Both are expansionist, supremacist, undemocratic, neoliberal and consider those not aligned with the project to be sub-human. It felt like an attack because it was. Two vast geopolitical entities openly sought our submission to their rule, and they were succeeding!

Our vernacular architecture was demolished, our landscape cleared for new housing. Our pubs and live music venues were legislated into the dustbin of history, whilst religious practices were exempted from regulatory compliance. If I committed bigamy or were responsible for a girl's genitals being mutilated then I would be arrested, why not apply the law equally to everyone? While homeless veterans begged, people rocking up in rubber dinghies from France were automatically housed; why not have the same housing policy for all humans? Our public spaces were encircled by bollards to prevent cars being driven into crowds of people. Our culture was deemed to be inferior and less worthy of support and protection than the cultures of those who sought our submission. If your average Brit felt assailed by this, they were not tilting windmills, but making fairly reasonable complaints based on observable facts. If hundreds of thousands of people are entering a country and seeking to establish their political system in which we have no say, and if your average Brit considers themselves to be under attack, then with what facts do I refute them? What actual evidence can I hold up to demonstrate they are wrong? I can't say there is no fear, I can't say there is no coercion, I can't say there is no strategy, I can't say there is no threat, I can't say there is no advance.

I put it to the reader that if anything deserves a civil rights protest it is surely the attempt to subject an entire population into submission to the rule of others. If anything constitutes intellectual violence it is surely the comprehensive, well-funded and relentless battle to prevent us from achieving our democratic control of our society. Which authorities sanctioned protests about that? None of them. Indeed, not only did the various authorities do nothing to support us, but these institutions (which we were always told, existed to uphold fair play) appeared to be openly conniving with those who sought our submission! Why? Because they don't work for us – we work for them.

Let's presume I have totally misjudged this and that when Islamists or rich unelected people seek to impose their political systems on us, that is somehow not an attack upon our society. Well, fine ok, but then we would seem to be using a definition of 'conquest' that does not allow us to condemn what happened to the Zoroastrians, Yazidis, Apache, Aborigines, Māori, Inca etc. We cannot apply these definitions selectively so we find ourselves challenged by the consequences of our enquiry. Throughout history attempts to destroy cultures are actually pretty common. Naturally attempts by Remainers and Islamists to take control were presented as mere tidying up procedures by the enlightened to civilise the savages.

The genuine enquirer must be suspicious if, even as EU law and Sharia law advance, the British are relentlessly assailed with accusations of prejudice. Accusations which routinely assume the perpetrators to be British and the victims to be otherwise. It's almost as if those who identify prejudice in others are guilty of the very thought crime they are so hasty to condemn. Is that the case? How could I know? I'm not a mind reader, but the empirical evidence does not refute it.

The attacks on the British after the 2016 referendum by EU supporters and Islamists were raw naked power grabs plain and simple. But the only civil rights campaigns seemed to be ones that assumed the British were sub human bigots. The hate campaigns against us didn't seem to count. If those taking the knee in 2021 were silent about the abuse of the British after 2016 then it is hard to see their condemnation of racism as sincere. Often they appear to be acts of self-interest embracing precisely the double standards they claim to reject. Our opponents were brilliant at spotting the prejudices of everyone else - their 'Gammon are racist' argument was comical in its hypocrisy.

When George Floyd was murdered there were worldwide protests and something was done about it. Good. But when far-right groups bribe and threaten and coerce and abuse and bomb and stab to bring about the submission of an entire nation who stands up? How come the terrorist murder of Jo Cox was (rightly) met with international condemnation, whilst the terrorist murder of David Amess was met with quiet reflection? Given that every side will always claim double standards, what determines whether an atrocity is quietly grieved or met with outrage? Sure it's a difficult question, but right now the determining factor seems to be that outrage is only legitimate when it assumes that those who want more democracy are perpetrators and those who want less are victims. It's almost as if those who are against democracy have hijacked this issue to advance their cause.

Indeed if I wanted to advance an authoritarian system the cleverest way to do it would be to pretend I was doing the opposite. I would start by accusing democrats of being racist or trans-phobic or some other vogue thought crime du jour. (Not to say that racism and trans-phobia are not problems.) That would pre-emptively silence counter argument, and allow me to masquerade as a moral crusader, it would tie my opponents in knots requiring them to explain themselves, appearing guilty even as they demonstrated their innocence. And that would give me cover as I went about separating people from power. The dictator's movie has a noble soundtrack!

If there is discrimination against a black person I am with the black person. If there is discrimination against a Muslim I am with the Muslim. If there is discrimination against a Jew I am with the Jew. And so on. I do this not *because* they are black or Muslim or Jew, but because they are human. I apply the general principle of human rights to humans generally, not to this or that group in particular. I am not against human rights - I am against campaigning for rights selectively out of self-interest. The clue is in the title '*human rights*' are by their very nature for humans generally so they should be applied generally not specifically. If we are to appeal to universal values (of anti-racism) then we must own the consequences of that and condemn all racism everywhere, even (indeed especially) when it is 'others' who are the victims. So I'm obliged (eager in fact) to condemn discrimination against 'others' and invite them as my fellow human beings to condemn the attacks on us. But because the position of EU supporters and Islamists are belief-based and supremacist, it is precisely that offer which they cannot reciprocate.

137

Imagine if taking a moral stand didn't mean you got slapped on the back and hailed as a civil rights hero, but that instead you became a vilified outcast, and your career ended? We Brexiteers don't have to *imagine* that. It happened to us. We were the ones it was ok to hate.

Obviously this is a sensitive subject, so at the risk of labouring the point I am going to clarify now, just so we are clear. If you are against prejudice and racism then I am with you. And although I have misgivings about taking the knee, I can respect that most people doing it have good intentions. And if you disagree with me on Brexit I'm not going to hate you for that, as it's a complex subject and lots of decent people take a different view to me. But … if you choose to remain silent about the blatant attempts by the European Union and the Islamic religion to make us submit to their rule … then please spare me your ethics lecture.

Conclusion
So we see that an issue which superficially seems simple, upon closer inspection is more difficult than first appears, and we must all be careful (myself definitely included) not to only see mental violence when it is convenient to do so. So what should we do? I'd say we should stop exhausting ourselves with public gestures of moral purity (however well intended) and instead concentrate our efforts on prosecuting racism wherever there is evidence to do so. In other words, stop wasting our time and energy worrying about the Kantian thing in itself, and instead conduct real action in the real world.

I don't enjoy writing these things. Speaking out against the EU has cost me and my family dearly, and by speaking out against Islam I am risking a lot. So why do I bother? Because when more people have more democratic control over more power, there is more chance of more good for more people.

Recipe For Endless War:
1, Set up a project that is belief-based and therefore impervious to empirical refutation.
2, Decree that virtuous acts are those which conserve, deepen or expand the project.
3, Prohibit dissent such that, to even air misgivings is assumed to reveal concealed depravity.
4, Project administered by small number of ideologically pure appointees.
5, Population taught the 'right' way to think.
6, Regard those outside to project as sub-human savages, to be civilised by their superiors.
7, Set up a legal sham that adjudicates on the basis of whether or not the project is advanced.
8, Smash the lives of critics.
9, Call it 'peace'.

In your society you will be assured (by the powerful) that those who uphold such projects are ethical and that those who critique are not. It's the other way round (again).

The Far-Right Religion
I wish every Muslim in the world peace, prosperity, happiness, good health and a long life. I don't hate anyone, I am merely, politely disagreeing with certain ideas. The reason why I disagree with Islam is precisely because I am a moderate, left-wing social democrat. Islam is anti-gay, creationist, patriarchal, mercantilist, supremacist, mono-cultural, territorial, expansionist, censorious, authoritarian, anti-trans, anti-democratic, anti-philosophy, socially conservative, coercive and segregated. No Islamic state in history has advocated free speech, minority rights, artistic expression, social mobility, women's rights, gay rights or any of the other touchstone issues of the left. Islam is an extreme right-wing ideology by every conceivable measure.

Note: Re Islam being mercantilist. Islamic states are not financially viable because they monetise their intellectual property the way other countries do, but because they monetise the territory conquered. So the OPEC states monetise the commodity of the territory (oil) whereas, for say Turkey and Egypt their economies are kept afloat by tourism which is a form of leasing access to territory.

You will notice when I claim that Islamic values and left-wing values are incompatible, that is based on empirical observations of every Islamic society that has ever existed in history. Naturally many will disagree and claim that it is perfectly possible to be both Islamic and left-wing. But that would be a solipsistic argument rather than an empirical one. Even if we accept that opinion as sincere, how do we know it is not mistaken? How is it demonstrated that left-wing values and Islamic values are compatible when every demonstration of support for the left in Islamic countries (gay rights, women's rights, workers' representation, minority rights, free speech etc) automatically results in conflict with the theologians? I try to make my arguments hyper empirical, as opposed to the hyper solipsistic arguments of my opponents.

Now let's contrast my position on this with that of a right-wing politician. For every Muslim in the world I want nothing but goodness and happiness. Right-wing politicians don't – for them being anti-Muslim is just a way to climb the political ladder. Regarding Islamic leaders, I think they are tyrants who should be subject to the approval of the people they rule. Right-wing politicians don't. They are happy to chill with dictators who are rich and powerful.

Here is Bojo having a tête-à-tête with the Sultan of Brunei.

139

...and here is Trump having a cosy fire side chat with Saudi royalty. (Clearly it's the poor Muslims they don't want around). Finally regarding Islamic ideology itself, I think its merits and demerits should be discussed politely and openly just like Christianity, Marxism, Capitalism, Post Modernism or any other set of ideas. Right-wing politicians don't. They see religion as either good (when it confirms prejudices) or evil (when it doesn't). So my position with regard to poor Muslims, rich Muslims and Islamic ideology is pretty much the opposite of say Trump or Johnson.

So once again if we look at the adjectives used in the popular narrative we see they are the ones that most completely misrepresent the empirical reality. The popular narrative is that the 'far-right' are 'Islamophobic' and that the liberal minded progressives are relaxed about society becoming more Islamic. The empirical reality is that Islam is a far-right ideology by every conceivable measure and those who indulge or embrace it are facilitating its attack on feminism, free speech, democracy, multiculturalism, diversity, gay rights philosophy etc. From whence cometh the popular narrative? Empiricism? No. Core beliefs? Yes. Classic Othello Syndrome.

But when this narrative that black is white has been expressed so vehemently, so often, who will dare put their head above the parapet to challenge it? I think two types of people: The first are the people like me, who out of sheer bloody mindedness spend years writing long essays explaining why things are the other way round (for which we receive no credit, no money and much abuse). The second are the antagonists, the genuinely odious, who don't care if they piss people off and revel in the notoriety. This in turn creates a vicious circle of ever-increasing polarisation making it increasingly difficult for moderate people like me to be seen to agree.

Ideas Are Not Colours (Unless You're Hilma af Klint)
Islam is not a race, there are Muslims of every colour, and yet an odd notion has been established that it is somehow racist to disagree with Islam. Buddha was Indian, but disagreeing with his philosophy is not hatred of Indians. Adam Smith was a Scot, but disagreeing with Capitalism is not prejudice against the Scottish. Marx and Christ were Jewish, but it is not anti-Semitic to disagree with Marxism or Christianity. I can disagree with Rousseau without being anti-French, and so on. It would be ludicrous to say that expressing misgivings about capitalism is an attack on everyone that has to earn money to support themselves and their families; similarly it's ludicrous to say disagreeing with Islam is an attack on Muslims. Obviously it's possible to be racist and disagree with this or that ideology, but to say 'People who criticise Islam are racist' is a clear-cut logical fallacy. There are various different logical fallacies; this one is called a 'non sequitur' (a statement that does not logically follow from what preceded it). But if this logical fallacy is so obvious why is it employed so often? I suspect that there are two reasons. Firstly apologists for Islam are making an unfalsifiable accusation to pre-emptively silence criticism. They ascribe racism promiscuously as a means of social control (See Foucault section). And secondly, those who are scared of Islam wish to make their cowardliness look like a courageous ethical stance.

Patterns to Study
The human race is very good at analysis and problem solving. But we are addressing ourselves to the wrong problems. Clever people on the left analyse the relationship between incomes and outcomes. Clever people on the right analyse the relationship between demand and supply. But the correlation we really need to analyse is between belief and deserts. There seem to take two basic forms of desert the world today: the destruction of nature by capitalism and the destruction of intellectual life by Islam. The former expands a physical desert, the latter expands an intellectual desert. Both utterly reject empiricism. Capitalists deny their responsibility for the destruction of nature and Islamists deny their role in the destruction of intellectual life. How do we reduce the physical deserts? By looking at the relationship between human actions and their effect on the planet. How do we reduce the intellectual deserts? By looking at the correlation between free speech and a thriving society. What should we fear? A lack of empiricism and an excess of subjectivity.

We see from Darwin that nature prospers through a process of natural selection - the future will be in the image of choices made by females. It is no surprise therefore that where men make all the decisions and women are powerless, civic life and biodiversity are destroyed. Sometimes there is a geographical desert, sometimes an intellectual desert, sometimes both.

Con-Fusing

Fusing is when a mischievous person fuses together a questionable argument and a good argument and assumes that to argue against the questionable is the same as arguing against the good.

For example let's say I am arguing with someone about tax, if I can fuse together the issue of tax and racism (for example that a particular tax policy unfairly discriminates against this or that community) then I get to automatically win the argument because the accusation of racism is so devastating it sweeps everything before it. As society has become more multicultural we would expect racism to become less and less of an issue, but precisely the opposite has happened. Why? Because racism is such a trump card, everybody is pissing their pants to fuse it together with their pet subject. Consequently good causes that initially we would have no difficulty in supporting (anti-racism, care for the environment etc) have become intellectual Trojan horses for all manner of dubious propositions. Fusing takes various common forms:

1, Fusing criticism of Islam with racism.
2, Fusing scepticism about state power with denial of climate science.
3, Fusing scepticism about officially endorsed anti-racism campaigns with racism itself.
4, Fusing concern for the environment with contempt for individual liberty.
5, Fusing concern about racism generally with contempt for 'us' specifically.

Example 1: Let's say I were to visit the house of a climate change denier and dump a load of industrial waste at the end of their street. I am sure they would quickly come out and remonstrate with me. Would that make them a hypocrite on the environment? Probably, but on a deeper level it would also show that they do actually care about the environment when the issue is immediate. Their scepticism about environmentalism is that mischievous people are using it as an excuse to coerce them into submitting to authoritarianism.

Example 2: Now let's take an example from the other side. What if Fred wanted to carry on driving his car, taking flights, and throwing plastic into a landfill site with no regard to the consequences of his actions? As environmentalists we want to make Fred consider the consequences of his actions upon everyone else. But if Fred can fuse together concern for the environment with authoritarian state power, he can get to carry on acting in a selfish way whilst claiming to defend the liberty of all. Liberty is a two-edged-sword. It is all too easy to see only the impositions on ourselves. A true Libertarian should ask "am I imposing myself?" as often as they ask "am I being imposed upon?" Again as with the section on Kant, we should cross-check more and be less fixated with the self.

Example 3: I can value the music of John Tavener or Bach without having to subscribe to their religious viewpoint. We should homogenise and specify until the conclusion drawn are proportional to the evidence provided, to do otherwise would be an unwarranted extension - fusing.

Example 4: One type of fusing we must carefully guard against is allowing disagreement with Islamic ideas to become antipathy towards Muslims. I have the pleasure of working with Muslims every day, and I couldn't ask for more pleasant, decent, professional colleagues. I don't know how I would cope without them! There has never been a single unpleasant word. Naturally I treat them with the respect and courtesy to which they are entitled. Why should any Muslim take criticism of Islam seriously if they suspect it is just the over-intellectualised front of a hater? I don't hate anyone, I (politely) disagree with bad ideas. We must clearly differentiate: it is NOT ok to hate Muslims, it *is* ok to disagree with ideas. Simple.

"Strong minds discuss ideas ... weak minds discuss people."— Socrates

There are so many other examples of fusing we are spoilt for choice. For example in October 2021 the BBC reported *"Senior government climate change advisers have warned Boris Johnson against more foreign aid cuts ahead of the COP26 environment summit. The group known as 'Friends of COP' said foreign aid cuts would show the UK was "neither committed to nor serious about helping countries vulnerable to climate change ... The ability of the UK to act as a genuine, trusted partner for developing countries is of crucial importance to COP26's success. Further implied cuts to overseas aid at the Comprehensive Spending Review (CSR) would send a signal that the UK is neither committed to, nor serious about, enabling a green global recovery from the pandemic, nor improving the resilience of the most vulnerable to climate change."*

You should know the drill by now ... so ... what was the empirical reality of what the 'Friends of COP' were calling for? The continued transfer of money from the UK to countries without democracy and free speech. That's right, they want the best governed countries to become poorer and the worst governed countries to become richer. It's hard to imagine a more obvious recipe for social and environmental catastrophe.

How exactly does the transfer of money from countries with democracy and free speech to countries without democracy and free speech reduce environmental damage? It's a practical question. All the empirical evidence tells us that the more rich and powerful authoritarian regimes are, the worse the environmental and social outcomes. All our observations of the modern world tell us that countries with democracy and free speech have better environmental, social and humanitarian policies. Indeed it is hard to imagine a course of action less likely to yield a better world than the enrichment of tyrannies or the impoverishment of democracies.

Clearly the signatories of this letter had conflated mutually exclusive things – they had fused good outcomes with bad methods. But was this confusion or insincerity? When the genuine enquirer sees a phrase like: *"The ability of the UK to act as a genuine, trusted partner for developing countries is of crucial importance to COP26's success"* they must instinctively smell a rat. What is the actual project here? To maintain the capacity of the planet to support life? Or to pay tyrants to like us? If FoCOP were genuinely interested in protecting the environment, then why not advocate (as I do) the total prohibition of pollution, 100% renewable energy, and the total boycott of tyrannies? Simple!

So who are FoCOP? I won't name names but looking down the list there are the usual suspects of Lords, CEOs Chairmen etc. So ... a bunch of wealthy, unelected, powerful people are calling for money to be transferred from tax payers to wealthy, unelected, powerful people. No surprise there then. Basically FoCOP are just another bunch of rich unelected powerful people trying to make democracies poorer and tyrannies richer. Naturally to conceal their scurrilous aims they masquerade as environmentalists, but hey-ho, what apologists for authoritarianism haven't pretended to be upstanding ethical heroes?

To apply 'Paul's Rule' do they want power over me? Yes. They want to seize and allocate my money such that people like them are empowered and people like me are de-powered. Once again, when we disregard the emotional response and instead consider the empirical reality, it is those claiming to be champions of social justice and the environment who are the real far-right. File under 'mental violence'. Still, on the bright side, it's always nice to find yourself up against a bunch of people calling themselves 'FoCOP' ... makes a nice change from 'Submission'.

When libertarians say environmentalism is a conspiracy to impose authoritarianism, it's important we can contradict their argument, but doing so becomes very difficult when rich unelected people use emotive appeals to expand their power and influence. Racism, gay rights and environmentalism ARE important issues we should all be concerned about, but mischievous people are using them as Trojan horses to advance authoritarianism. For example, there are many people who are happy to support gay rights but feel threatened by the contemporary debate about gender because the feel infertility is being selectively fetishized to eradicate unfashionable ethnic groups. The consequence of this is that lots of perfectly decent people who deplore racism, homophobia and environmental damage have become cynical about causes they should have no difficulty in supporting.

Why Brexiteers should support Extinction Rebellion

This is a rant I published in 2019

I've lost quite a few 'friends' because of my Brexiting … so might as well go for the clean sweep … I support Extinction Rebellion! So I'm asking all Brexiteers to pause for thought before condemning them.

Firstly I think Brexiteers are conflating XR with 'Remain' and 'People's Vote' but XR are primarily concerned with physics and biology whereas EU supporters are primarily concerned with political union. Those are two different things. Conversely the aims of Brexiteers and XR are not mutually exclusive. We want to live in an independent democracy and they want to save the environment. Are there any two positions more obviously in accord? I want the maximum number of people to have the maximum amount of scrutiny over the maximum amount of power. If there was any sure way of generating good environmental laws that's it! The EU is about the minimum number of people deciding the fate of the maximum number of people in secret. If ever there was a sure way of incubating plutocracy that's it! No wonder EU pollution has increased despite declining EU birth rates, declining manufacturing and greener technologies!

Next the accusation that XR are 'virtue signalling'. Well, it seems to me there are only two ways of avoiding this accusation, either:
1, Never do anything virtuous. Or…
2, Only do virtuous deeds anonymously to avoid being credited for it.
Given that someone has to do something to maintain our ecosystem it seems unreasonable to expect XR to rock up dressed as Zorro.

Next, I'm supposed to hate these people because they're trouble makers? They want to change society. How do you suggest they achieve that – by voting? If there is anything Brexiteers have surely grasped by now it is that winning votes doesn't count.

1, In 2013 David Cameron promised a simple in/out referendum and was rewarded with a working majority in 2015.
2, Parliament quickly approved the Referendum Bill by 544 votes to 53.
3, The British people then participated in the referendum in greater numbers than any other vote in our history (17,410,742 to 16,141,241).
4, Following Gina Miller's legal action the Commons voted to give the Government power to trigger Article 50 by 498 votes to 114.
5, Theresa May then asked the Commons to agree to a general election. They did.
6, 84.2% of the votes in that election were for parties that promised to honour the referendum result.
7, Theresa May's attempt to keep us in the EU by technocratic stealth was then defeated in all THREE 'meaningful' votes.

Where has winning all those votes got us? Nowhere. If anything Britain is now less democratic and less independent than we were before the referendum! But in just 1000 days, EU supporters, by intellectually terrorising their opponents have managed to stop the most voted-for thing in British history and reduce one of the world's great democracies to a laughing stock. You may be disgusted by this (as I am) but you have to admit Remain's campaign *worked*. And I'm supposed to hate XR for getting in their opponent's faces? Brexiteers have spent the last four years winning votes, handing out leaflets, writing rants, lobbying MPs and *not* rioting. XR obviously looked at our campaign and concluded (rightly) that we've been wasting our time, so they're employing a functional method of achieving their goals rather than the non-functional method we Brexiteers have been persevering with.

I've seen several Brexiteers point out that at our big demo on 29th March there were only 5 arrests whereas over 750 XR members have been arrested over the last week. So what? Which of those causes is getting somewhere with their campaign? The one that causes the most trouble obviously.

Now apparently XR are going to target Heathrow. Three cheers! Does any Brexiteer seriously dispute that there is an excess of people going hither and thither? Too many people travel too far, too often; it's bad for the environment, spreads disease, increases terrorism, depresses wages, places a strain on housing and public services and decimates the traditional indigenous communities who tend to produce the least pollution. Why are Brexiteers not slapping XR on the back?

So remind me again, why am I supposed to hate these people? Because they dress differently to me, listen to different music, eat different food and mix in different circles? For the last four years I have patiently defended the proposition that Britain should be an independent democracy, only to find that the person I'm talking to thinks I'm actually arguing that racism and war are ok, that human rights are bad and that Boris Johnson is a wonderful human being. I then have to explain what a non sequitur is. XR want to prevent lots of species of plants and animals from becoming extinct. What's wrong with that? And if someone from a different social tribe supports them, does that somehow make it ok for plants and animals to be killed?

Here is Leo McKinstry writing in the Telegraph last week:
"If any satirists wanted to mock the green movement, they could not have come up with anything more absurd than this week's infantile protests in London. As the demonstrators continue to bring gridlock to the capital, their laughable middle-class preciousness has been on full display. The disruption, organised by the Extinction Rebellion campaign, might be a severe aggravation for workers who actually have to earn their living, but it has been one long street party for an army of well-heeled social parasites."

Ahh so they are middle class *and* unemployed parasites? For the last four years people have tried to sneer Brexiteers into silence with precisely this type of diatribe designed to induce a mind-closing spasm of rejection. I am not going to accept McKinstry's attack just because its directed at 'them' not 'us'. All fact-free opinion is an attack on all of us.

Here is a quote from XR's Declaration of Rebellion:
"We, in alignment with our consciences and our reasoning, declare ourselves in rebellion against our Government and the corrupted, inept institutions that threaten our future. The wilful complicity displayed by our government has shattered meaningful democracy and cast aside the common interest in favour of short-term gain and private profits."

Seriously, how can any Brexiteer have a problem with that? It's fucking true and I'm not going to deny it because it's said by someone with a funny haircut and tattoos. XR is reason-based. It is reasonable to want to prevent the extinction of species and it is reasonable to employ methods that work to achieve it. There is a ruling elite in this country who would like nothing better than for XR and Brexiteers to attack one-another, but I know exactly who we should be attacking – the deaf 'leaders' who are pathologically opposed to democratic oversight of the powerful.

The rules are the rules (Sometimes)
The EU is not a rules-based entity. EU supporters are sticklers only for the rules that advance their project. They operate according to the Thrasymachus doctrine: "Justice is nothing other than the advantage of the stronger". For example:

1, If the EU were rules-based, then when it came to picking the President of the Commission they would simply look up in their brilliant rule book who it should be. Well they tried that and the rules said it should be Manfred Weber, but France didn't like him. So weeks of horse trading ensued and eventually Ursula von der Leyen was crowned winner. Brexiteers won 52% of the vote and the result was endlessly contested. Ursula von der Leyen was 'elected' with 52% of the vote in a 'contest' where she was the only candidate and the result was quietly accepted! Being a less legitimate president than Trump takes some doing but somehow Ursula von der Leyen managed it! Still, always nice to get a moral lecture from the democracy haters. If the EU had been a rules-based entity then there would have been no need for any haggling, the very fact that negotiations took place demonstrated they were with Thrasymachus.
2, The rules were disregarded when the treatment of Catalonia broke Articles 1, 6, 11, 12 and 54 of the European Charter of Fundamental Rights (and probably 21 and 22 too).
3, The rule that member states must be democracies was disregarded when Greece was crushed and austerity was imposed on it in defiance of what its voters had instructed.
4, The rules were disregarded when countries that rejected the EU constitution had it imposed on them anyway via the Lisbon Treaty.
5, When small member states breached the Stability and Growth Pact they were crushed - When France breached it nothing happened.
6, The EU has systematically refused to comply with the judgements of the World Trade Organisation, flouting rulings on GMO crops, hormone beef, and Airbus subsidies.
7, In Portugal v Council, the European Court ruled that the EU has no obligation to follow WTO law if it narrows the European Commission's scope for manoeuvre.
8, During Brexit negotiations the EU said it could not agree to us leaving unilaterally, so they were in breach of their own Article 50.
9, The ECJ ruled in the Kadi-Barakaat case that the EU should disregard the UN Charter (the highest text of international law) if the Charter is at odds with the EU's internal constitutional order.
10, Article 1-i and Article 1-iii of the Northern Ireland Peace Agreement state that "*it would be wrong to make any change in the status of Northern Ireland save with the consent of a majority of its people*". The Withdrawal Agreement does indeed change the constitutional status of Northern Ireland without the consent of its people and is therefore a breach of international law. But hey ho, the 'law' seems to be whatever is in the interests of the powerful.

So we see it's standard procedure for EU supporters to see as legitimate, only the rules that advance their domination of territory. For example, Erskine May (the document which sets out the running of parliament) states that the same bill cannot be put before the Commons more than once in a parliamentary session. But John Bercow (the Speaker who openly supported Remain) granted *three* 'meaningful votes' on the 'Withdrawal Agreement' to try to get it through.

Science Bit
The predictions of Cameron, Osborne and Carney et al collapsed because they deliberately confused a priori and a posteriori knowledge.

For example Osborne's 'Project Fear' claimed that Brexit would shrink GDP by at least 0.1% in each of the next three quarters (it went up by 0.5%, 0.7% and 0.2%). He said unemployment would increase by 1.6% over the next year (it reduced by 1%). He said house prices would crash by 18% (they increased 5.6%). He said borrowing would rise by £12.2bn (it fell £20bn).

A priori knowledge can be demonstrated with proofs so it can be confidently applied to the future (for example Euclid and Newton's laws will still be valid tomorrow) whereas a posteriori knowledge is based on observation (for example it rained yesterday). Osborne's claims were not demonstrable in the way maths and geometry are demonstrable, therefore they had to be a posteriori or they were nothing, but they were claims about the future, so they could not be a posteriori … so they were indeed nothing.

How were Osborne's computer models less valid that climate models? Simple, weather forecasting models are based on a vast amount of empirical evidence that increases every day. We see that desert planets cannot support life and that Earth's deserts are increasing in size so it is valid to draw the general conclusion from the general observations. Where is the equivalent empirical evidence that becoming an independent democracy makes a country poorer? If it existed there would be fewer and fewer countries rather than more and more as is actually the case.

They were just a bunch of rich conservatives at the pinnacle of society masquerading as prophets. All the elements of the judgement myth were there replete with our supposed post-judgement descent into a lake of fire. The only difference was that their predictions were draped in secular statistical garb; their doctored computer models were the contemporary equivalent of tea leaves, oracles or crystal balls, but the arguments were essentially no different to the prophecies of doom the establishment has always rolled out to ensure nothing changes. In 1633 Galileo was threatened with torture if he did not recant helio-centrism. How were the treats made against us democrats any different? I would maintain they were not.

Sorry if I am repeating myself but you in your time will be assailed by similar arguments, so it's important you know why they are not valid.

The Fear was Real
Do you think Galileo was mad to be scared of speaking the truth to the Church? And that he just should have just stuck it to them? Think again, because fear is rarely unjustified. In 2018 I was at a party talking to an art historian, he taught at one of the most prestigious colleges in the country, he was a Marxist and had just published a book on Warhol. He confided in me that he had voted leave. As our discussions of Brexit continued he hissed: "Keep your voice down, don't you know what it could do to my career if people knew?" The fear was real and it was justified, even now years later, this book could lose me my job and my friends, it could affect my wife's buisness and cause problems for my children at school.

Following the vote to leave we were told that we were subhuman bigots, uncultured savages too stupid to understand the reality; that we would be nothing without our enlightened former leaders; that we should be permanently locked into a political system where our votes were meaningless; that we should live in fear of even being seen to question our betters; that our human rights of free speech and self-determination should be disregarded; that institutions we never voted for should be able to help themselves to our money; that our superiors should be put in charge for our own good, to make us better people; and that our culture, way of life and history were something we should be ashamed of and apologise for. How is that not a hate attack? How is that not a replication of pretty much every hate campaign in history? It was a very clever takeover strategy – to achieve territorial domination via psychological abuse, but to insist, even as the abuse was taking place, that they were against the haters.

NIESR Not Nice
On the 1st November 2017 the Guardian published an article entitled '*Brexit vote has cost each household more than £600 a year says NIESR*'. NIESR stands for the National Institute of Economic and Social Research. Obviously the title of the Guardian piece is a logical fallacy as it attempts to compare something we can observe with something we can only speculate about. A central feature of economics is precisely that we can't observe two different policies applied to the same people at the same time. But hey, let's leave that to one side for now.

Being a curious chap I did a couple of minutes digging on NIESR. I went to their website, downloaded the previous year's annual report, pressed Ctrl F and did a search for the word 'European'. The reader will be astonished to learn that in the previous year European Commission institutions had funded the NIESR to the tune of £421,526. But hey, that's probably just an isolated incident right? Wrong. Three weeks later the Guardian published a similar article, this time citing a report by the IFS. Again I did a couple of minutes digging and found that in the previous year the IFS had received £704,657 from the European Research Council and £22,302 from the European Commission. Additionally the IFS was being funded by the World Bank, PWC and the LSE, all of whom also receive money from the EU.

My research took minutes, it was astonishing how easy it was to follow the money. But the important point is that these 'news articles' were not news at all but the propaganda of interested parties. A bunch of millionaires who didn't like democracy had formed a mutually-funded, mutually-supporting, mutually-promoting union. They give themselves august titles and acronyms to cultivate the appearance of dispassionate authority, but they are nothing but a bunch of unelected and greedy apologists for authoritarianism. They are rich, and they like being rich so they try their level best to keep everything exactly how it is. To this end they swamp media outlets (that should know better) with Foucaultian normalising power. It was a coordinated attack of psychological abuse on an entire population. Fighting it damaged my career, my health, my family and my marriage. I will never forgive and forget what happened to us, and how could I forgive when there's never been an apology?

Brexit / Disorderly departure could damage UK's economic recovery from Covid, says OECD

Guardian 14.10.20

"The EU is a major contributor to the overall OECD budget with EU funds representing a quarter of all voluntary funding given to the Organisation in 2019. In addition, the 22 EU Member States provide about 40% of the assessed contributions." Source – Europa.EU. By *'disorderly departure'* they mean democratic independence.

Why were Remain's Economic Predictions So Inaccurate?
The Remainers' preferred economic model was called the 'Gravity Model'. One of the most infamous examples of this came courtesy of George Osborne, who 66 days before the Brexit referendum claimed that becoming an independent democracy would make us 6% poorer over the next 14 years. Obviously any serious economist making predictions about things in 14 years' time would go out of their way to stress the high degree of uncertainty involved, and would at least demonstrate an awareness of alternative economic models that predicted otherwise. Not Osborne, he just trotted out his silly gravity model and the Remainer media compliantly assumed that because he was rich and powerful he knew what he was talking about.

We can conceptualise the gravity model by picturing the Newtonian Solar System. The idea is that the EU is the radiant Sun, and that countries most deeply integrated (closest) benefit most from membership. So Italy and France would be like Mercury or Venus and glow with prosperity whilst Norway and Switzerland would be out in the cold like Pluto. So Osborne's theory was that the UK would be like Uranus – but there were several holes in it!

1, The collapse of UK exports since joining the EU was completely inconsistent with his model.
2, He assumed that despite being the 5th largest economy we wouldn't be able to negotiate new trade deals with anyone.
3, The rapid growth of independent democracies in Europe was wholly inconsistent with the model.
4, He assumed there would be no political response to any transitional disruption.
5, Osborne confused GDP per household with household income.
6, He assumed (wrongly) that remaining a member would not entail increases in budgetary contributions.
7, He was committing a basic logical fallacy of trying to compare something that could be observed with something that could only be speculated about.

If Osborne's gravity model was so brilliant, how come it couldn't explain the plummeting GDP growth, declining trade balance, 10 year pay freeze, increased debt and increased inequality? It's a practical question. Here is a man who had no plan for the biggest event of his political life that was about to happen in 66 days, but was happy to pontificate about what would happen in 14 years' time!

Remain's economic predictions all turned to dust is because they were all based on the same flawed gravity models. Their gravity models estimated the aggregate benefits of EU membership and assumed they would be wholly or largely reversed on leaving the EU. Read that sentence again and think about it. If an economist is tasked with evaluating the costs/benefits of membership of some club … and they base their investigation on the assumption that membership is good … then they are not engaged in a genuine investigation at all … instead they are beginning with the conclusion and using that to generate the method … when the correct approach is to use the method to generate the conclusion. The technical term for this is *'getting things arse-about-face'*. Why did the Treasury and the BoE and all the other Remainers make such an obvious error? Because they were stupid? No. On the contrary they were highly intelligent people. They got it wrong because the *wanted* to get it wrong. Their gravity model sounded impressive, appeared clever and allowed them to advance political bullshit masquerading as impartial economic analysis; whereas a clear accurate assessment would have undermined their war on democracy.

If the sun in their gravity model had represented democracy and free speech then their model might have yielded approximately accurate figures. Because as we have seen, worldwide over many years there is an approximate correlation between democracy and prosperity. But instead the Treasury, the BoE, IMF and OECD all assumed that the more we were governed by a tiny number of unelected people operating in secret, the more prosperous we would be. Their gravity models were founded on the assumption that democracy and prosperity were inversely proportional rather than directly proportional.

So don't kid yourself that the BoE, IMF, OECD etc are disinterested parties, like some type of economic referee ensuring fair play. They are unelected, rich and powerful and they want to keep it that way, so naturally they pursue a political program which does precisely that. They think British people having more democratic control over our society would make us poorer eh? Well they would say that wouldn't they! (see Christine Keeler – the Profumo affair) These outfits are simply the contemporary equivalents of feudal barons and aristocrats of the past, the primary difference being that they are better at masquerading as honest brokers. File under: 'Rich Democracy-Haters' (again).

Incidentally when checking some details about the Gravity Model the first paper that appeared on Google was 'The role of gravity models in estimating the economic impact of Brexit' published by the Centre for Business Research, University of Cambridge. In the first paragraph about gravity models the report focuses on higher tariffs but fails to mention reduced membership fees. Additionally the first paragraph fixates on 'additional costs of administration and potential border delays' whilst omitting to mention that this would be a natural consequence of us democratically determining our own laws, which would obviously make us more prosperous. Being a Brexiteer makes me instinctively suspicious of any outfit calling itself the 'Centre for Business Research'. So I went to their website and downloaded their annual report from 2016 (the year of the referendum) and, you guessed it, the EU had just given them £848,399. Just like all the others they were producing the information (propaganda) their employers were *paying* them to produce. Always nice to get an impartial view. The report gently suggests that Osborne's forecasts might be 'overly pessimistic' but surely the job of economists at this time was to scream the most obvious fact from the rooftops: If the forecasting methods of the IMF, OECD, BoE and Treasury were valid then then how come they couldn't explain the collapse of the trade balance, GDP growth, or wages as we became more integrated? Or the correlation of EU integration with increased debt, inequality, terrorism, pollution and collapse of public services? (Do those somehow not count as economic criteria worthy of consideration?)

IMF / World Bank / EU / WEF ETC

The IMF consists of 189 countries that collectively decide what the IMF does. Within it, a country's voting power is proportional to how much it pays in membership fees, so wealth is directly proportional to power. When the IMF 'gives' money, if does so on the precondition that free-market policies are implemented. The poor, weak communities don't tell them what to do – it's the other way round.

The IMF like the World Bank is a child of the FDR age. It is about control, it's centralised, undemocratic, neoliberal and within it the powerful and the wealthy are the same people. It was set up just after the Second World War and conflates its mission with peace, order, stability etc. This is obviously very similar to the EU which is probably why they teamed up to destroy Greece.

UK economy will shrink without Brexit deal, IMF warns

So they formed an incestuous mutually-supporting clique, and I should be happy about that because I like the idea of collective action right? But what does their union actually do? They do exactly what you would expect – they prevent the democratic control of power. Basically the IMF are just a bunch of loan sharks who lend money on the precondition that crappy economic policies are adopted which make people poorer. They are just another centralised, top-down institution seeking to prevent decentralised, bottom-up politics. For example, at the time of writing the Argentinian Peso is devaluing at 50% per year. Naturally the Argentines want to protect themselves from this so in May 2022 Argentina's two largest banks agreed to allow Argentines to open Bitcoin accounts using this decentralised protocol to protect savers from fiat devaluation. Straight away the IMF reminded the Argentinian government that IMF loans were contingent on discouraging cryptocurrencies.

Above are some press cuttings showing how the IMF openly supported the EU's continuing control of the UK. Just as with Greece and Argentina (there are many other examples I could give) the soundtrack was sound economics but the actuality was a war against democracy. They're expansionist, they project their values on us, their leaders are appointed and they want to control how we live. Don't let the secular capitalism fool you - they're churches.

Ditto the World Economic Forum (WEF). Authors of the now infamous "You'll own nothing."

Acronym? Check.
Top down? Check.
Stacked with rich unelected powerful people? Check.
You don't have a vote? Check.
Central figure? Check. (Klaus Schwab has been in charge for over 50 years).
Want to control how you live? Check.

Seeks expansion of power/influence? Check.
Seeks to project their beliefs on us? Check.
Hypocritical? (They own assets, we don't) Check.
Usurps good causes as Trojan horses for authoritarianism? Check.
Tax exempt? Check.

They are just another church. The fact that they prioritise seducing the rich and powerful gives them the appearance of intellectual credibility they simply do not deserve. Naturally, being a church means they are much more sanguine than empiricists are about cruelty. In 2022 they issued a communique saying: "should you implant a tracking chip in your child? There are solid, rational reasons for it". The WEF image even looks religious. We could substitute their logo in the top right hand corner for the name of any other cult and it would work just as well.

Birds of a Feather Flock Together
Rich unelected powerful people will naturally be sympathetic to wealthy, undemocratic powerful institutions. It was ever thus. Men who want power and exemption from criticism have always gravitated to religions in which men have power and are exempt from criticism, which preach unsurprisingly, that we should worship a powerful man who is exempt from criticism.

Truck Off
Sometimes I had to wonder whether Remainers were even aware of how silly their arguments sounded. One particular issue that seemed to exercise them was lorries. Sometimes apparently Brexit was shit because it would mean there would be lots of lorries in traffic jams…

Post-Brexit lorry queues could make Kent 'toilet of England'
12 Nov 2020

Vast Brexit customs clearance centre to be built in Kent
10 Jul 2020

Chris Grayling's glassy-eyed confidence doesn't help with Brexit debacle
9 Feb 2019

No-deal Brexit rehearsal in Kent 'a waste of time'
7 Jan 2019

152

No-deal Brexit: transport crisis could leave cities short of police
12 Mar 2019

Anti-terror checks deliver fresh Brexit threat for UK hauliers
13 Feb 2019

M20 could be giant lorry park for years in event of no-deal Brexit – report
31 Jul 2018

No plan for surge in driving permits after no-deal Brexit, say auditors
19 Jul 2018

(Guardian)

On other occasions Remainers were pissing their pants that Brexit would mean not having enough lorry drivers…

Retail industry

● This article is more than **1 month old**

HGV driver shortages could 'cancel' Christmas, warns Iceland boss

Richard Walker urges UK government to relax immigration rules to ease shortfall of skilled staff

153

The fact that we cannot have both an excess of lorries on roads <u>and</u> a lack of drivers never seemed to occur to them. Obviously as an environmentalist, I'm happy for the lorries to fuck off. I think lorries are a problem rather than a solution, that trading local produce is good, and that transporting cheap consumer goods half way around the planet to shopping centres is insanity, but hey, let's leave that to one side for now.

The proposition I am defending is that Britain should be an independent democracy with total democratic control over *all* our laws. Let's call this *'Proposition A'* for short. In order to defend proposition A, I am not obliged to first of all anticipate and explain every hypothetical technicality that might arise. Looking around the world I see that countries that are independent democracies are superior to those that are not. So I work from the general to the particular. I say democratic independence should come first and technicalities about freight and transport policies should dance a waltz around that. Remainers mischievously put the cart before the horse. Because they were opposed to us being an independent democracy *in principle*, they attempted to make the generalities contingent on the particulars. Or in layman's language, they claimed (inevitable) teething problems in the transition to independence constituted a credible argument *against* independence itself! So we shouldn't become an independent democracy because there might be a traffic jam? Or because we might have to train some people to drive lorries? Or because we may have to give lorry drivers better pay and conditions? Or because we might have less cheap plastic crap in shops? Call that an argument?

This was a common tactic, for example, it is also the case that to defend Proposition A, I am not obliged to first of all defend the character of Nigel Farage or Boris Johnson. Whether Johnson or Farage are good or bad has nothing to do with whether Proposition A is right or wrong. To claim that Farage and Johnson are dreadful and that it therefore follows that Brexit must also be dreadful is, again, to make the error of making generalities dependent on particulars. The apologists of authoritarianism repeatedly sought to conceal what they were up to by urging us to look away from the general good and fixate on emotive details.

(Note: Additionally, if you think Brexit is shit because it will mean too many lorries *and* too few drivers then clearly you have drawn your conclusion prior to your investigation. That's not a scientific method but an article of faith.)

Shit!

Kent / Roadside portable loos planned for lorry drivers delayed by Brexit checks

Guardian 14.10.20

Propaganda
And here are some more…

154

Brexit / Kent council leader says no deal would spread chaos across country

Paul Carter says no-deal gridlock in Dover would cost national economy almost £1.75bn a week and require 'boots on the ground'

Guardian 07.12.18

Brexit / Cabinet Office compares no deal to Iceland ash cloud chaos

Eyjafjallajökull seen as nearest recent example of what civil service could have to cope with

Guardian 25.01.19

Brexit / No deal would mean shortages and price rises, say retailers

Bosses of Sainsbury's, Asda, M&S, Co-op and Waitrose write letter to government

Guardian 28.01.19

Brexit / No deal would mean shortages and price rises, say retailers

Bosses of Sainsbury's, Asda, M&S, Co-op and Waitrose write letter to government

Guardian 28.01.19

Exclusive / 'Trauma packs' being stockpiled in UK over fears of no deal

Pharmaceutical giant Johnson & Johnson fears border delays could disrupt flow of vital medical supplies

Guardian 31.01.19

Brexit / Risk to progress on school dinners from food shortages

Exclusive 'Trauma packs' being stockpiled in UK over no-deal Brexit fears

Guardian 31.01.19

Brexit / UK police 'will be unable to cope' if no-deal cuts EU data sharing

Guardian 20.10.20

❚❚ Brexit was never a grassroots movement, but an elitist political takeover
Aditya Chakrabortty

19m ago 💬 9

Guardian 09.12.20
(Remain was never a grassroots movement but an elitist political takeover).

Above is the cover of a report by the University of Manchester entitled 'The Arts After Brexit'. 2020. And below are two screen grabs from the BBC 'news' website. Note the dates. The first shows the cause, the second the effect.

Brexit uncertainty is a disgrace, says Airbus

◯ 24 January 2019 🏳 4384   f 💬 🐦 ✉ < Share

Brexit

Airbus has warned that it could move wing-building out of the UK in the future if there is a no-deal Brexit.

The planemaker's chief executive, Tom Enders, said Airbus "will have to make potentially very harmful decisions for the UK" in the event of no deal.

…so Airbus pocketed illegal subsidies from the EU and then campaigned against us becoming an independent democracy. How is that not corruption?

We now have a word for this type of information attack: 'FUD' (fear, uncertainty and doubt). Obviously it can be good to be mindful of potential problems, but FUD can also be a propaganda tool, and it certainly was for the Remain campaign. The BBC was the national monopoly state broadcaster (stacked with wealthy, unelected EU supporters) and in every 'news' bulletin, every hour on every channel the narrative was pumped that the Remain coup was a Brexit crisis; that our national humiliation was caused by the people demanding democratic independence not the refusal of those in power to deliver it. The crisis was not that we were leaving but that we weren't! EU supporters did everything they could to ensure Brexit negotiations were a catastrophe and then had the audacity to claim that Brexit had caused the crisis! 'How's Brexit going?' Friends would sneer. Well it was going a whole lot better for the UK than remaining was going for Italy, which at the time was governed by unelected central banker Mario Draghi.

They Don't Serve You…
On the 28th November 2018 the Bank of England published a report trotting out the usual nightmarish conjectural propaganda about how Brexit was going to fuck everything. It listed the various scenarios along with claims about how much worse off we would be under each one.

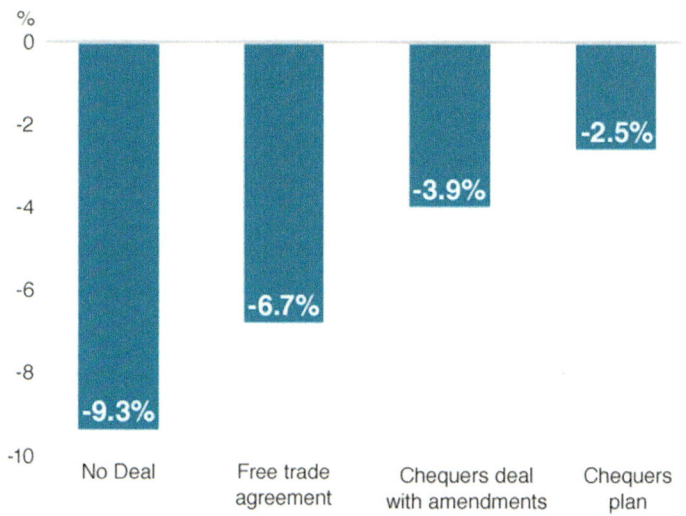

It would be too kind to call these predictions 'guesses' because genuine guesses might at least have been approximately accurate. For example, if the BoE really thought Brexit could make the UK economy shrink by 8% why didn't it give examples of countries that had become independent democracies and suffered a similar fate? The BoE claimed that Brexit would cause unemployment to rise to 7.5% (didn't happen) house prices to fall by 30% (didn't happen) and commercial property prices to collapse by 48% (didn't happen). The empirical evidence we now have demolishes all these claims, but that's not what I want to talk about here. The BoE claimed that economically the various options ranked as follows:

1, Chequers
2, Chequers with amendments.
3, Free trade agreement.
4, No deal.

Let's now take these four scenarios and rank them according to which ones allow the most people to have the most democratic control over the most power, and we see they rank as follows:

1, No deal.
2, Free trade agreement.
3, Chequers with amendments
4, Chequers.

Spot the pattern? No deal would have meant directly elected MPs would be completely responsible for all laws (including laws re goods, services, labour and capital) whereas the Chequers agreement would have effectively maintained external rule. So what the BoE were saying wasn't simply inaccurate, it wasn't just counter-factual, it was a denial of all the evidence of the modern world. When we observe the modern world we see that when lots of people have lots of democratic control over lots of power lots of them prosper, whereas when a small number of appointees make decisions in secret, more people become less prosperous (and less people become more prosperous). The BoE report claimed the opposite was the case - that democracy and prosperity were inversely proportional rather than directly proportional.

So the BoE were asserting that the less democratic we were, the more prosperous we would be. Think about that. Like which other countries? Names? The reader is no doubt scratching their heads wondering how such an illustrious institution could produce findings that seem to defy all the evidence of the modern world. What possible explanation could there be? It's all very simple. Here is a picture of my desk:

What do you suppose I *do* at my desk all day? That's right. I produce the information my employer PAYS me to produce. You probably do the same. Who commissioned the BoE's report? The House of Commons Treasury Committee. This committee has 11 members, I've gone through the names and at the time at least seven of them were Remainers – in fact I would be astonished if more than two of the eleven voted for Brexit. The BoE boss was appointed to his £874,000 p/a job by George Osborne (Remainer) and retained in the position by Phillip Hammond (Remainer).

What makes me suspect bias? Simple – the empirical evidence. When I observe many countries over many years, I see that when more people have more democratic control over more power, then there is a more good life for more people. And that conversely, when a small number of rich people decide things in secret there is decline. An elite committee stacked with an unrepresentative number of EU supporters asked a bunch of millionaires, appointed by EU supporters to produce a report saying democracy and prosperity are inversely proportional. The report was duly produced, and then another bunch of rich appointees in control of the BBC circulated the 'news'. I am completely within my rights to call out bullshit here. The above were not objective honest brokers but partisan propagandists.

Bank warns no-deal could see UK sink into recession

By Jill Treanor
Business reporter, BBC News

28 November 2018 | Comments

Brexit

(Footnote: Every news bulletin by the BBC (the monopoly state broadcaster) was pro EU propaganda designed to demoralise and crush the resistance of the British to EU rule. Additionally every BBC political discussion program was stacked with Remainers and chaired by Remainers. To give examples would fill several volumes so I will simply refer the reader to the BBC website where the archives are in the public domain.)

So the BoE was simply doing what we all do every day – they were producing the information they were PAID to produce. This is how the ruling elite went about their coup d'état by stealth. The EU and their stooges mutually funded, promoted and supported until their agents occupied every conceivable position of political influence. In 2018 EU supporters controlled the Tory party, the Labour party, the Lib-Dem, SNP, Plaid Cymru and Green Party, the House of Lords, the civil service, the Supreme Court, the BoE, BBC, the CBI, the TUC, NFU, LSE, the Arts Council, the British Chambers of Commerce, every trade lobby group, the Electoral Commission, the Committee for Standards in Public Life, even the Parliamentary Committee for Exiting the EU (!) Additionally the Speaker and Deputy Speaker voted for EU rule. Remain were the majority everywhere except among the electorate. Coincidence or corruption?

Brexit / No-deal to cost more than Covid, Bank of England governor says

Guardian November 20

And what of the monarchy? When the endemic corruption was too obvious to be deniable did they side with us? Three years after we voted to leave our Prime Minister openly colluded with foreign powers, cancelled our exit and actually extended our membership! Did Elizabeth Windsor sack her Prime Minister and dissolve parliament as she should have done? No the monarchy silently acquiesced. File under *'rich democracy-sceptics'*. Your precious royal family do not serve you. You serve them.

(Note: We are frequently told that having a monarchy gives us a constitutional subtlety that republics lack. That in times of constitutional crisis the monarchy gives some ambiguous wriggle room that allows us to muddle through. Well if ever there was such a crisis it was March 2019. What did the Liz do? Fuck all. Sure the Queen was old and her husband was in poor health, but that's no excuse for abandoning us which is basically what she did. If ever there was a time for the royal family to demonstrate their worth, then March 2019 was it, but they don't which is why Chaz accepts money from the bin Laden family. There is no argument why we shouldn't have a head of state with exactly the same powers as the Queen – but elected).

And the above are just the *national* institutions that were bought off by the EU. On the international level the EU were funding the IMF, the IFS, the OECD, the World Bank and the credit rating agencies, all of whom duly produced anti-Brexit propaganda. Additionally student bursaries helped keep the universities quiet. How was the EU paying for all this? With our membership contributions! We were being abused with propaganda paid for with our own money! Even I have to admit, it was a very very clever power-grab strategy.

The above are all just tentacles of the same beast and if you think they prospered via meritocracy you are credulous. They are all just a bunch of millionaires who are unenthusiastic about democracy. They prospered under the existing system, so they assume the existing system to be benign and meritocratic, it naturally follows that a system in which things could be fundamentally altered by voting scares them. So they close ranks, mutually fund, mutually support and mutually promote in order to prevent the restoration of democracy. Look at these people close up, where are their big ideas? What are their actual achievements? What interesting books have they written? What are their great deeds? By what right are they above you? The above are characterised by low responsibility, high salary and mediocre ability. If you think they serve you, you are credulous. It's the other way round (again). They don't represent our interests, they pursue their interests. We support their interests and their words are of no interest.

I am a teacher so if I receive gifts that could compromise my ability to do my job fairly then I am obliged by my code of conduct to declare it. But codes of conduct only seem to apply to the little people. Before the eyes of the world our entire political system revealed itself to be an incestuous conspiracy, designed to prevent the most voted-for thing in our history. It was the crime of the century.

De-Fi AOK

Given what I've said about our illustrious central bank it's nice to know that the age of central banks is over, and that pretty soon Bitcoin will dump them in the dustbin of history where they belong. It is interesting to note that Bitcoin is validated in the same way I think knowledge should be validated – by external cross-checking. So BTC is Kantian in so far as its value resides in our beliefs about it, but it is absolutely not Kantian insofar as its validation is hyper-objective and achieved by cross-checking decentralised external ledgers around the world. Each of which has no motive to say anything other than how they see it. Maybe it's even fair to say that decentralised finance is fighting a financial war in the same way that I say we should fight a knowledge war – the centralisers seek to project their design on the world, whereas the de-centralisers establish value through mutual agreement of disinterested parties. And in a sense the whole of this book can be seen as a critique of centralisation:

1, Power should be decentralised, so voters explain to the executive rather than the executive explain to the voters.
2, Morality should be decentralised, so we maximise our consideration of others instead of prioritising a moral law within that may be mistaken.
3, Instead of the world around us conforming to our way of seeing it, knowledge should be mutually agreed and peer reviewed.
4, Central banks have devalued fiat money which has made the owners of assets much richer than the wage earners. De-Fi (decentralised finance) allows poor people a store of value that can't be devalued by those in power or seized by the corrupt.
5, Our attacks on racism should be a celebration of all humanity rather than preferring one group at the expense of another.
6, Bakunin was right to see that the shortcoming of Marxism is not its emphasis on collective action, but its tendency to establish a centralised authority. How exactly do the workers correct any excesses of the executive if the executive considers itself to be the embodiment of the will of the workers?
7, Bizarrely my critique of capitalism is almost identical to my critique of Marxism! How do we get off the railroad to Grand Central? The shortcoming of capitalism is not its emphasis on the profit motive but its tendency to see humanity as isolated competing *individuals* with risk/reward decisions centralised in each of us. Capitalism wrongly assumes we are individuals when actually we are conflicted members of a community, and it advances by isolating us from one another. Also capitalism attempts to divorce power from votes with centralised bodies like the IMF and the central banks. It could be said that markets cross-check and that they often get the price wrong, and that would be true, but mainly only in the short term; over the longer time period, much more accurate values emerge. For example, fuel is only under-valued because we are not factoring in the long term consequences of burning it.
8, Tom Paine's is the only revolution still standing because it advocates a bottom-up power structure.
9, We should define countries not by projecting our inner beliefs upon geography, but by us being persuaded by our observations of geography.

10, Centralised knowledge is just belief. When decision making is centralised, what prevents the decision makers confusing the good with what they think is good? Nothing. When power is centralised among a small number of people, then however good their intentions, the general population are vulnerable to their errors. Much better that the leaders be vulnerable to the errors of the voters.

11, The goodness of morality became formalised in social structures called religions, which set up power structures where there was no oversight of the centre, instead the centre oversaw.

12, We see that as power is centralised so the sanctimony of those who wield it increases. As does the cruelty they employ to maintain it. They become increasingly incapable of recognising their failings. Being right becomes a simple matter of believing they are right. And because they only have to answer to themselves anything can be excused with the words "I believed it was the right thing to do".

13, When did Europe contribute the most to the arts, sciences and philosophy? When it was decentralised.

So I think we should establish knowledge and morality by cross-checking. It should be noted that, when we do this, if we only cross-check with specific groups of people then that will not yield valid results. Indeed, carefully selecting with whom we cross-check would be one way of rigging outcomes.

Nominalism

Nominalism, the view that only individuals are real, is an enormously important concept for right-wing intellectuals. But I maintain that thought, like love, sex or DNA is two intertwining things, despite not being one individual thing, they are not only real, but the most real things of all. If we are faced with a choice between an ecological product that is expensive and a polluting product that is cheap, the nominalist, being individual-centric will naturally choose the latter. But whereas individual-centric decisions give one person pleasure and prosperity for a moment, consideration of others is not only proportional to virtue, but ultimately, the most enriching for everyone.

Decentralised Network of Centralised Bodies

I have mentioned a few times that I prefer decentralisation to centralisation. But I've also mentioned that centralised bodies mutually supported one another. But surely I should be in favour of that right? because they formed a network and employed collective action to advance their interests? Well, yes, they got the network bit right, and they got the collective action bit right, that's why they were terrifyingly successful. But what is the empirical reality of what they sought to achieve? And once we set aside all the fine words about sound economic management, maintaining stability and making the world better etc, we see they are simply concerned with insulating power from votes. They are not working together to cross-check ideas but to impose beliefs. Similarly Islam has proven to be a very successful means for the domination of territory because it is decentralised geographically but centralised mentally, allowing each subscriber to deny its failure as a social system.

Easter Bunny, Where's My Money?

Pope Leo X wrote to Copernicus with a curious question: 'When is Easter Sunday?" It's great fun to imagine the famous mathematician reading it and thinking: 'Mate, you're the Pope, *you* tell *me* when it's Easter Sunday!' But it wasn't a good idea to be cheeky to the Pope and besides, his holiness had a practical problem. The church was using an archaic calendar from the time of Caesar, which calculated dates using a Duckworth-Lewis type formula, so Easter Sunday was cropping up on wildly differing dates from year to year. So Copernicus applied himself and tried a thought experiment – What if the Sun were at the centre rather that the Earth? Then the years suddenly would become marvellously orderly! It's hard to overstate the importance of Copernicus' achievement. He had established a new objective datum for space and time.

Bitcoin is a Copernican revolution for money. It establishes a new objective datum. More gold could be discovered, the dollar could be devalued but BTC is unique in that its quantity is hard-wired into the protocol and beyond the control of any central authority however powerful they may be. Consequently BTC is the pessimist's Eldorado, the cynics' long, a hedge on stupidity! Don't trust banks? Buy BTC.

Don't trust fiat or the government? Buy BTC. Unemployment up? Buy BTC, Inflation? War? Buy BTC. What would crash its price? Responsible government. The EU try to ban Bitcoin precisely because it is a rules-based entity with no corruptible human being in control.

If we can establish knowledge and morality in a similar way, with independent disinterested validators in various locations cross-checking values, then this would be another Copernican revolution which could help answer Bakunin's critique of Marx, or maybe resolve Adam Smith's problem with restraining the excesses of self-interest. So the bad news is that democracy will always be under attack from the centralisers, who become increasingly rotten, but the good news is that by their very nature, centralisers constantly diminish in number.

Was the Referendum Advisory?

No. I downloaded the *European Union Referendum Act 2015* and did a word search for 'advisory'. How many times do you suppose that word appears in the 67 page document? None. EU supporters said the referendum was binding before they lost and advisory after they lost. What do we call someone who decides which votes are legitimate? '*Your Majesty*'. Of course the referendum wasn't advisory, if it had been then people would have been less scared of voting leave and our majority would have been even bigger! The whole point was to terrify people into voting to keep the existing system. So the democracy haters said the referendum would be binding before they lost, but refused to be bound by it after they lost.

Nice ...

The EU was utterly ruthless in its negotiating approach, treating us as a policeman might treat a miscreant, and using all the tools at their disposal to exert maximum control over us. It is curious that EU supporters in the UK could not bring themselves to acknowledge that their precious, progressive EU was engaged in a classic power play in which the bigger bullied the smaller.

How to Spot the Democracy Haters. (Adapted from 2018 Blog)

EU supporters are engaged in total war against democracy. Their dream is to dismantle British democracy before the eyes of the world and reduce us to a society where no meaningful votes are ever held; where voting only exists to confirm decisions already made by the ruling elite, and where the biggest vote in our history is indefinitely disregarded. Because they don't have the courage or integrity to come right out and admit this, they endlessly devise ways of attacking democracy by stealth, with dog-whistle phrases like '*populism*'. This essay is about how they seek to destroy democracy whilst pretending to be simply concerned with mundane trade technicalities.

After they lost the referendum EU supporters sought to keep us in the Single Market. When it was gently pointed out that would mean us not democratically governing ourselves they called for us to instead remain in the EEA but that was open to the same objection; so then it was The Customs Union, then *a* customs union, then '*a customs partnership*' and so on. They continually call for '*full access*', '*frictionless trade*', '*harmonisation*' and '*alignment*'. And what could be wrong with that? Having '*access*' sounds like a good thing right? And friction sounds like a bad thing? And who could object to '*harmonising*' things to make them all nice and harmonious? And what on earth could be wrong with '*protecting the four freedoms*'? I will explain:

I live in East Sussex. East Sussex has '*fully aligned*', '*frictionless*' trade with West Sussex. Between the two there is free movement of goods, services, labour and capital. People from East Sussex can work in West Sussex. Goods, services and capital traded in one can be traded in the other just as easily. This is because they are part of the *same nation*. We can be an independent democracy or we can have '*fully aligned frictionless trade*' but not both. To be independent is to have your own system. To share the same system is to be *not* independent. It is therefore oxymoronic to claim to respect the referendum result whilst calling for '*alignment*', '*full access*' or '*frictionless trade*': to have these things is to *not* have the democratic independence we voted for, and to campaign *for* them is to campaign against democracy itself.

If you have harmonised free movement about something (say goods) you are agreeing that, rather than vote for better laws about goods you will instead align your laws with those of another country. So you are fettering yourself, taking your democratic control of that particular issue off the table. So democracy and the free movement are inversely proportional - the more free movement, the fewer things are left to vote about. And if you accept the free movement of goods, services, labour and capital then that's everything, so effectively you are no longer a democracy at all. A free movement maximalist is a democracy minimalist. They claim they are giving you wondrous freedoms, whilst depriving you of the most important freedom of all – the power to vote for a better society.

Seriously, is their offer that we would still be able to vote for better laws – just so long as those laws have nothing to do with goods, services, labour and capital? But that's everything! A border is where two different political systems abut. If the laws that pertain to goods, services, labour and capital are identical on both sides of that line then there *is* no border, and there are no *two* countries, only a single country comprising a dominant region and a dominated colony. And who do the EU think should decide which of our laws should be allowed to stand, and which ones should be struck down (because they pertain to goods, services, labour and capital)? Their unelected officials obviously.

So don't think calls for '*harmonisation*' are innocuous technicalities. They are not. The EU seeks to control how we trade in order to achieve their ultimate goal of controlling every aspect of our society. Their calls for '*aligned, frictionless, harmonised, access*', are a mendacious attempt to achieve through technocratic stealth what they cannot achieve through democratic vote.

A Brief History of Modern British Prime Ministers
Imagine a Brexiteer becoming PM, not because lots of people voted for them but because theirs was the only name on the ballot paper. It's unimaginable right? But in recent British history EU supporters have done that – three times!

Initially Mrs Thatcher supported the EEC (EU) but when she saw that it wasn't simply about free trade, but about them ruling us, she became sceptical about the project. Naturally she had to go, so three EU supporters (Howe, Heseltine and Clarke) brought her down. There were three candidates in the leadership contest to replace her, Heseltine, Major and Hurd. All three were EU supporters. Hobson's choice, just how the Remainers like it – you can 'choose' whichever EU supporter you like! In the second ballot of Tory MPs a simple majority was required (187 of the 372 MPs) John Major only secured 185 votes, but Hurd and Heseltine then withdrew so no further votes were held. So John Major became PM not because he won the leadership vote, but on a procedural technicality – he was the only candidate on the ballot! He ascended to the highest office in the land not through the votes of the electorate, not through the votes of party members, but on the basis of just 185 votes – he didn't even win the support of a majority of Tory MPs!

In 1997 Major was replaced by Blair who rose to power as a Euro-sceptic.

General Election
Thursday, 9th June 1983

SEDGEFIELD
THE NEW CONSTITUENCY

VOTE LABOUR

TONY BLAIR

- We'll protect British Industry against **unfair** foreign competition.
- We'll negotiate a withdrawal from the E.E.C. which has drained our natural resources and destroyed jobs.

Blair's election was legitimate. But it's worth remembering that Labour were more Eurosceptic than the Tories at the time. The great John Smith had striven to stop the Tories imposing the Maastricht Treaty, and at least (unlike Major) New Labour did not actively seek handing control of monetary policy and interest rates to the EU (although this was principally because it would have reduced Gordon Brown's power). But then Blair became rich and powerful, got in with the Davos gang and started to see things different. In 2004 Blair promised that Labour would put the EU constitution to a referendum. After the general election the next year he decided not to honour that promise.

Blair was replaced by Brown. How did Brown ascend to the highest office in the land? Again it was a stitch up. He didn't become PM in a general election, He didn't win a vote among Labour party members. He didn't even win a vote of Labour MPs! He became PM because his was the only name on the ballot. Just the way EU supporters like it. Like Blair he dishonoured Labour's manifesto pledge to have a referendum on the European Constitution.

In 2010 Brown was succeeded by Cameron who also had also promised a referendum on the Lisbon Treaty … but then decided not to have one when he became PM. Spooked by the rise of UKIP Cameron promised an in/out referendum if he won a majority in 2015. The electorate duly gave him his majority. After Cameron led the Remain campaign to a stunning defeat in 2016 he was replaced by May. How did May come to ascend to the highest office in the land? Do you really need me to tell you? Did she become PM in a general election? No. Through a vote of Tory party members? No. May became PM after receiving 199 votes from 329 Tory MPs. There was meant to be another round of voting among the Tory party membership with May against Leadsom (which obviously Leadsom would have won as she was the more Pro-Brexit of the two) but Leadsom was pressured to pull out of the race. Just like Major and Brown before her, May became PM by virtue of the fact that hers was the only name on the ballot paper.

Spot the pattern? When a new PM was voted in by the people we chose the most pro-Brexit option. When it was rigged in secret we got the most pro EU option. Again and again we voted for the most pro Brexit option on the ticket (See also section on XR) yet somehow the extent of EU rule kept increasing. This reached its nadir in 2019 when, after decades of consistently voting for the most pro Brexit option we found ourselves governed by a body we had voted to leave 3 years previously, over whom we had no influence and with whom we were supposed to be negotiating!

Then came Boris Johnson, who won all four rounds of preliminary voting among Tory MPs and then went on to beat Jeremy Hunt in the leadership election by 92,153 votes to 46,656. Johnson may be incompetent and facile, but at least his premiership is democratically legitimate. The previous five PMs all ascended to the premiership either via a procedural stitch up, or by making promises on Europe that they dishonoured once safely in office. Obviously most of the rigging of these contests takes place before the leadership elections even take place, which is why, despite Brexit being the majority preference in the country there never seems to be an actual Brexiteer on the ballot paper. But my basic point is that three of the last six PMs were ascended to the highest office in the land because their name was the only name on the ballot paper, and it just so happened that they were also raving EU fanatics. Coincidence or endemic corruption?

Cameron
Lied that he would give us a referendum on the Lisbon Treaty, 'negotiated' a 'deal' with the EU that left them in complete control of our society. Called a referendum, lied that he would implement the result, and did everything he possibly could to win the referendum for the EU. His 2016 referendum campaign was a shameful attempt to intimidate the very people he was supposed to represent. But deserves some credit for managing, against all the odds, to lead the EU side to a spectacular defeat.

Groundhog May
I don't have the energy to forensically detail the full extent of Theresa May's failings, and even if I did the reader wouldn't have the energy to read it. Fortunately an overview will do, for which I will be drawing mostly on the legal analysis of Martin Howe QC.

In her resignation speech Theresa May said:
For many years the great humanitarian Sir Nicholas Winton – who saved the lives of hundreds of children by arranging their evacuation from Nazi-occupied Czechoslovakia through the Kindertransport – was my constituent in Maidenhead. At another time of political controversy, a few years before his death, he took me to one side at a local event and gave me a piece of advice. He said, 'Never forget that compromise is not a dirty word. Life depends on compromise.' He was right."

Here we see Theresa May seeking to associate herself, and the act of compromise, with the most noble cause imaginable. She went on:
"I have striven to make the United Kingdom a country that works not just for a privileged few, but for everyone ... the unique privilege of this office is to use this platform to give a voice to the voiceless, to fight the burning injustices that still scar our society."

So May's self-justification was emphatically a belief-based appeal to values. As we have seen, claims of moral virtue are often red flags indicating a disdain for empirical reality. Was May an unlucky technocrat who tried, but failed, to achieve a happy compromise or was she a liar who betrayed us? You should know the drill by now. We are going to disregard the words and look at the actions.

May's deal would have locked Great Britain into a vassal-state customs union with the EU until the EU chose to release us. Its 'level playing field' committed us to aligning our rules to EU rules. Furthermore it forbade the UK from negotiating trade deals with third parties.

May's deal subjected the UK to the rulings of the ECJ, which, following exit would be a foreign court, owing no loyalty to us, and an organ of the opposite party with whom we may be in dispute. The (normally independent) arbitration panel would have had to refer any issues of EU law to the ECJ and would be bound by the result. So not only would we be compelled to abide by EU rules but also to any 'reinterpretations' the ECJ might choose to make in the future. Dr Carl Baudenbacher, a Swiss lawyer who had recently retired as president of the EFTA Court, said *'It is absolutely unbelievable that a country like the UK, which was the first country to accept independent courts, would subject itself to this.'*

As Will Podmore pointed out: "Article 4 of the agreement [she negotiated] would require us to give 'direct effect' to EU law, overriding our law. Article 4(5) obliges UK judicial and administrative authorities to "have due regard to relevant case law of the Court of Justice of the European Union handed down after the end of the transition period". The Article makes it very clear that relevant provisions of the Withdrawal Agreement and of EU law will have supremacy over UK law. This Article is not limited to the transition period, so EU law will have direct effect and supremacy after the transition period ends."

When would the transition period end? At a time of the EU's choosing. May's deal contained a 'backstop' with no article 50 mechanism for leaving unilaterally. So effectively we would be bound by EU rules over which we had no vote or veto, paying whatever costs the EU chose to impose, until such a time as they decided to release us. But they couldn't just demand money right? Wrong. May's withdrawal agreement imposed financial obligations on the UK which went well beyond the UK's obligations under international law. The amount was generally referred to as "£39bn". In fact, the obligation was not defined in the WA as an amount of money, but as a series of vague forms of words which were open to interpretation. And in one of her maddest acts, Theresa May agreed a clause under which the UK's financial obligations were to be unilaterally decided upon by the ECJ instead of by an independent arbitration mechanism. And that that money would be unconditionally payable.

The impression people got was of a powerful EU crushing the helpless UK negotiators. Actually the UK negotiators held all the cards. All we had to do was nothing and under international law we would have automatically reverted to an independent democracy, with no obligations to the EU, no £39bn payment, no £13bn annual membership fees, total control of our money, laws, borders, hugely enlarged fishing grounds, and the freedom to strike trade deals with anyone, anywhere, anytime. Additionally the WTO Treaty, the Trade Facilitation Agreement and Lisbon Treaty would have prevented the EU from punishing us with retaliatory measures. Professional UK negotiators could have crushed the EU or at least achieved a deal that was mutually beneficial. So why didn't they? Because they couldn't? No. They *wanted* to fail.

Clearly May's intention was to impose an 'exit' 'deal' that would humiliate the country so much that there would appear to be a causal relationship between being an independent democracy and being downtrodden; and that we would lose the will to consider ourselves worthy of self-determination. She did not capitulate, she colluded. Her talks with the EU were not negotiations between two parties seeking a mutual agreement, but discussions between two parts of the same organisation committed to the same outcome – the preservation of the established order which had enriched them and impoverished us.

May's deal would have forced us into 'full alignment' with the rules of the EU's Single Market and Customs Union, so when the 2017 Tory manifesto pledged "We will no longer be members of the single market or customs union" that was a lie. And when May said (White Paper July 2018) that her deal "takes back control of our laws, ending the jurisdiction of the ECJ in the United Kingdom" she was lying. Predictably, Blair praised civil servant Oliver Robbins (May's chief Brexit negotiator) for 'camouflaging' May's deal.

In her Lancaster House speech (January 2017) May said "No deal is better than a bad deal" Then after the general election (5 months later) the narrative changed to 'any deal is better than no deal'. So just like all the others it was pro-Brexit words *before* the election and anti-Brexit actions *after* the election. Additionally in the Lancaster House speech May said that staying in the single market and the customs union "*would mean complying with the EU's rules and regulations ... without having a vote on what those rules and regulations are ... It would to all intents and purposes mean not leaving the EU at all ... We will not have truly left the European Union if we are not in control of our own laws.*" That was absolutely true, and May was right to say it. But why did she say the truth at that particular time? Because it was just *before* the general election. Again, pro-Brexit words before the election, anti-Brexit actions after the election. But what is important here is that it shows May was not naïve but devious, she understood perfectly well that an 'exit' deal could be struck which maintained or even increased EU control. She saw the 'negotiation process' as her chance to prevent the Brexit that she never wanted.

The empirical reality of what May pursued was the polar opposite of what she had promised before the 2017 election. She insisted the preservation of EU control was a necessary compromise essential to achieving a deal, when the empirical reality obvious to the world was that passing her deal and delivering Brexit were mutually exclusive. When the other side insists that they rule you, there can be no '*Withdrawal Agreement*' because to agree is to *not* withdraw. Our right to democratically decide our own laws was something Theresa May was not entitled to even put on the negotiating table to begin with. The fact that even a buffoon like Johnson could secure a much better deal proves that May didn't even try to negotiate.

Not once did May demand a major concession from the EU. Why? Because she was incapable of being ruthless? Not at all! May was relentless and unyielding in her attempts to get her deal approved by the House of Commons, three times she tried to get it passed, each time with a three line whip - the maximum coercion a UK government can impose. Again and again she warned us it was that or nothing. Not once did she tell the EU it was that or nothing. She treated them how she should have treated us, and she treated us how she should have treated them. Why? Because she was one of them.

It would take a whole other book to flesh out my reasons, but of all the protagonists involved it was Theresa May who presided over the darkest days. It was her administration that was the most devious, and her conduct that was the most unforgivable - and that's from a pretty crowded field! Still today I am astonished by the number of perfectly intelligent people who seem to think May had the misfortune of trying, but failing, to strike a compromise in difficult circumstances. Theresa May was not a failed technocrat. She masqueraded as a technocrat to conceal the monumental failings of her ideology which was every bit as fanatical as Major's or Blair's. Yes Blair was a rabid Europhile but at least he was politically shrewd enough to avoid unpopular policies. Not so May. She was utterly committed to 'The Project' but concealed her fanaticism with deadening verbiage. She was prepared to sacrifice anything, absolutely anything, her place in history, her party, even her country in order to preserve EU control. Relentless and cold-blooded, May used every tool at her disposal to make Brexit as slow, expensive, miserable and demoralising as possible. Even as our national humiliation reduced Tory support to 18% she clung tenaciously to power, imposing three line whips on her opponents, striving heart and soul to retain EU rule. In May the EU had a true believer in Downing Street. She served them unstintingly till the last hour of the last day. She never represented us to them – she represented them to us. Her resignation speech contained not a scintilla of apology; her tears were only for herself.

Imagine if you and I signed a contract obliging me to abide by your interpretation of your rules ... rules over which I had no vote or veto ... and that if you decided I was in breach of your rules, you could demand as much money as you liked from me … and that I had no right of appeal … and no mechanism for unilaterally exiting the arrangement. Under such an arrangement I would be a slave and you would be a slave owner. Slavery is illegal and certainly prohibited by the ECHR. But apparently when such an arrangement is foisted upon an entire nation, instead of calling it 'slavery' it is called 'Withdrawal Agreement' and the person seeking to impose it is not called 'traitor', they are called Prime Minister.

Obviously I don't enjoy being critical of a lady, but dark days require dark descriptions. Words such as 'liar' or 'betrayal' exist to be applied correctly, and not calling out failure invites repetition. The awful truth that many still don't want to admit is that not only were we lied to and betrayed by a manifestly corrupt political system, but that such events are actually pretty common. I could have written an equally damning appraisal of several other Prime Ministers, but it was May who swore blind she would do precisely the opposite of what she actually did, it was May who presided over the crisis, it was May who appointed the poachers as gamekeepers, it was May who deliberately failed, it was May who employed tautological sophistry to conceal her deviousness. And if you think her politics was bad, then I'm guessing you haven't seen the robot dance! And no, this has nothing to do with her gender, background, or any other circumstantial point. It has everything to do with her actions. May was not guilty of some technical error, she was stone cold determined to deliver the opposite of what we voted for.

(Anti Brexit T shirt Amazon, just £16.99!)

Imagine if any of us little people did the opposite of what we promised at our job interview? Imagine if we did the opposite of what was in our employment contract? Imagine! But rules only seem to be for the little people. Before the eyes of the world Theresa May relentlessly pursued her goal of placing the

UK completely under the control of the EU. My seven year old son recently said to me "*To get the sack you have to do the opposite of what you are supposed to do and talk about potatoes.*" I concede that May did not talk about potatoes.

In March 2019 May promised to resign if her 'Withdrawal' Agreement was passed, this was because then she would then be able to retire, content in the knowledge that her betrayal was complete. The good thing about British politics is that you get to read your obituary without having to die first. I wish Theresa May a long and healthy life that she may fully ingest history's verdict.

The Cooper-Letwin Bill
The Cooper-Letwin Bill (2019) imposed an obligation on May to seek an extension in the event of no-deal. Of it Martin Howe QC wrote:

"The progress of the Cooper-Letwin Bill illustrates a further aspect of the Prime Minister's conduct, which is to claim that she is being forced by others to do things which she wants to do anyway. The government at first formally opposed the Bill on sound constitutional grounds. However, it emerged from the amendments they tabled that their real concern was not to stop the Bill, but to correct some of its inept drafting that could have accidentally stopped the government from agreeing to an Article 50 extension which it wants to agree to ... So if we do stay in the EU for an extended period, that will be the result of the voluntary act and decision of the Prime Minister, not forced upon her, for which she should be held fully accountable."

The government agreed an extension and the Act then lapsed. But crucially the Cooper-Letwin Bill muddied the waters sufficiently for May to cancel our exit (which had already been enshrined in international law with huge votes) whilst denying culpability.

The Benn Act (Miscellaneous chapter from 2019 Blog)
The Benn Act placed an obligation on the government to seek an extension in the event of no deal being reached. But because no deal and Brexit were the same thing it effectively made it a crime to implement the referendum result. Did the Tories attempt to oppose it, amend it or filibuster it? No, because it gave them cover to dishonour the referendum result, so it sailed on the statute book unopposed. This is why Johnson should have defied the Benn Act:

1, What is supreme, the law or the vote? If a policeman asks me to do something, how is that instruction different to the demand of a gangster who will punch me if I refuse? The answer of course is that the policeman speaks with the authority of the law. But from whence cometh the law? From Parliament. But from whence cometh the authority of Parliament? From its members of parliament. But from whence cometh the authority of the members of parliament? From the fact that they were elected. But from whence cometh those votes? From the electorate. At this point I cannot repeat my question because we have reached the fountainhead. The vote generates, whereas the law is merely generated. The vote is the parent, the law the offspring.

I can enquire where the authority of the policeman comes from, I can enquire where the authority of the judge comes from, I can question where the authority of the law or constitution comes from, but no one can enquire where the authority of the electorate comes from. How do we decide what constitution to have? By voting. And how do we decide constitutional amendments? Voting. Similarly, we can question who should vote, what question to ask, and how it should be counted, but we cannot question the vote *itself*. What authority would we invoke in doing so? The voters may be stupid, bad or misinformed, but for all its tawdry imperfection, the decision of the electorate is the supreme political act.

So the electorate are supreme, Parliament merely the representatives. And once the supreme authority had handed down its judgement, it was Parliament's job to implement it, not to interpret it, or deliberate about it, or negotiate about it, but to implement it. You can declare independence or negotiate the extent to which laws (about goods, services, labour or capital) are harmonised, but you cannot do both. You cannot negotiate independence; to negotiate it is to *not* be independent. Once we had voted to become an independent democracy, to even negotiate what we could vote about was to be in contempt of the judgement handed down by the supreme authority.

No judge, politician or law had any authority to impose external rule. If they claimed they did then I could simply, quietly and politely enquire from whence their authority came. And a few short questions later we would find their argument is actually: *"Votes that give me power are valid, votes that give you power are not"*. To which I would reply: *"Where is the formula that says which votes count and which don't?"* Let's say they produce such a formula from somewhere, I then simply ask *"Who voted for that?"* QED.

Votes gave them the power to disregard votes? Call that an argument? Why should votes for the Benn Act be punctiliously implemented but greater numbers of votes by the electorate be ignored for years? The answer of course is corruption. There was one sort of votes for them and another for us.

What if a judge instructed you to do something, and you took the judgement to be a suggestion, and did the opposite; you would be 'in contempt of court' right? What if an employer instructed you to separate two things and you waffled about the process of separation as you conjoined them, that would be professional misconduct right? What if you made a promise to a friend or lover, broke it, and attempted to pass it off as a technicality? That would be betrayal right? Well precisely that was happening between 2016 and 2019 but on a much much bigger scale. What they described as a 'process of leaving' was in reality a process of *not* leaving. We have a word to describe this sort of behaviour: 'lying'. Did our well-paid employees apologise? Did they show a scintilla of contrition? On the contrary they masqueraded as the most upstanding heroes imaginable. They actually acted as if *they* were trying to solve *our* problem, when it was them that was the problem! They saw the electorate not as the highest rung of the ladder but the lowest, and they saw themselves not as our servants but our masters. They assumed only the highly educated would be able to see through their charade when it was obvious to the world they were conspiring to transfer power from us.

Parliament took it upon itself to interpret a referendum result that was not up for interpretation. And Parliament decided that when we voted to be an independent democracy, that the result could be implemented by striking a deal in which the EU remained in control. We must not be naïve about how dark the situation was. It was a coup d'état. We were being attacked, not by foreign aggression but by internal corruption. What the hell did they think they were doing? Why on earth did these mere representatives think they had any authority to negotiate what we were allowed to vote about in exchange for access to the Single Market? The decision had already been made very clearly, very publicly by the highest authority in the land.

Once the supreme authority had handed down its judgement, laws incompatible with our declaration of independence (DoI) ceased to be legitimate. If the DoI was not automatically put into the statute (and laws incompatible with it removed) then the body politic should apologise for its failure to do its job, not attack the vote or the voters. Their failure to do so was not some technical hiccup but a revolt by them against us.

Generally votes contradict laws (that's the whole point, it's why votes exist) and when they contradict laws it is the laws that must be corrected. That's how we improve our world. The error the EU side made was that once they lost the referendum they assumed there was something wrong with the vote itself. But if something that has been voted for is not on the statute then it is the statute that must be corrected, not the vote. When disregarding our judgement, what authority could they invoke? They found themselves making oxymoronic arguments that invoked the legitimacy of democracy selectively: apparently votes that gave them power were automatically binding, whilst our vote to be an independent democracy was merely a suggestion that could be honoured by spending years making us less independent and less democratic.

If two mutually exclusive things have been voted for we should ask ourselves which vote put the clearest proposition to the greatest number of people? Which one was debated most widely, most publicly for the most time? Which one was endorsed by the most electors? And of course, we should favour votes passed by the primary body (the electorate) over the secondary body (the representatives). Clearly the referendum trumps a bill allowed by a partisan speaker, carried by a majority of 28 by the most discredited parliament in history and left completely un-amended.

So there, I have asked a serious question and attempted to answer it giving my reasons. This is altogether different to the EU side for whom votes are meaningful when they are for the EU, meaningless when against. And laws are binding when convenient and optional when inconvenient. However wrong you think I may be on this, at least I am grappling with a problem and attempting to address it, for EU supporters what matters is neither the vote nor the law but whether their purposes are served. They are with Thrasymachus.

2, Clearly MPs who voted for the Benn Act didn't understand what they were doing, they were blinded by lies and manipulated by foreigners, so they should vote again till they get it right. Obviously I'm saying this as a joke, it's an absurdity, but the point is it is no more absurd than pro-EU arguments that were being advanced in seriousness!

3, It's not as if we are up against a rules-based entity here. (For examples see section entitled '*The Rules Are The Rules – Sometimes*') EU supporters believe the EU to be good, therefore anything that advances the EU can't be bad – even if it involves bending the rules and crushing democracy! Even if there was nothing questionable about this position it would still seem to disqualify them from accusing others of not following the rules.

4, Parliament had already accepted the terms and conditions of Article 50 (which was international law) which clearly established what was to happen in the event of no deal. That vote was won 498 votes to 114.

5, The counter argument is that the law is the law and must be obeyed. I admit it's a good argument, but the trouble with it is that it doesn't allow us to condemn bad law. What about the racial segregation laws? Was it immoral to disobey those? Of course not! Technically Rosa Parks, Gandhi and Mandela were all criminals, but criminality is not necessarily villainy. To conflate what is law with what should be done obliges us to tolerate rotten governors. But if we say the vote is supreme then we are free to favour that which is most democratic.

6, We voted to leave, the Benn Act was about preventing that from happening. If Parliament is going to treat our votes with contempt, why shouldn't we treat their laws with contempt? If they are going to pick and choose what votes are legitimate, why shouldn't we pick and choose what laws are legitimate? If Parliament says '*to hell with the people's decision*' then why shouldn't people say '*to hell with Parliament's laws*'?

7, British law prohibits 'bad' behaviour rather than compelling 'good' behaviour. The Benn Act turns this on its head. By its tenet presumably Johnson could sit in his room, do nothing, wait for Article 50 to elapse, and go from being an innocent man to a guilty man – an absurdity.

8, Imagine there is a husband and wife, and that one day, one says to the other "*I don't love you anymore.*" In the eyes of the law nothing has changed, but in reality everything has changed. Sure there are a few legal technicalities to deal with but the substantive act has already *happened*. EU supporters mischievously confused substantive acts with technicalities. It is the substantive decisions that determine the technicalities, not the other way round.

9, It was claimed that to ignore the Benn Act would cause a constitutional crisis. But that assumed a constitutional crisis did not exist already. People making this argument were merely denying the existence of any crisis that didn't confirm their prejudices. So Remainers pissed their pants that we might 'crash out' of the EU but were completely sanguine about the electorate crashing out of having democratic control of lawmakers. They speculated that all sorts of scary monsters were lurking just around the corner, in an unknown and unknowable future. But when a Theresa May grovelled to foreign bureaucrats for permission to postpone our independence, they chose not to see the real constitutional crisis – the victory of authoritarianism – that was right in front of them.

10, If to ignore the Benn Act was a crime then so what? How could any punishment for this 'crime' be worse than remaining a subjugated vassal state?

11, Votes generate laws right? Well the most voted-for thing in British history is that we should be an independent democracy, but somehow it was precisely that which we were being told was illegal!

12, It was illegal to have a Christmas party during the Covid Lockdown, but Johnson didn't have any qualms about that law did he?

Johnson referred to the Benn Act as *'The Surrender Act'* and refused to sign his letter requesting an extension, but even in 2020 when Johnson could (and should) have walked out of talks he placed an obligation on himself to strike a deal, proving that the Benn Act did not place any obligation on himself that he didn't want anyway. Johnson's dislike of the Benn Act had been a charade - he was a dealer all along.

Johnson.
Regarding Johnson. He doesn't deserve much of a mention. He could (and should) have been the greatest PM since Attlee. He held the greatest political victory imaginable in the palm of his hand, all he had to do to achieve it was nothing, and still he spunked it! Because he was cowardly? in cahoots? incompetent? Who cares - I have no interest in psychoanalysing him. All that matters is that he fucked it up in a way that appears habitual.

He negotiated the non-negotiable which was unforgivable. Before the election he swore blind he would 'get Brexit done' – after the election he delivered nothing more than a crappy trade agreement. He actually sat down and discussed the terms and conditions of our independence with people pathologically opposed to it. The EU scorned us, belittled us, intimidated us and threatened us, and the man with no shame just sat at the negotiation table like a lemon, wittering on about technicalities when he should have told them to fuck off to hell where they belonged. But it would not be fair to describe the UK Brexit negotiators as a bunch of whores; after all, prostitutes tend to be professional negotiators who actually do the job they are paid to do.

Johnson's failings on Brexit were twofold. Firstly he negotiated and signed a deal with the EU which by its very nature compromised our capacity to democratically govern ourselves. And secondly he left unchallenged and in situ the entire political and electoral system that had so obviously conspired against us. So after five prime ministers determined that we should never be an independent democracy, we finally got one who was amenable to it, but incapable of doing a good job of it (or much else for that matter). Terrific.

Johnson is the man ethics forgot, and I have no intention of voting for him, but maybe there is hope, albeit a glimmer. Firstly it is better to be 'ethically flexible' than a zealot for a bad religion. Secondly, if someone is one magnet short of a moral compass then the more incompetent they are, the safer for us all. Thirdly, at least a venal desire for power compels him to pursue policies the electorate want. And lastly, an incompetent, amoral buffoon is still a significant improvement on the predecessors. I know it's not much of a silver lining but I'm afraid that's the best I can do.

Labour Likes Losing
The most pro Brexit side won the 1987 election, the 1997 election, the 2010 election, the 2014 EU election, the 2015 election, the 2016 referendum, the 2017 election, the 2019 EU election and the 2019 election. What does Labour do? It chooses Keir Starmer as leader! Someone who, like May, is utterly opposed to us being an independent democracy, and who would lay down his life to restore EU control. Political masochism.

Time Line Summary
I'm going to summarise events again because this is important.
1, When Thatcher became Euro-sceptic she was brought down by three EU supporters. The candidates to replace her were three EU supporters. John Major became PM on the basis of just 185 votes in a sham leadership contest.
2, Major was replaced by Blair who rose to power promising EU withdrawal. New Labour were more Euro-sceptic than the Tories under Major, because Labour advocated retaining control of monetary policy. Before the 2005 Election Blair lied that he would give us a referendum on the European Constitution.
3, Blair was succeeded by Brown. We can't accuse Brown of winning a sham leadership contest - because there wasn't actually any leadership contest at all! Like Blair, Brown dishonoured Labour's manifesto pledge to have a referendum on the EU Constitution
4, In 2014 UKIP won the European elections.
5, Cameron was more Euro-sceptic than Brown so he won the 2010 election. In 2013 he promised an in/out referendum and so won the 2015 election with a majority. During the 2016 referendum campaign Cameron sent a booklet to every home in the country containing this lie:

A once in a generation decision

The referendum on Thursday, 23rd June is your chance to decide if we should remain in or leave the European Union.

The Government believes it is in the best interests of the UK to remain in the EU.

This is the way to protect jobs, provide security, and strengthen the UK's economy for every family in this country – a clear path into the future, in contrast to the uncertainty of leaving.

This is your decision. The Government will implement what you decide.

If you're aged 18 or over by 23rd June and are entitled to vote, this is your chance to decide.

Registration ends on 7th June. Find out how to register at *Aboutmyvote.co.uk* and register online at *Gov.uk/register-to-vote*

If you would like to know more about any of the information in this leaflet, go to: *EUReferendum.gov.uk*

6, Cameron was succeeded by another Manchurian candidate, Theresa May in yet another Euro-sham leadership contest.
7, The HoC then voted to trigger Article 50 by 498 votes to 114.
8, 84.2% of the votes in the 2017 general election were for parties that promised to honour the referendum result. But because May was obviously trying to get out of delivering Brexit she failed to win a majority.

9, May placed Remainers in charge of the 'negotiating process' which was another sham. May's betrayal was put to the Commons and was rejected it in the 'meaningful vote'.
10, The rule book of the House of Commons (Erskine May) states that the same thing can't be put to a vote more than once in each parliamentary session. But obviously for EU supporters, the only rules that count are the ones that advance their project, so John Bercow (the openly pro-Remain Speaker) agreed to THREE 'meaningful votes' on Theresa May's 'deal'. Obviously calling these 'meaningful votes' is laughable because the only votes that really seemed to count were the ones that enshrined EU control. Votes that rejected submission to the EU were disregarded. May lost all three 'meaningful' votes.
11, In 2019 the Brexit Party won the European Election.
12, Then in March 2019 when, three years after we voted (VO-TED) to leave, a small number of EU supporters with no democratic right to represent us, met in a closed session in Brussels and agreed to suspend Article 50 (which was international law) extend our membership, and that the EU should continue to rule us with laws over which we had no vote or veto. Who led the British delegation? Theresa May, who had never actually won a proper leadership election or general election majority.

There are several patterns we can observe:
1, Over this period of about 20 years the most pro-Brexit side won virtually all of the major votes.
2, Over the same period of time EU control of the UK steadily increased.
3, Before major votes Blair, Brown, Cameron and May all promised that they would either grant an EU referendum or implement the result of an EU referendum. Promises they dishonoured after the voting had taken place.
4, Again and again EU supporters ascended to the highest echelons of political power without actually winning a proper leadership vote or general election.

Every time the people had a choice they chose the most pro-Brexit option (Thatcher, Blair, Cameron & Johnson) which is why all the EU supporters were installed by circumventing the electorate (Major, Brown, May, all the officials, top civil servants, governors, regulators, heads of committees etc) So the great innovation of the Brexit battle was on the Remain side, They had achieved every political strategist's fantasy – a project that advanced even as people voted against it! We never consented, but the EU had developed a strategy for incremental conquest that was deniable and actually paid for by those it attacked. It advanced irrespective of how people voted and to even air disagreement was to be guilty of a hate crime. It appeared completely benign as it advanced authoritarianism in the name of progressive values. It appealed to a romanticised view of Europe whilst claiming to reject nationalism. A type of secular Calvinism, its appeal to beliefs and values allowed its advocates to simply deny a mountain of empirical evidence. Those who were for it were the minority. They didn't pay for it, it paid for them. They mutually funded and promoted one another to power, prestige and prosperity. Those who were against it were the majority who paid for it. The minority then used their superior wealth, status and power to abuse the majority into acquiescence with a hate campaign of righteous discrimination, all the while insisting it was themselves who were against discrimination! It was the perfect takeover strategy, appearing to be cosmopolitan and worldly even as democracy was crushed and the poor were psychologically abused with Foucaultian normalising power. Why on earth would those in power not want this to continue? Our country had been sold out by precisely the political system supposedly there to safeguard our interests. I maintain this is prima facie evidence of endemic corruption.

So on the face of it the Remain coup was a simple land-grab, a fairly ordinary seizure of power, but it was the method employed to achieve it that was innovative – Othello Syndrome was weaponised on an industrial scale.

Obviously for each of the above events the apologists for authoritarianism will assert that it was simply a technical anomaly, that just so happened to have yielded a pro EU outcome again and again, and that we are too stupid to understand. But I'm not interested in *why* the system failed. All that matters is that it did. How many pro-EU technical anomalies before I'm allowed to call out corruption? That is why

March 2019 was the darkest chapter in modern British history, because that was when the primary means by which we could peacefully effect change was removed from the table. No Brexiteer ever said to me that they had decided to take up the armed struggle, to throw bricks or petrol bombs. But if they had it would have been crucial that I could say to them "No. There is a better way". In March 2019 "No. There is a better way" pretty much ceased to be a credible argument. What are you allowed to do ('*do*' being the operative word)? What are you allowed to actually DO if your society is taken over? If you speak out you are committing a hate crime, if you don't speak out you lose. If you win a vote it is part of a process that never goes anywhere, but if you lose a vote it's automatically implemented. What do you actually *do*? It's a practical question.

From Nelson Mandela leaving prison to becoming South Africa's president took 4 years and 86 days. Four and a half years after we voted to be an independent democracy we were *still* bound by EU judgements and regulations over which we had no vote or veto. That's right - an apartheid state in Africa managed to become an independent democracy faster than the UK under the Tories! This wasn't the result of technicalities; it wasn't some procedural quirk of fate. The entire British political establishment united in their total refusal to implement the most voted-for thing in British history. In 1000 days Africans turned a failed state into a beacon of hope. In 1000 days British Remainers achieved the opposite.

Summary of that bit.
Let's ignore Thatcher, Callaghan and Wilson as they are dead and were elected before EU integration. There are six living people who have been PM: Major, Blair, Brown, Cameron, May and Johnson. Three were put in Downing Street by the electorate, three by party apparatchiks. The three who were put in Downing Street by the electorate defeated more pro-EU opponents. The three put in Downing Street by apparatchiks were insanely pro-EU. Spot the pattern? EU supporters prosper by excluding the maximum number of voters. Theirs is an anti-democratic philosophy that uses and anti-democratic-method to achieve an anti-democratic outcome.

The Grumblers
So who emerged from Brexit with the least credit? Johnson? May? Cameron? Well of a crowded field I was most disappointed and ashamed of the British themselves who watched the news and grumbled. Many times I found myself on my own, handing out homemade leaflets, being sworn at. And in the depths of my despair I had to wonder whether the British really deserved the democracy I was fighting for.

Remainers Fail Up
Why did the media ignore intelligent moderate Brexiteers like Mark Hill, Will Podmore, Brendan Chilton, Jenny Jones, Doug Nichols, Fawzi Ibrahim, Lee Jones, Martin Howe, Lucy Harris, Dominic Frisby, Jonathan Isaby and Michael Lightfoot? And instead fixate on Johnson and Farage? Because it was easier to demonise a couple of Thatcherites. By fusing together Brexit, Farage and Johnson a narrative could be presented in which the shortcomings of one were the shortcomings of all. And notice how the great Labour leavers Kate Hoey, Gisela Stuart and Dennis Skinner are now out of politics? Corbyn voted leave and his career is now over. Whereas, Starmer, who fought tooth and nail to prevent Brexit was duly knighted and is now the leader of the Labour party. On the Tory side, Javid is back, Paterson is finished, Amess is assassinated, Patel looks finished and there is a clear campaign to remove Johnson less than 2 years after he won a democratic mandate. (His crime apparently that he attended a public gathering). No Tory MP ever had the courage to publicly call on May to resign, but they do it to Johnson all the time. Why? Because he is some type of Brexiteer so it's critical for the EU that he be removed from power and supplanted by a Rejoiner in another sham contest as quickly as possible. And the last I heard of Farage he was selling financial services in YouTube videos. Notice the pattern? Brexiteers just so happen to have shit careers whilst the Remainers fail up. You will probably notice this in your time and place – if you are a rational democrat you will be scrutinised and judged, if you're not, you'll get a pass.

However much you may disagree with my position that we should have left with no deal, you must acknowledge it is a position that I have produced an argument for, which has some merit, and that I was broadly right to campaign against Johnson's unlovable trade deal. How many people in positions of power in the UK today agree with me that we should have left with no deal? None. How many people in positions of power in the UK today think there should have been some sort of deal that compromised our ability to democratically govern ourselves? All of them. Coincidence or corruption?

In the 5 years I spent fighting for Brexit my pay went down from £42k to £34k but in the two years since, despite Covid, I've managed to turn things around. Obviously my personal story is irrelevant, the point I am making is that the sacrifices made by us Brexiteers were real and substantial.

Double Standards
Before the last general election, till the last hour of the last day I was putting leaflets through people's doors urging them not to vote for Johnson and the Tories. But this has to be said: Heath lied that joining the EEC would not affect our sovereignty. Blair, Brown and Cameron lied they would grant a referendum on the Lisbon Treaty. Cameron and May lied that they would implement the referendum result. Johnson lied about attending a Christmas party.

All the above lies changed the course of our history - except one.
All the above lies dishonoured written manifesto promises – except one.
All the above opposed us being an independent democracy - except one.
None of the above faced repeated calls from backbenchers to resign - except one.

The way Tory backbenchers treat Johnson anyone would think he had invaded Iraq, bailed out failed capitalists or bombed Libya! However dreadful we may find Johnson we have to wonder whether he is being judged by the same standards as previous prime ministers. Clearly EU supporters are desperate to replace him with a Rejoiner in another sham leadership contest, so that at the next election we have another Hobson's 'choice' between a Rejoiner and a Rejoiner. They know they must do this now so the decision is made in secret by their people, rather than publically by the electorate, who will always choose the maximum democracy option. Sure, his handling of Brexit and Covid were a disgrace, and my gut instinct urges me to condemn him without reservation, but would I swap him for May? No. Cameron? No. Brown? No. Blair? No. Major? No. I'm not saying the contempt is unwarranted, but that it is greatest among the forgetful.

Democracy Maximalist (Pending Refutation)
Do I fear democratic errors? Not much because they can be easily corrected, so I fear undemocratic errors more. But this isn't an article of faith for me. If someone could produce an evidence-based argument that more people having more democratic control over more power results in a worse world, then I would happily swap sides. Or that the concentration of power in the hands of a small number of ideologically pure appointees didn't result in people and nature being crushed, again I'm open to persuasion. But people have had years to produce such an argument and haven't managed it yet, so I'm not expecting that to change any time soon.

Judge Judges.
All power should be contingent on votes. Even judges should be elected so we can DO something if they fail - after all the rest of us are appraised by our employers. A critic might reasonably say 'but what if the voters fail?' I would answer:
1, That's unlikely as votes involve lots of public cross-checking.
2, Voters decisions could always be amended at the next judicial elections.
3, Who is qualified to say the voters have failed? And from whence does their authority emanate?
4, The question assumes (wrongly) that problems are democratic and solutions are undemocratic. All the empirical evidence suggests the opposite is the case.

The Path to a Better World
When knowledge contradicts belief we correct the belief.
When science contradicts religion we correct the religion.
When votes contradict the statute we correct the statute.
When more people have more control over more power it results in a world that is more good.

On Liberty.
If I am responsible for pollution then (indirectly and imperceptibly) I am inflicting problems on everyone else. What about *their* freedom? What about *their* liberty? No one who imposes shit on other people likes regulation but the second they have to put up with other people's shit they see things different. Everyone hates regulation till their toaster breaks.

Meditation V Going Down the Pub.
Al-Ghazali was obviously a brilliant thinker but in choosing to spend years meditating in isolation he picked a method hard-wired to produce an extreme religious outcome. Meditating is by its very nature inward looking. It's bollocks. How is me thinking about myself going to make the world better? Small wonder that where introspection is the norm tyranny prospers. Contrast meditation with going to the pub and having a pint with someone. Going to the pub is conversational, a feedback loop is established, in which our personalities come up against an external reality. This is why our reflections as we walk home from the pub are more profound than what we think when meditating.

Power to the People?
If power must exist then dictatorship by the electorate, though flawed, is surely preferable to the alternatives. This is a particular point of disagreement between myself and several of my Brexiteer friends who do not accept that power should exist in the first place.

The Real Far-Right
So if we look again at this picture of the March for Europe. The participants consider themselves to be cosmopolitan, rejecting nationalism, and advocating peace, prosperity and human rights. Why? Because those are the values they associate with their cause. But when I look at the same photograph I see delirious nationalism, a war on democracy and an absolute rejection of a political system that genuinely gave us peace, prosperity and human rights. Furthermore these people are fetishising a political system in which we live in fear of religious judgement.

How does the reasonable, undecided person differentiate between these two diametrically opposed interpretations? Simple, I look at not in. I base my position on empirical reality not subjective values. It's not about *how* we see things. If it were purely about how the mind organised the sense perception then however many flags they waved, no evidence could persuade an EU supporter that this is an extreme right-wing movement by every conceivable measure. And even when EU supporters are empirical, on closer examination we see they are trying to establish generalities with specific examples, whereas I look at the broadest swathe of empirical evidence available, and am persuaded by that. They tailor the empiricism to the value; I do the opposite.

Contra Climate Sceptics

Imagine if I were locked in a garage with a car and the engine was running. Eventually I would suffocate. Similarly if I were locked in a garage with two cars with their engines running, I would die more quickly. Three cars and I would die quicker still. And so on. Polution and life appear to be inversely proportional. Humans are burning 100 million barrels of oil a day which seems to be erasing life on earth. The more we burn, the larger the deserts and the greater the extinction. Because polution and extinction appear directly proportional the onus is on the polluters to produce a factual argument why pollution should not be outlawed. Until such an argument is produced, we have a 'Pascal's Wager' - If we are confronted with a choice, where one path could mean salvation, the other total calamity, naturally we should err on the side of caution. What's the worst that could happen? A few tyrants go bankrupt? That's not a problem, that's a solution! Additionally, why should the polluter's liabilities be limited when ours are not?

Is Religion a Human Right?

There are various versions of human rights on offer, for example there's the UN declaration of Human Rights (1948) which was mostly plagiarised by the European Convention of Human Rights (1953). But these are written in an additive way. We start reading them and they are inspiring, but by Article 29 we find ourselves scratching our heads, and feel it's a bit of a boot fair of nice ideas. As a Brit, it pains me to say it, but the most electrifying human rights document is the original French Declaration of the Rights of Man of 1789. Its greatness lies in its economy. Just 17 articles in 650 words.

Article 10 simply states: "No one may be disquieted for his opinions, even religious ones, provided that their manifestation does not trouble the public order established by the law."

So people have the human right to believe whatever mumbo jumbo they like, so long as they do so within the confines of the law. It's very clear. It is not the law that should accommodate beliefs, it's the other way round (again) belief does not exempt you from equal treatment. And if your belief obliges you to break the law, fine, but at least have the integrity (as Gandhi and Rosa Parks did) to accept that the law must treat you like everyone else, and accept its judgement with good grace. But right now we have the worst of all possible worlds - a Kafkaesque legalistic labyrinth from which we exempt the most credulous, irrational people.

Why aren't religions regulated?

Employers are regulated, schools have league tables, teachers are assessed, manufacturers comply with standards, professionals have codes of conduct and pubs are licensed. Every other section of society has an ombudsman or a regulatory body to whom complaints can be made – so why are religious groups exempt?

Here is an excerpt from Building Regulations Part L2A:

1. New buildings other than dwellings which are roofed constructions having walls and which use energy to condition the indoor climate must comply with the energy efficiency requirements unless they are exempt as set out at regulation 21(3) of the Building Regulations. For the purposes of the energy efficiency requirements of the Building Regulations a building means the whole of a building or parts of it designed or altered to be used separately. The following classes of new buildings or parts of new buildings other than dwellings are exempt:

    a. buildings which are used primarily or solely as places of worship;

So here in black and white is proof that believers get preferential treatment. Apparently you MUST comply with the law … unless you believe in a load of old mumbo jumbo in which case you don't! But that is just a minor example; the worst aspect is that across the regulatory world the believers get an easier ride. They have the human right to advocate their beliefs which we don't have the human right to critique. Their culture enjoys protection, ours is modernised. Not only are we failing to treat people equally but we are favouring the most dangerous! If there's one bunch of loonies who should definitely not be exempt from compliance with the law, it is the irrational, credulous, fanatics with their crappy wars.

In order to make a planning submission architects must submit a 'Design and Access Statement' to the local authority, so why shouldn't every religious group have to submit a 'Peaceful Coexistence Statement' (PCS) such that, an inspection is carried out to check the 'PCS' being complied with? Building sites are required by law to clearly display health and safety signage. In a similar way the PCS assessor would check there is clear, prominent information calling for peaceful coexistence with the rest of society, if there is none then the doors get locked. Every football club must participate in the 'Kick It Out' anti-racism program, why shouldn't every religious group have to sign up to an anti-abuse program? No compliance? Then the doors get locked. Every office has a picture board showing the managers and giving their job titles. If there is no equal opportunities program in place whereby a sufficient number of women are promoted to positions of authority, then the doors should get locked. Once the religious group thinks the necessary reforms have been made, they can simply pay to apply for their theology licence to be reinstated. These are perfectly sensible recommendations to prevent people from being hurt, based on the indisputable observation that theological doctrine is behind most of the conflicts in the world today.

Home > Housing and local services > Owning and renting a property

Buildings that do not need an EPC

These include:

- places of worship

People discussing economics on YouTube are obliged to stress they are not financial advisors, Failure to do so will result in their channels being taken down. Councillors cannot advise. Theologians do nothing but advise, yet they are free to lecture the most vulnerable. People were being killed in car crashes so drink-driving was prohibited and seatbelts made mandatory. It worked. So why does the law suddenly cease to apply when lives are being destroyed by religion?

I recently put on a cabaret show and had to comply with endless technical requirements just to play some comedy songs on stage. There were registration forms, music licensing forms, insurance forms and tech spec forms. I needed a special pass to hand out leaflets on the street, and once it was over I had to fill in another form to get my money from the ticket sales! It's no surprise that throughout Britain, pubs and live music venues are closing down in huge numbers – in the last 10 years half of Britain's night clubs have closed and in the last couple of years alone, the heart of London culture has been purged, with Madam Jojos, the Astoria, the 12 Bar, the Bull and Gate, and many other legendary live music venues shutting their doors. They have now been developed into shops and flats. Our music scene is facing death by a thousand regulations, declining from vibrant culture to sonic neo-liberalism. But drinking alcohol and playing music have been part of our way of life for longer than Christianity or Islam, additionally alcohol and music have given more people more profound revelations than Christianity or Islam, and have killed fewer people too! So why is one glorious culture legislated into the dustbin of history whilst more dangerous ones proceed unchecked?

Of course rationalism can't apply to religion – the whole point of religion is to be irrational, but that is no reason why the law should not apply to religions. Naturally religious groups will claim that any curtailment of their activity infringes their right to free speech, but the same could be said of the press, and they have a complaints commission. This is the funny thing about religion – if nothing else it should be about having consistent moral beliefs, but here it becomes precisely the opposite: their critique of us is 'ethics' but our opinion of them is 'hate'. Similarly their requirements of us are 'moral' but our requirements of them are 'censorship'. Thus religious groups are often fair-weathered friends of liberty, usurping the language of the civil rights movement only when it's in their self-interest to do so. Sometimes I wonder whether religious groups are not embarrassed to enjoy exemption from the law whilst advocating one morality for all. Oh well, always nice to get an ethics lecture from the double-standards gang.

As we grow out of childhood we all yearn to be exempt from boring rules, and wish that reasonable behaviour be required of everyone except ourselves; but religions have actually managed to pull off the coup, demanding liberty and the right of free expression for themselves which they simultaneously deny everyone else. All of us work in highly regulated fields and have to deal with technical procedure every day. Why do we legislate to deal with every threat to humanity – except the one that has killed the most people?

Fiction and Non-Fiction
Let's contrast mythical beasts (like unicorns, dragons or goblins) with species as classified by Aristotle (birds, dogs, fish etc). The former are imagined whilst the latter are observed. With the former we create them internally and assume them to exist in the world. With the latter we are ignorant of them until they become known to us. With the former the process goes from the brain to the world. With the latter the process goes from the world to the brain.

Similarly, alchemy is about imagination whereas chemistry is about observation. Astrology requires imagination, astronomy requires observation. Magic requires imagination, physics requires observation. Luck is imagined, probability is observed. And so on. We see with these pairs, the former belong to the infancy of our species; as humans matured the imagination-based stuff retained its importance, but only in an allegorical way. So fables were imagined, history observed. Gods imagined, nature observed. Beliefs required imagination, knowledge required observation. Religion was imagined, philosophy was observed.

Similarly, in the infancy of our species humans projected what we were familiar with onto the universe, so we called constellations things like 'Plough' or 'Bear' and created gods in our image (more specifically in the image of beardy old clerics). We worked *from* the mind *to* the universe, taking what we understood and sticking it on what we didn't understand. But real progress was not made untill the process was flipped and the external informed the internal.

Kant's monumental development was to create a philosophy that operated like a religion – from the inside to the outside. Yes he critiqued various beliefs, but belief itself he not only retained but established in a greater form. In so doing Kant awarded supremacy to a method that throughout history produced the most ludicrous monsters imaginable. His achievement was mighty but it opened the door to human regression to infancy. We are now suffering the consequences of beliefs enjoying a status they simply do not deserve. Across the world we see the catastrophe of according preeminent status to phantasms unsupported by observations. If I wanted to destroy the world, I could do no better than create societies in which empiricists are abused into silence for fear they will be accused of thought crimes, where statements of belief are free speech, and critiques of belief are hate speech, where the law discriminates in favour of believers, and where the most irrational credulous people are exempted from having to produce a valid argument. As empiricism retreats, the mental health crisis expands, the geographical deserts expand and the belief desert expands. Additionally exemption from legal compliance incentivises more people to choose the easy path of belief. A vicious circle is established.

Hulk Smash!
Modern popular culture, especially from the US is awash with secular miracle stories. They usually run like this: Our downtrodden hero bottles up moral indignation, a bad event happens causing an explosive spasm which imbues our long-suffering protagonist with powers beyond the norms of what is physically possible. One example could be the Country and Western song '*Coward of the County*' by Kenny Rogers which can be seen as a metaphor for American military adventures generally.

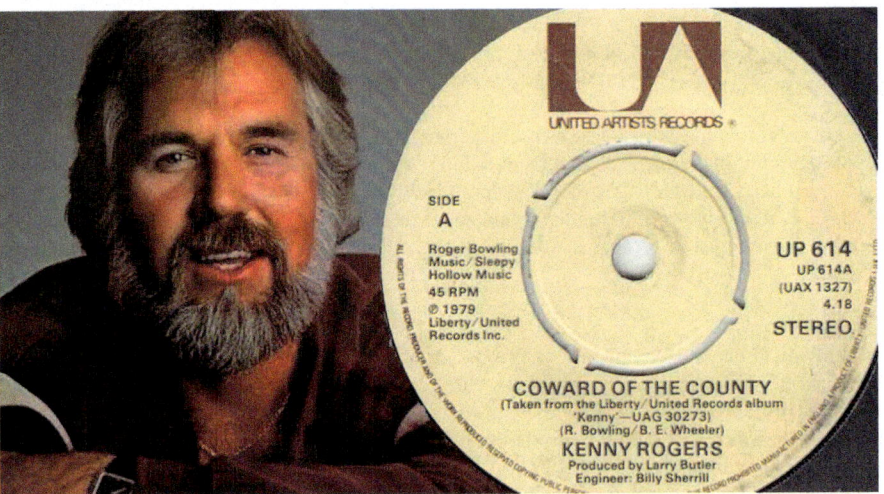

Here is Eleven from 'Stranger Things' who by dredging trauma, is able to overrule the laws of Newtonian physics.

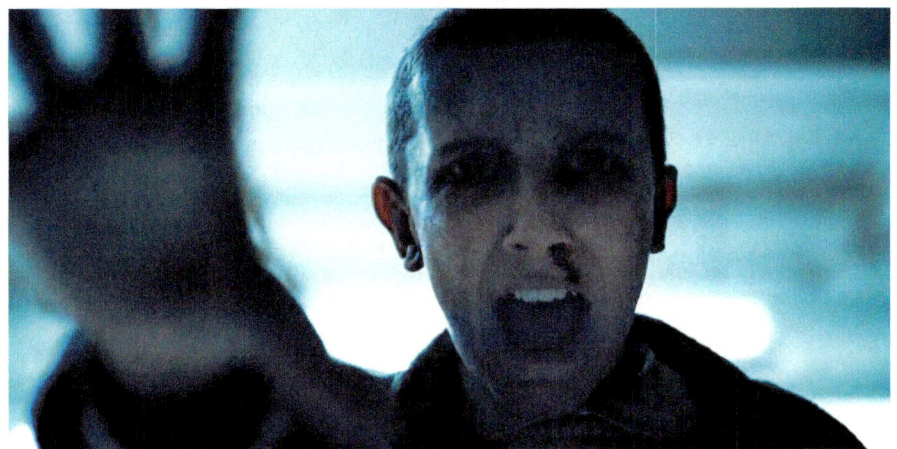

Another example can be seen in these panels from Spiderman where our hero is trapped under tonnes of machinery he cannot lift. But then his rage at past tragedies gives him the power to achieve the impossible.

These are presented as triumphs of the will over the phenomenal realm. They also represent precisely what does not happen in our everyday lives. Similarly, every contemporary film seems to culminate with a spasm in the noumenal realm establishing order and morality in the phenomenal realm.

America was founded by atheists. None of the founding fathers (except possibly Maddison) had a priest at their bedside when they died. Jefferson was an Epicurean and the great architect of it all Tom Paine was a Deist who wrote *'The Age of Reason'*. But as the US has gone from a young country to middle age, just like an aging human who has less and less to gain from this world, and more and more to gain from a spiritual world, we have seen the establishment of a secular belief system in which the same absurd appeals to credulity that we find in religion are presented to us for example, by superheroes. The difference being that what was formally attributed to divine intervention is now attributed to moral necessity, radioactive spiders, gamma rays or some other such codswallop. When Bruce Banner gets angry, transforms into the Hulk and bashes the baddie this is a standard Biblical morality tale presented as entertainment. These tales can be fun, even educational, but they can also constitute dangerous nonsense that the beauty of our world is of secondary importance, and that justice can be served by spasmodic outbursts. Who invented the idea of a moral belief system without organised religion, in which the noumenal realm prevails over physical world? Kant. Because his system is a technical labyrinth people have not spotted its huge social impact. Kant is the missing piece of the jigsaw that helps us understand why we feel we live in a mad world. I hope I have been some help here.

Belief / Reason Discrimination
Some minds opperate on the basis of belief, others on the basis of reason. If the believers can claim any critique is criminal mental violence then they enjoy immunity from criticism, and have every motive to become more extreme in their beliefs. But those who use reason cannot make a similar claim because reason by its very nature invites critique. We therefore find ourselves in a legalistic apartheid state where the least rational are least confronted whilst the most rational endure criticism without limit. If the law discriminates in favour of the least rational, why would anyone be rational?

Underwater!
Our local municipal swimming baths sells a fixed number of tickets for every hour slot. It's not a perfect system and it can be frustrating, but I accept if they didn't, then the pool would get overcrowded and there would be ridiculous queues for the limited number of showers and changing rooms. Imagine if they operated a policy of free movement, whereby anyone could enter whenever they liked? How would the staff cope? Similarly, in order to function, every theatre and cinema must carefully regulate how many come and go. Another example, I tried to join Extinction Rebellion but they obviously put my name into Google and I quickly found myself ejected. In order to function, every social institution must control entry. But when it comes to society as a whole there appears to be no system!

Recently when buying some wood I asked the timber merchant to demonstrate it had not been sourced from the Brazilian rainforest. They explained that for every delivery of wood there is a record of which saw mill cut it, and ultimately which forest the tree came from. So for every piece of wood in every timber yard in Britain we have records of type, quantity and origin ... but when it comes to human beings it's a different story! The government does not appear to know how many are here, why they are here or where they came from. We have an organised system for bits of wood but not humans! It is easier to enter the country without ID than it is to get on a 53 bus without scanning your microchip! The former gets you housed, the latter gets you ejected! Why not allow people on busses and trains for free? It sounds crazy right? But it is no *more* crazy than the policy we have for the entire country!

Clearly we are being selective about our aplication of free movement. Why is it that some of us are monitored, regulated and controlled in a way that Stalin could not have imagined in his wildest dreams, whilst for others there is free movement? This is easy to answer, we simply follow the money. When freedom of movement is convenient for the people at the top it is applied, when it isn't, say hello to contactless data harvesting. This brings us to a second question. Why would any society allow this to happen? Again it's an easy question to answer. No society would. It has not come to pass because our society made the wrong choice but because the power to choose was taken from us by stealth.

Obviously as a democrat I am not that bothered what immigration system we have so long as we have a vote on it. Sure we may vote for free movement, but I would prefer a fallible democratic system that can recognise and correct its errors, to an imposed system that assumes itself to be ethically supreme.

Bad values or none?
There are two wings of the Tory party: Ideologues and non-ideologues. The Ideologues are into Hayek, Friedman, Reagan, Thatcher etc. Whereas the non-ideologues say: *'forget values, screw beliefs, bollocks to morality, what do we have to <u>do</u> to win?'* Paradoxically this amoral group is actually the better half of the Tory party because it compels them to listen to what voters actually want. Labour don't have this, their certainty that they are ethically supreme renders them the explaining party, permanently nonplussed by rejection.

How do we critique something we *believe* to be good? It's a practical question. To even begin feels like a concession to evil.

The TLDR
Life on Earth is imperilled by a mass psychosis which I call Othello Syndrome. Othello Syndrome is when our beliefs (imagination, desires and fears) impose themselves on the empirical evidence we receive, overwhelming it, and we wrongly assume reality is what we think it is. We counter Othello Syndrome by cross-checking. Those who cross-check invent, create and discover. They enrich and are enriched; they learn more, earn more, hurt fewer people and help more people. Those who don't cross-check impose their beliefs and are therefore more likely to cause damage. Every gangster, thug, abuser, dictator and crook says the same thing: "don't talk" they know that cross-checking is fatal for villainy.

Right-wingers think the basic social unit is the individual but it is questionable whether their idea of the individual even exists. Because our dreams are full of surprises we know our minds must contain at least two active parts. So 'I' can't be an individual. It is natural for humans to cross-check within ourselves and between ourselves. This takes place in all fruitful human activity from reading to sex. This is why Hamlet is such a powerful metaphor for the human condition; as a species we cross-check as we inch forward. We are the cross-checking animal. The lives of even close friends and family will constantly surprise because others are themselves not what we suppose them to be. Life is full of surprises each one of which confronts belief.

When an opinion is not cross-checked, we call this a belief. It is the believers who imperil the world with their denial of climate science and their religions which are often cunningly disguised as secular organisations simply concerned with benign economic management. Naturally religions discourage cross-checking. Dictatorships are belief-based secular religions that also prohibit cross-checking (democracy) for similar reasons. Central control is wrong.

Philosophies predicated on the individual fail because the individual does not exist. We are conflicted members of groups. But social systems also tend to fail if they attempt to organise humanity whilst denying humans. What is important is not the social system or the individual but the interrelationship between them.

Democracy is the least bad political system and the best democracies are proportional as they allow fringe ideas to be critiqued openly and quickly. Censorship of political opinion should be prohibited. Because peace is our objective, a large number of small countries is preferable to a small number of large countries. Nature should impose the borders on us rather than us impose borders on nature. Countries should cooperate militarily (as per Ukraine) but this requires no political union.

If something is apparent or there is a general correlation the onus is on those disputing to produce an argument. When rules are applied inconsistently we should first apply *'Paul's Rule'* and enquire who stands to gain from people being treated differently.

How do you change something?
It's a practical question. Let's say we want to ban something that is dangerous, make taxes fairer or introduce a better way of doing things; what do you actually *do* to bring the better world about? And in that sentence 'do' is the operative word. Let's say you *vote* to change something. But what if what is ultimately implemented is the opposite of what was voted for? Then you would have to accept that when the vote was taking place you were not involved in a meaningful battle of ideas at all but a sham, a preordained procession orchestrated by the powerful for the powerful. So we find ourselves repeating the question. What do we do? What do we *do*? I'll tell you what you do. You choose, between submission and self-defence.

More words of wisdom from my son:
"You don't even understand how economics works."

Phobia Phobia.
A phobia is an irrational fear so we begin with the question: Is there a reason to be scared? Yes or no? If yes, it's not a phobia. If no, we proceed to the next question: Is the phobia causing real problems in the world?

Imagine there is a spider in my room and I have arachnophobia; so I take a book and squash it. If it were a poisonous spider then the phobia may have saved my life. If the spider was harmless then it was my inability to rationalise my fears, and physical actions in the real world that killed it. Either way the phobia itself is something to discuss rather than proof of evil.

Phobias probably prevent more injuries than they cause so why assume they are bad? Humans have evolved to be apprehensive of what might be dangerous, so why has every questionable proposition suddenly sprouted this suffix? I suspect it's because people wishing to impose their will want a scientific sounding accusation with which to accuse their opponents of being less than sane. (See also section on Foucault and madness)

Imagine if criticism of capitalism was deemed to be 'capitalism-phobic' or criticism of Marxism was considered 'Marxism-phobic'? (Unfortunately this often requires no imagination whatsoever) Do you think that would:

A, generate a fruitful civilised debate … or
B, incubate the most heinous tendencies of those ideologies?

The answer is B obviously. I have argued with many capitalists and Marxists. Often we haven't got on, but I've never met a capitalist or a Marxist so pathetic at arguing or so insecure in their beliefs that they thought disagreement should be criminalised.

Nouns verb.
The ultimate reality is not, as Heraclitus suggests, a verb, because verbs can't exist without nouns. Nor is it a noun (individual/society/universe etc) because nouns must verb. The ultimate reality (like love, sex, DNA, looking at a painting, listening to music, or reading a book) is a conjunction, a unity, an intercourse involving at least two nouns and one verb.

And Another Thing...
Sorry if I've come across as pedantic but if I am going to write this book I want to make sure I've shut down all the obvious counter arguments and made it absolutely clear how serious the situation was. 2016-20 was an attempted coup d'état, a war. Yes we were subject to *mental* violence, but it was an onslaught nonetheless. We were under attack from powerful, well-funded, well organised aggressors who waged a relentless information war in pursuit of their power grab. And if you think I am being

alarmist then you are being naïve - it is you who should be more alarmed. On 29th March 2019 the EU came within just 58 votes of total conquest, with Johnson, Gove, Davis, Fox, Raab, Duncan Smith and Rees-Mogg all capitulating. And if you think it's done and dusted, think again, the victory of the Brexiteers was by no means clear cut, fanatics don't stop believing, the democracy haters still enjoy their privileged status; and to this day parliament has never formally acknowledged our declaration of independence. The anti-democrats successfully overturned Denmark's vote against Maastricht, France's vote against the EU constitution and Greece's vote against austerity, why should they think our referendum any different? Yes I have written the death blow for the re-join campaign, but I doubt many people will read this, and for me, now this war must be over. Too many equally deserving causes have been on the back burner for too long. It's now time for me to exhaust myself on some other unpopular folly.

And Another Thing...
If we look again at the graph on pages 18 and 19 we see that many other countries were damaged by EU membership to a much greater extent than the UK. Yet still we were among the first (after Greenland) to leave. Why? If the answer is geographical, that Greenland left first, then the UK, because we are islands, then that opens the electrifying prospect of an independent, democratic and united Ireland being next. If on the other hand the answer is philosophical, that the decisive factor was our tradition of practicalities over ideologies, then that would make Bacon, Locke and Hume the architects of our departure rather than Johnson or Farage.

And Another Thing...
Brexit, Trump, Covid, race, environmentalism, gender - notice how every political issue automatically becomes radioactive? But if reality and morality is determined by the core of the mind then any opinion that doesn't confirm what we think is bound to feel like an attack on our character, and raise our hackles. This has rendered us incapable of discussing the simplest difference of opinion. What sort of politician is likely to prosper in such an environment? Someone who thoughtfully picks their way through an argument? No. The shameless, insincere or inconsiderate? Yes.

And Another Thing...
Because the forces of authoritarianism cannot call upon empirical evidence to justify their position, they advance by mutual promotion and by character assassinations of their opponents. So you will notice in your country in your time that those who want more democratic cross-checking by more people will be the ones it is ok to hate, apparently they are evil beneath the surface. Conversely those who are for authoritarianism will be portrayed as professional and suited to power in order that we associate them with prosperity and high status. Generally, monstrous democrats are pressured to step aside for charming democracy haters.

I am being careful not to defend the characters of prominent Brexiteers who I do not admire, but the point I am making is that if Johnson or Farage or Greta Thunberg or Meghan Markle or Extinction Rebellion are being sneered at then we must be scrupulous in applying the same standards to say Mario Draghi, Christine Lagarde, Ursula von Der Leyen, Guy Verhofstadt, Donald Tusk etc. When people are portrayed as monsters we should first ask who stands to gain from the character assassination. And sure enough, when France votes against the European Constitution or Greece votes against austerity, or Britain votes for independence, or Denmark votes against the Maastricht Treaty, like a whodunit, we suddenly find out who are the real bad guys - though as a general rule we should hate bad ideas rather than those who harbour them.

And Another Thing...
Some readers may be puzzled that I have not said a kind word about Farage, Johnson or Trump. Well, in a close contest it's always nice to get support from wherever it may come. But they supported Brexit because it elicited an emotional response in themselves; I prefer to be persuaded by evidence rather than follow beliefs. We found ourselves on the same side by sheer coincidence.

And Another Thing…
Before publishing I double-checked the latest figures for GDP growth, pay and trade. And by mid-2022, despite Covid, despite the Ukraine war and despite being governed by amoral, incompetent Tories, the UK had the highest GDP growth for 30 years, the biggest increase in pay for over 20 years and the biggest improvement of our trade balance ever in our history ever. For the first time ever there were more vacancies than unemployed people. We didn't vote to become poorer. How was this astonishing improvement in our trade balance reported? As a 'collapse of imports'!

And Another Thing…
If we had voted to remain, then the European Union and Islamic religion would have simply continued their conquest of our society, and no vote we could ever cast would have had any effect on their advance. We would have had the same control over the powerful that the people of Hong Kong have over the Chinese Communist Party – None. The deal we ended up with was abysmal, but at least it gave us a glimmer of hope.

Ayn Another Thing…
Nietzsche vehemently attacked those to whom he owed the most: Schopenhauer and Wagner. Ayn Rand did something similar - bizarrely, she described Kant as 'the most evil man in mankind's history'. I disagree with Kant but would never embarrass myself by calling the great man names. What had he done to deserve such abuse? Apparently his ethics opposed the self-interests of human beings. But Rand's ethical philosophy is basically the Categorical Imperative but without the effort. We can simultaneously be ethical *and* selfish? It's easy to see why her work has seduced so many. If there was ever a misnomer it is Ayn Rand's description of her philosophy as 'Objectivism' when a more subjectivist philosophy is hard to imagine. Kant critiqued reason itself, but the only thing Rand's philosophy can truly critique is insufficient selfishness. There is no contradiction between following your interests and helping others? Kant undermined reason? Laissez-faire capitalism is the only moral

social system? Capitalism is good because it protects our property … but the initiation of force is evil and irrational? It was fortunate for her the great man wasn't around to defend himself!

And Another Thing…
Generally the people backing Remain were wealthy, unelected and powerful, Richard Branson, Christine Lagarde, Tony Blair, George Soros, Mark Carney, Olly Robins, Baron Hall of Birkenhead, Lord Kerr, Lord Rose of Monewden, Donald Tusk, Ursula von der Leyen etc. As the free movement of goods, services, labour and capital increased, they became more wealthy and powerful. The leavers were the shelf stackers, the broom pushers the van drivers. As the free movement of goods, services, labour and capital increased, they became poorer and more powerless.

And Another Thing…
Who do I attack? The powerful: the clerics, lords, CEOs, appointees, governors, chairmen and central bankers. Who do they think should have more power? Themselves. Who do they attack? Those with the least power and money. Who do I think should have more power? Voters.

And Another Thing…
We were told we were not threatened, so we should shut up and stop being offensive. Obviously that argument was oxymoronic. The very fact we were pressured to be silent and self-censor confirmed the threat was real.

And Another Thing...
My aim for this book has been to show that like bitcoin, knowledge and morality should be mutually agreed by decentralised, disinterested parties. The political system that does this best is called democracy. The best democracies are the ones in which there is a proportional correlation between votes and power, and the legitimacy of law is proportional to the extent to which it was democratically agreed. Obviously the laws generated by this system should be equally applicable to everyone without exception. When power is centralised this has a corrupting effect. And as the corruption increases so does the sanctimony of those who have an interest in preserving the existing condition, increasingly they will abandon empirical arguments and evolve into a type of religion.

And Another Thing …
This is possibly the first manifesto ever written that doesn't advocate any policy, but instead merely advocates a *method* of deciding policy.

And Another Thing …
A critic of my first draft accused me of sweeping generalisations. This is a fair criticism, but I don't see how other than by generalising the big picture can be established. I have tried to structure this as clearly as I am able. If I appear to be thrashing around that is probably an inevitable consequence of dealing with interconnected issues. An overview will, by its very nature address several subjects, each of which is better known to specialists. Should overviews not be written for fear of incurring the scorn of specialists? I say no, because there is much to be gained from generalising. Indeed it seems to be the specialists who often miss the obvious.

And Another Thing…
I have little to gain and much to lose from this book. I am publishing it anonymously for the minimum price so I can expect neither fame nor fortune. It's a book almost everyone will find disagreement with. Some will disagree vehemently, and some of them will be rich and powerful or even violent. Specialists will line up to scoff at my generalisations. If a major error is found the book will be forgotten and if one isn't found it will become a battleground. Even Brexiteers will take issue with my critique of libertarianism, my support for XR and my refusal to write a kind word about Farage, Johnson or Trump. I doubt it will change anyone's mind. It hasn't exactly been a barrel of laughs to write, in fact it's been an albatross round my neck for several years, and to cap it all it could damage

my career, family and friendships. So, while I'm sure attacks will come, at least the accusation of self-interest won't be one of them! Hopefully Schopenhauer was right that "Every writer writes badly as soon as he starts writing for gain."

And Another Thing …
I have taken on a broad subject and I'm sure I will have made some embarrassing errors that others will be quick to point out. Great! Criticism welcome! After all it's obviously an essential part of my system. But if you believe that Jesus walked on water, that the sea parted for Moses, that Mohammad flew to the moon on a winged horse, or that the EU gave us peace prosperity and human rights, then please spare me the lecture about fact checking. And if you think the British are provincial bigots who would be improved by foreign law being imposed on them, then please unsubscribe me from the racism lectures. And if you are against free speech then I'm not interested in your opinion about human rights.

And Another Thing …
Because some people might selectively dip into particular sections I have repeated several justifications. Sorry if this bored those who did me the courtesy of reading the whole thing.

And Another Thing…
I have a diary of the Brexit struggle from 2017 to 2021. Which records my personal struggle, and the toll the Brexit took on my health, career, marriage and family. If there is interest I might cobble that together for a final instalment, but the TLDR is that I will never forgive and forget what happened in March 2019. In this book I have played down the bitterness I feel, but I am expressing 1% of it here as a point of record. There have been a handful of times in my life when I declared war. Usually, subsequently, I regretted having done so. Brexit is one of the few instances where, even years later, there are no regrets. Finally I would like to pay tribute to the inspirational Vickie Davies who is sadly missed. I would like to thank V for putting up with me, Will and Rosaleen for their invaluable peer review, Joe and Nick for arguing with me, and my fellow Brexiteers, Peter, Paul, Ian, Wayne, Robert, Michael and Gary.

And Another Thing…
I could rant on for ever, but for now that is the best I can do. Thanks for reading. S-

Printed in Great Britain
by Amazon